A SHEARWATER BOOK

# LIVES PER GALLON

# LIVES PER GALLON

## THE TRUE COST OF OUR OIL ADDICTION

Terry Tamminen

ISLANDPRESS / SHEARWATER BOOKS

Washington • Covelo • London

*A Shearwater Book*
*Published by Island Press*

Copyright © 2006 Terry Tamminen

SHEARWATER BOOKS is a trademark
of The Center for Resource Economics.

*Library of Congress Cataloging-in-Publication data.*


Tamminen, Terry.
  Lives per gallon : the true cost of our oil addiction / Terry Tamminen.
    p. cm.
  Includes bibliographical references and index.
  ISBN 1-59726-101-7 (cloth : alk. paper)
  1. Energy consumption—Environmental aspects. 2. Energy policy—United States. 3. Petroleum industry and trade. 4. Middle East—History, Military.   I. Title.

  HD9502.A2T34 2006
  333.8'232--dc22

                                        2006014156



*British Cataloguing-in-Publication data available.*


Printed on recycled, acid-free paper ♻

Design by Maureen Gately

Manufactured in the United States of America

10  9  8  7  6  5  4  3  2  1

To Art Arndt, Kyle Damitz, and all of the other parents and children whose breath has been lost to our petroleum addiction.

# CONTENTS

# Prologue

Here we have a serious problem: America is addicted to oil, which is often imported from unstable parts of the world.

*President George W. Bush,*
*"State of the Union Address"*
*January 31, 2006* [1]

Great beasts, fantastically shaped, armored skin. Lumbering giants that ceaselessly roam the land to plunder every natural resource within their grasp, devouring the weak, the slow. Their breath is hot, cloying, steeped in deliberate destruction and death.

Jurassic Park? A lost colony of tyrannosaurs left over from 65 million years ago? No, it's any modern U.S. city and the inexorable daily stampede of steel machines on rivers of asphalt, belching toxic fumes that foul the lives of every living being, a beast that kills as surely as the senseless, serrated teeth of a T. rex.

Yet according to a growing body of evidence, petroleum-powered transportation is about to fade to black. We have profited much from the Oil Age, but for years have chosen to ignore its limitations and its true cost. Like an aging actor, the Oil Age will yield to players of greater gifts who even now wait in the wings to make welcome entrances, if we are smart enough to give the cue.

Innumerable clues indicate that change is urgently needed and that our window of opportunity to shape a future beyond oil addiction is narrowing. Since the U.S. invasion of Iraq in the spring of 2003, the price of a barrel of oil has shot past $75, tripling the average price that had prevailed for decades. Experts predict that this trend will continue, while overall uncertainty about the price of oil—and the ability of refineries worldwide to supply enough finished products—has already begun to erode international economic stability. Competition for these scarce resources may even foreshadow a new cold war, with China striding the globe in search of energy to fuel its torrid economic growth, while the United States seeks to checkmate those moves and guarantee supplies of its own to protect domestic prosperity. These dramas are beginning to play out against the backdrop of a steady stream of revelations that air pollution is shortening lives and costing governments billions of dollars, rupees, pounds, and euros in health-care costs.

Consider how much of your life is dependent, if not outright addicted, to petroleum, not only the daily commute and delivery of the kids to soccer practice, but the broccoli in the produce aisle that got there because of petroleum-based fertilizers, diesel fuel in the tractor and harvester, bunker fuel in the ship, and yet more diesel in the train and big-rig that delivered it to the supermarket. You probably can't smell the petroleum fumes from the cars in the parking lot, polluting from their engines and gas tanks even when the engine isn't running, but they're in the air you are breathing. You take the broccoli home in a plastic bag and pop it into a plastic container, both made from petroleum, then store it in the refrigerator's plastic perishables bin.

You buy those fresh fruits and vegetables thinking of your family's health, but does a member of your own family suffer from asthma or emphysema that may have been caused or exacerbated by petroleum pollution? Perhaps a loved one or neighbor has died in a foreign war that was waged, at least in part, to protect our supply of the petroleum drug to which the President suggests we are addicted.

A century from now, will our descendants view this dependence on oil with bemused contempt in the same manner that we now scoff at those who thought the only way to cure disease was to bleed a patient to remove "ill humors" from the body? Will they also wonder why we didn't step back sooner to see the true price we pay for this addiction, especially knowing that at some point petroleum's wellspring would run dry?

It has taken me a long time to understand our oil addiction and to learn why it's so difficult to shake. My passion for the environment and the urge to write this book grew out of a series of four "aha" days, the ones that make you see things more clearly. The realization on each of those days had something in common.

At the age of twelve I wanted to be Mike Nelson of *Sea Hunt* and took my first scuba dive off the coast of Southern California. I was truly awestruck by the towering kelp beds and their abundant, alien sea life. I harvested my first abalone and watched my mother pound it into something roughly edible. A decade later, I returned to Los Angeles from a life in Australia and Europe to dive those waters again, to reclaim my youthful *Sea Hunt* and Jacques Cousteau–inspired enthusiasm.

What I found instead was a desolate wasteland of rock and mussels, of purple urchins and Styrofoam cups. No densely populated kelp beds, sculpted by the unseen hand of ocean currents, just a moonscape of barren rock covered in silt. What had happened to the lush kelp beds, the abalone, the sea bass, the lobster, the octopus?

My second epiphany was at the time of the death of my father, Art Arndt. He served in the Marines at Peleliu and the other bloodiest battles of World War II in the Pacific. He died of emphysema at the age of seventy, after a decade of wheezing and dragging an oxygen tank behind him, the result of smoking and living in one of the world's smoggiest cities. Not Los Angeles or Houston, but

Milwaukee, Wisconsin, covered much of the time in green-gray smoke from upwind Rust Belt industries and millions of vehicle tailpipes. The day we buried him, aging veterans in bulging, faded uniforms offering their twenty-one-gun salute, I asked myself, How could *this* happen?

Then there was the day I met a Hopi elder named Vernon Masayesva. He opened the door for me to a civilization that has continuously occupied the same land, indeed the same dwellings, for more than 10,000 years, living sustainably in one of the most unforgiving, stingy landscapes on Earth. Of the many reasons for the Hopi's remarkable success, two features of their culture exemplify their approach to life. First, the Hopi have no word or idea that describes "wilderness," but they do have a word for wild, or crazy, people. To them, the land is not wild, but people who harm it are. The land is simply their home.

"Western science looks at the world in which we live, separates the human from the environment, and then studies the parts—the air, the water, the land, the animals—as if they had little to do with one another," Vernon explained with a sad resignation. "But traditional science looks at the world in which we live, recognizes the essential connection of all of the parts—the air, the water, the land, the other animals, and the human—and from it develops culture and a way of being. The world is sacred and the human is its steward."

Another trait that explains much about the Hopi culture of sustainability can be discerned from their simple daily customs. When they eat, they thank not only the person who cooked the food, but the land, sun, water, farmers, even their parents—all the elements that made the meal possible. They say something unpronounceable to the European ear, but it might look like *kwak-kwak . . . eetem . . . new-new-sa*, which means *thank you, we have eaten*. The Hopi recognize that if you don't feed all living things, there would be no food to eat and no survival in the desert land.[2]

The fourth of these remarkable days in my life was meeting Jo

Anne Van Tilburg, the anthropologist whose team helped solve the mystery of the civilization that once flourished on an island off the coast of Chile. Rapa Nui, better known as Easter Island, is also home to the equally enigmatic tiki-like "moai," effigies carved from volcanic rock, standing as much as 70 feet tall and weighing up to 165 tons apiece.[3]

"I thought I was just studying an ancient civilization," she told me, gazing out to sea from her home in Malibu, California. "Then I realized we were looking in the mirror."

Rapa Nui today looks oddly like Ireland, green and tawny, although devoid of large plant or animal life to sustain any substantial human population. This island, though, was once a lush, subtropical paradise, reminiscent of the South Pacific islands that the first Polynesian settlers on Rapa Nui had once called home. Those lucky immigrants found abundant plant and animal life, including giant palms that made outstanding oceangoing canoes for hunting marine mammals. Every step brought fruits, edible roots, and medicinal plants.

So generous were the land and sea that a sophisticated, robust population emerged, including priests and artisans who carved, transported, and erected the moai, ultimately numbering nearly a thousand mute, forbidding sentinels. As the growing population depleted traditional food sources, however, islanders worked their way down the food chain, in turn exhausting the supply of shellfish, sea snails, even grasses. Porpoise bones suddenly disappeared from garbage heaps as islanders no longer had large trees to make oceangoing canoes. Even garden crops declined as topsoil washed into the sea, a victim of deforestation. Ominously, the bones of birds, seals, and porpoises were rapidly replaced by those of rats and finally humans as islanders devolved into warring tribes, fighting over the only remaining food source of any significance—each other.

Did any islander see what was happening and try to warn others? One can only imagine that those who spoke out would have been ostracized by a complacent populace accustomed to seemingly endless bounty, unwilling to face the new reality. Vested interests of clan leaders, chiefs, and statue carvers might have drowned out the cries for moderation as the ruling class feared losing prestige and wealth. With no written histories, photos, or satellite views to guide them, islanders of one generation would have little idea of what life had been like in the land of their forebearers. Oral histories of great abundance may have seemed like myth instead of fact. At some point, no one would have even noticed the decay of the last ocean-going canoe, the fall of the last great palm tree, or even the roasting of the last rat.

It seemed oddly appropriate to hear Jo Anne spin her tale in the shadow of Malibu's sprawling palaces, 10,000-square-foot McMansions, modern moai that dot the hillsides, each a greater display of clan wealth than the next, each erected on the dust of an earlier clan's display of ostentation.

"Easter Island is Earth writ small," says Jared Diamond, another UCLA researcher and author of numerous thoughtful books on how modern society has arrived at the brink of its own crisis. "Today, again, a rising population confronts shrinking resources . . . and we can no more escape into space than the Easter Islanders could flee into the ocean."[4]

That simple conclusion succinctly summarizes the lessons I take away from my four personal epiphany days and describes the crossroads where modern civilization now stands: rising population confronting shrinking resources, including the declining supply of fossil fuels and compromised supplies of clean air, clean water, public health, and a vibrant economic future. It reminds us that we are very mortal, clinging to life on a planet that may not remain hospitable to us and that certainly doesn't care as much about our well-being as we must. It also highlights that natural habitats are shrinking and that populations of species are declining around the globe because of human activity.

Paleontologists estimate that some 98 percent of all plant and animal species that once lived on Earth became extinct before the dawn of Industrial Man.[5] Scientists agree that mass extinctions are linked to drastic changes in the environment, such as those caused by the effect of an asteroid strike or the warming of Earth's climate by man-made pollution. Yet it can also be something as dim-witted as eating all the food or poisoning the air and water.

World-renowned paleontologist Richard Leakey tells us that five major waves of mass extinction have washed over Earth since the first living creature emerged from the primordial ooze, the most recent of which was the passing of the dinosaurs. The most startling fact in what Dr. Leakey calls the "sixth extinction" is the *rate* of today's extinctions. He warns that if the trend continues, we will lose half of all plant and animal life on Earth within this century.[6]

"Whatever way you look at it, we're destroying the Earth at a rate comparable with the impact of a giant asteroid slamming into the planet, or even a shower of vast heavenly bodies," Leakey says.[7]

The lessons of those four days in my life were a catalyst to a career as an environmental advocate, researcher, and the head of California's Environmental Protection Agency, which in turn led me to the conclusion that the crossroads in question today are nowhere more sharply defined than with respect to our addiction to oil. Such thinking does not lead me to the conclusion that we must return to some idealized existence akin to our Native American ancestors, but rather that we need to choose the road to sustainable living in a twenty-first-century context.

Nor do I conclude that *Homo sapiens* is necessarily one of those species facing imminent extinction. The decline of civilizations like that of Rapa Nui and the loss of species from the planet are cautionary tales, offering us a chance to learn and adapt, to demand better thinking from our corporations, our government, and ourselves. The lost kelp beds of Southern California teach us how quickly things can change if we don't pay attention to the evidence. The

Hopi teach us that there is a better way to thrive on a planet with limited resources. Rapa Nui—and our fellow human beings today, who struggle with respiratory illnesses for each breath—teach us that there are some fates that may be worse than extinction.

The modern "asteroid" may not be a heavenly body that wreaks instant planetary disaster, but may instead be a steady erosion of our quality of life from the continued burning of fossil fuels, especially petroleum, if we fail to shake our addiction. The price we pay includes illness, death, a changing climate, and our own sustainability on this island we call Earth. The price may also include further injury to our body politic as we pursue ever more extraordinary lengths to secure another "fix" of oil.

How can we fail to see our civilization as heading down the path of the Rapa Nui islanders, a twenty-first-century version of warring clans clinging to life in caves and eating one another? We have started from the same place as they did—consuming our resources and fouling our nest without seeing the incremental losses—but unlike the ancients, we have written text, films, and science to know what we are losing and to enable us to make changes.

If we continue to burn oil for much of our energy needs, despite our science and foreknowledge, we could still end up like them. There are many alternatives to oil and many strategies we can use to ensure that those alternatives compete on a level playing field. But, like any addiction, we must first admit that we have a problem and then make the decision to solve it.

# CHAPTER I

# The Breath of Our Fathers

H ave you ever really thought about the 3,000 gallons of air you breathe each day? If so, then you know that 99 per-cent of it is oxygen and nitrogen, which can be metabo-lized or otherwise transformed in the human body. What might have escaped your notice is the other 1 percent, which is inert argon gas that is not modified, but simply inhaled and exhaled. Because of the finite, unalterable supply of argon in the atmosphere, we share it with every other living thing on our planet and we always have.

Harvard researchers have thought a lot about this 1 percent. They calculate that by the age of twenty, each of us has inhaled argon atoms that were literally exhaled by dinosaurs, Gandhi, Shake-speare, and a carpenter from Bethlehem.[1] This surprising fact about argon illustrates that we literally share the same air with all living things on the planet, both past and present, making it a unique resource. So how do we treat our air, something that is arguably sacred?

One hundred percent of the air we breathe is contaminated with human-made pollutants, fouled with a toxic stew of oil-related ingredients bearing acronyms like PAHs, PM 2.5, BTEX compounds, and GHGs. In some instances, amounts may be negligible, but the majority of Americans live in areas of air pollution that exceed even the most basic state or federal standards that are designed to protect public health. Although you probably know people who have broken a limb or succumbed to cancer, you may not think you know anyone who actually suffers from disease related to air pollution.

Those who sued tobacco companies for hiding the harms of their products were told by the companies that cigarette smoking alone could not be held responsible for the illness and deaths of people like my father. These people, the companies said, were also routinely exposed to other sources of hazardous air pollution, especially from cars. And indeed they were. Research conducted on half a million Americans between 1982 and 1998 confirmed that a lifetime exposure to petroleum pollution exacerbated the effects of smoking, resulting in "enhanced mortality."[2] In short, not just tobacco but petroleum literally began to take away the breath of my father and millions of Americans like him from the day they were born.

Yet it is not tobacco that is the biggest threat to human health from the smoke it blows in our faces. It is the petroleum industry that is listed by the Geneva Protocol on Air Pollution as the largest single source of harmful air pollution worldwide.[3] Have we made a Faustian deal with the Devil? Are we now indefinitely obliged to pay our part of the bargain in human lives? Fast, seemingly cheap, independent transportation in exchange for higher rates of birth defects, asthma, emphysema, and years shaved from our lives?

"It required no science to see that there was something produced in great cities which was not found in the country," opined Dr. Henry Antoine Des Voeux in his 1905 paper "Fog and Smoke," the first scientific article to use the term *smog*.[4] For more than a hundred years we have known something about air pollution in general. When did we learn about the specific contribution to smog made by motor vehicles?

## What Did Ozzie and Harriet Know?
## A Brief History of Smog

By 1957, when black-and-white television sets broadcast *Ozzie and Harriet* and *Leave it to Beaver*—iconic images of a pure American lifestyle in which the greatest problem was a milkman who forgot to deliver the cheese—Congress had already become concerned about the health effects of vehicle pollution. Legislation was introduced that would prohibit *any* motor vehicle from U.S. roadways that discharged pollution in excess of levels found dangerous by the U.S. Surgeon General.[5] Needless to say, that legislation didn't pass, and by 1961, the U.S. Department of Health estimated that 90 percent of all Americans lived in localities with harmful air pollution that was directly linked to vehicle exhaust.[6]

By the time the nation lost JFK two years later, our rose-colored glasses began to clear and government agencies told us that every day in the United States, automobiles were discharging 430 tons of nitrogen dioxide ($NO_2$), a harmful pollutant and component of smog.[7] Little was done by the federal government to address this growing problem, however, and when Richard Nixon won the White House in 1968, those emissions had increased by more than 50 percent above the levels of just five years earlier.

As bras were burned and a war in Southeast Asia was fought and protested, researchers uncovered a correlation between higher death rates and higher smog levels.[8] They also found that our elders suffered smog-related illnesses, such as asthma and bronchitis, ten times that of middle-aged Americans and that people in poor health at any age were much more likely to die prematurely if they breathed smog.[9] By the time an actor from California left the White House in 1988, evidence from around the world showed that smog hastened the death of thousands of people every year and caused or aggravated bronchitis, cancers, heart disease, and asthma in millions more.[10]

My family first moved to Los Angeles in 1963. We lived in an apartment on land that had once belonged to Edgar Rice Burroughs in a suburb called Tarzana, not far from glamorous Hollywood. We sat by the swimming pool, while our relatives in the Midwest shoveled snow from their frozen driveways, mesmerized by the tales of old Hollywood provided by our neighbor Harry, a retired stuntman for Eddie Foy.

"That's haze," Harry would correct us, if we dared ask about the obscured skyline above the palm trees. "We don't have smog in Hollywood."

Fortunately, in those days, scientists had more credibility with government regulators than did stuntmen. Although the federal government failed to act, the State of California recognized that weather patterns and mountainous geography conspired to create and magnify a serious smog problem in places such as the Los Angeles basin.[11] State officials had formed county air pollution control districts as early as 1947 to combat the growing threat.

As a result, and because the federal government ultimately followed California's legislative lead and enacted national laws and pollution standards, there have been remarkable air quality improvements in the intervening years. Nonetheless, some pollution measurements in the Los Angeles region today remain more than double the U.S. Environmental Protection Agency (USEPA) standards and therefore continue to pose significant health risks.[12] Many of the chemicals found in petroleum products—and the air pollution caused by their manufacture, storage, distribution, and combustion—are defined by the USEPA as "materials that cause death, disease, or birth defects in organisms that ingest or absorb them."[13] Although much of this discussion draws on the California experience for examples, there are, as the American Lung Association pointed out in early 2006, more than 152 million people who live in areas of the United States where the air quality puts their health at risk.[14] Sorry, Harry, but that includes Hollywood.

## Secondhand Petroleum Smoke:
## The Six Most Dangerous Pollutants in Smog

After more than a hundred years of research, many of the health effects of smog are well understood, yet they are still very much out of control, both in the United States and in a growing number of cities around the globe. Detailed descriptions of the effects on human health and the environment are described later in this chapter, but first let's examine the six most toxic constituents of the inescapable secondhand smoke we create by the combustion of millions of barrels of petroleum in the United States every day.[15]

1. *Particulate matter.* Have you ever sat in traffic behind a big truck or an old school bus and experienced the black soot that belches from the smokestack or tailpipe when it starts up or accelerates? That's particulate matter (PM), measured as large particles of 10 microns or less, and small ones of 2.5 microns or less, called PM 10 and PM 2.5, respectively. To get an idea of this scale, consider that the human eye can detect objects as small as 35 microns (or millionths of a meter) and that a grain of table salt is about 100 microns.

   Soot from fires and dust from unpaved roads, agriculture, or construction generate significant amounts of PM 10 in addition to the amount pumped into our air by the incomplete burning of petroleum fuels. That's what the soot from the school bus really is—petroleum that hasn't burned in the engine, especially a diesel engine.

   The smaller particles, PM 2.5, that are even more insidious in terms of human health are generated from some industrial smokestacks, but the major culprits are emissions from vehicle tailpipes and the exhaust of planes, ships, trucks, and trains.[16] These fine particles are especially toxic, causing respiratory ailments, cardiopulmonary disease, premature death, low birthweight babies, and infant deaths. Research reveals that illnesses, such as asthma and lung cancer, and death rates rise on days when the amount of particulate matter in the air also rises. Conversely, evidence shows the benefits of decreasing particulate matter in the air: illnesses and death rates drop.[17]

2. *Volatile organic compounds.* Volatile organic compounds (VOCs) include a wide variety of products that easily evaporate, hence the term *volatile.* The fumes from paint, pesticides, cosmetics, and solvents and the distinctive odor you notice when you pump gasoline are examples of VOCs. The VOCs in petroleum products, including benzene, 1,3-butadiene, and polycyclic aromatic hydrocarbons (PAHs), are particularly toxic and are known to cause cancer.

Petroleum VOCs are especially insidious because they are not only emitted from the tailpipe while the engine is running, but they also fill the air above most parked vehicles, especially on hot days as the fuel expands in the engine and fuel lines. VOCs are known carcinogens and reproductive toxins causing leukemia, lymphatic tissue cancers, birth defects, bronchitis, and emphysema. Benzene is the "bad boy" of VOCs, with a growing body of evidence showing that health harms from inhaling it are significant even at very low levels.[18]

3. *Ozone.* "Asthma now hits 1 in 10 children, study says," blares the headline from the *Canadian Globe and Mail* on January 27, 2006. The newspaper article describes the surprise of regulators and researchers alike, but Canadians could have read even more ominous findings in the *Fresno Bee* as early as December 2002, when that paper ran the story "Last Gasp," describing that one in six children in Fresno, California, carries an asthma inhaler to school.

Or during the 2000 Summer Olympics in Atlanta, Georgia, when researchers discovered that decreased traffic in the metropolitan area over that two-week period of the games correlated to decreases in ozone levels and fewer hospital emergency visits by children complaining of breathing difficulties.[19]

Although ozone in the upper atmosphere shields Earth from the sun's harmful ultraviolet radiation, high concentrations at ground level are a threat to human health, animal health, and plant life. Ozone is formed when reactive organic gas (ROG) and nitrogen oxides react with sunlight. ROG comes from a variety of organic sources. For example, emissions from cows around Fresno supply almost as much ROG as does the refining and burning of fossil fuels in the same area. Of course, in most modern cities without a great deal of livestock, the bad actor is petroleum-based ROG, not the dairy herd.

Ozone acts like an acid on the lungs, causing and aggravating asthma, but it doesn't stop there. It also causes other respiratory ailments and impairs lung function, harms the immune system, aggravates heart disease and emphysema, and can cause fetal heart malfunctions.

4. *Nitrogen dioxide.* One of the charming bromides of Harry, the aging stuntman from the golden era of Hollywood, was an unwitting response to nitrogen dioxide, or $NO_2$. "I don't trust air I can't see," he would say, laughing and pounding his fist on the rusted metal patio table. It didn't strike me as odd at the time, but he always wheezed as he laughed.

Harry had a lot to trust in his hometown. The brownish tinge to Los Angeles's skies in the 1960s, and the skies over many other metropolitan areas today, comes from $NO_2$, a highly reactive organic gas that irritates the lungs and causes both bronchitis and pneumonia. It can also aggravate respiratory disease and lower resistance to respiratory infections. $NO2$ is one of many oxides of nitrogen (NO$_x$), all of which are a part of those ROGs that help form ozone.

5. *Carbon monoxide.* As unsavory as the first four air pollutants on this list are, carbon monoxide (CO) is especially insidious because it is colorless, odorless, and highly poisonous. In short, it is a sneak thief of breath.

Having read this far, you will not be surprised to learn that the majority of CO in the air comes from vehicles burning petroleum fuels. A smaller amount comes from wood-burning stoves, industrial smokestacks, and even the use of natural gas in your kitchen oven. No matter the source, this sneak thief robs the blood of oxygen, which ultimately can cause asphyxiation and death. When inhaled by pregnant women, CO can threaten fetal growth and mental development of the child.

6. *Lead.* Although lead was eliminated from most gasoline in the United States starting in the 1970s, it continues to be used in aviation and other specialty fuels today. When it was ubiquitous in gasoline, lead from fuel exhaust polluted soils along roadways. Those polluted soils dry out and become airborne, so lead is still thereby readily inhaled.[20] In addition, coal-burning power plants dump significant volumes of lead into the air each year.

Lead pollution delivers one of the more Darwinian consequences of all the self-inflicted wounds wrought by human-made air pollution. In men, it reduces sperm count and creates abnormalities in what's left. In women, it reduces fertility and can cause miscarriages. Children are especially vulnerable because they absorb lead more readily than do adults. As their brains and nervous systems develop, children may suffer significant learning disabilities and hyperactivity as a result of lead exposure.

For children and adults, lead is a neurotoxin even at very low levels, affecting the circulatory, reproductive, nervous, and renal (kidney) systems. Furthermore, those low levels "bioaccumulate" in bone and other tissues, meaning that part of each dose is stored in the body and is a poison that "keeps on giving." Although these effects have been well understood for decades, oil companies continued to sell leaded gasoline around the world long after the United States phased it out. Venezuela got the lead out in late 2005, for instance, but it is still found in the gasoline of at least twenty other countries today.[21]

## Smoking Guns:
## The Surprising Similarities of Tobacco and Oil

Of the constituents in secondhand petroleum smoke, lead is the only one that isn't also found in tobacco smoke. The health damage caused by both tobacco and petroleum are also similar in many ways. Table 1.1 lists the most common and the most toxic constituents that are found in both tobacco smoke and vehicle exhaust. Whether you inhale from a cigarette, breathe in secondhand tobacco smoke, or simply breathe the air in most parts of the industrialized world, you

#### TABLE 1.1. HUMAN HEALTH TOXINS FOUND
#### IN BOTH TOBACCO SMOKE AND VEHICLE EXHAUST

| Pollutant | Associated Health Effects |
| --- | --- |
| Benzene | Cancer; respiratory and reproductive toxicity |
| PAHs (polycyclic aromatic hydrocarbons) | Cancer; immune system toxicity |
| 1,3-butadiene | Cancer |
| Formaldehyde and acrolein | Respiratory illness, cancers |
| Carbon monoxide (CO) | Respiratory illness; cardiovascular toxicity; asphyxiation |
| Heavy metals | Cancer; neurotoxicity |
| Hexane | Neurotoxicity |
| Acids | Lung irritation and damage |

*Source*: "How Do Tobacco Smoke and Car Exhaust Compare?" *Energy Independence Now*, 2003. Available online at www.EnergyIndependenceNow.org.

are inhaling benzene, polycyclic aromatic hydrocarbons, carbon monoxide, and a host of other toxins. No matter the source, inhaling these pollutants can cause cancer, respiratory illness, and damage to your heart, lungs, and reproductive system.

Given these facts, it is not surprising that researchers have determined that living in a place with as much petroleum air pollution as Los Angeles is a lot like living with a smoker.[22] Living in Madrid, Spain, is the equivalent of smoking half a pack of cigarettes a day, and a third of Spain's entire population lives under what they call "the grey beret" of smog.[23] The Jakarta, Indonesia, city government simultaneously addressed its problems with tobacco and petroleum smoke by passing a law that banned smoking in public and another that required a smog check of all vehicles. Those bold steps were taken when air quality standards were met on only twenty-eight days in 2005, pushing Jakarta into third place, behind Mexico City, Mexico, and Bangkok, Thailand, as the smoggiest cities in the world.[24]

Tobacco and petroleum smoke are linked in still another insidious manner. Children born into households of smokers, who are also exposed to air pollution from combustion of motor fuels, have a 7 percent lower birth weight and a 3 percent smaller head circumference than average, conditions that are linked to learning disabilities later in life.[25] Evidence for these sobering statistics was found in the blood of umbilical cords, where petroleum-based toxins (including carcinogens such as polycyclic aromatic hydrocarbons, benzene, and toluene) were discovered. Let me repeat that: cancer-causing toxins from oil and tobacco were found in the blood of umbilical cords.

"My advice to pregnant women is don't let people in your household smoke," warns Dr. Frederica P. Perera, senior author of the study that made this discovery. Perera suggested reducing risk to children by eliminating their exposure to secondhand tobacco smoke because she knew that there is no effective means of eliminating exposure to secondhand petroleum smoke. That's where the similarities between tobacco smoke and smog end. Although tobacco is addicting and quitting is extremely difficult, smokers can stop inhaling toxic tobacco smoke. We can also walk away from secondhand tobacco smoke in many instances. Petroleum pollution, however, is impossible to escape in most modern cities. We are involuntarily subjected to the toxins created by petroleum 100 percent of the time and along every step on the journey of life. What do we know with relative certainty about the effects of petroleum toxins on our health at various points in our lives?

## Petroleum Threats from Womb to Tomb

In truth, the risks do not wait for us to come into the world, but rather begin their assault in the womb. Looking at thousands of Los Angeles–area expectant mothers, researchers at the University of California at Los Angeles found that those exposed for as little as a month to high levels of smog (mostly ozone and carbon monoxide) were three times more likely to have babies with physical deformities, including cleft lips and palates and defective heart valves, when compared with national averages for birth defects. Perhaps more alarming is that most of these women lived in areas that meet federal standards for ozone and carbon monoxide, standards that are supposed to protect public health.[26]

As they grow older, our children go to school, and many of them will make the trip in a familiar American icon, the lumbering yellow school bus. Like most states, nearly 70 percent of the 24,372 school buses in California run on diesel fuel, making them some of the dirtiest vehicles on the road.[27] Researchers found that a child riding inside a diesel school bus may be exposed to as much as four times the level of toxic diesel exhaust as someone riding in a car ahead of it. These exposures pose up to forty-six times the cancer risk considered significant under federal law.[28]

"We always thought air pollution had acute effects: If yo"

breathed bad air one day, you felt crappy that night," said University of Southern California professor James Gauderman. In one of his studies on the health effects of air pollution, completed in 2004, he confirmed years of research that observed a total of more than 5,000 California kids.[29] "Long-term exposure, day-in, day-out, in an area like Los Angeles, really appears to have detrimental effects on all kinds of chronic conditions." Gauderman also discovered that on days when ozone levels are rated "high," kids who play extensively outdoors are up to four times more likely to have an asthma attack than those who spend more time watching TV inside, where ozone levels are lower.

"Kids like me with asthma . . . during ozone days I will almost always have an asthma attack if I go outside," testified eight-year-old Kyle Damitz in December 2002 at a USEPA hearing on proposed diesel standards that would include reducing emissions from school buses. "On good days, I take 2 pills in the morning and 3 pills at bedtime. I do an IV treatment every 2 weeks. On a bad asthma day, I take 4 pills in the morning, more at lunch, and again, more at bedtime. I came here today to . . . ask you to help. . . . If you make our air cleaner, I will be able to live longer."[30] Cleaner standards for diesel-powered buses and trucks were ultimately adopted by the USEPA, over the objections of the American Petroleum Institute and numerous vehicle and engine manufacturers.

Looking at children and adults combined, a 1997 study estimates that smog pollution is responsible for more than 6 million asthma attacks in the United States each year plus 159,000 emergency room visits and 53,000 hospitalizations. These illnesses are not precipitated by outdoor smog exposure alone.[31] Does that mean that our children are not safe from petroleum pollution inside the home or at school?

"The message is . . . about not planning . . . schools close to a major freeway," declared Gauderman, discussing research conducted between 1993 and 2004 in Southern California related to asthma incidence and proximity to busy roadways. The research found that children living within a quarter mile of a freeway had an 89 percent higher risk of developing asthma than those who lived a mile away. For adults, the results indicated higher incidence of heart disease and deaths related to respiratory illness.[32] Similar results have been found in Vancouver, Denver, and a host of other cities around the world.[33]

If our children aren't safe indoors, at home, or at school, can they escape harmful petroleum smoke when they are in the car with the windows rolled up and the air conditioning on? No; in fact, as the school bus research showed, confined areas can concentrate air pollution and increase exposure levels. Research also reveals that levels of benzene, toluene, formaldehyde, and methyl tertiary butyl ether (MTBE), as well as carbon monoxide, were up to ten times higher inside vehicles than at fixed outdoor monitoring stations.[34] All these toxins have links to respiratory ailments and cancer.

To be sure, not all indoor air pollution is caused by vehicle emissions. Some fumes are emitted by plastics made from petroleum that are used inside the vehicle. Yet because the majority of the toxins are coming from the outdoor air around the vehicle, the simple act of opening a window to get "fresh air" does not improve the quality of the air you breathe. Unfortunately, there is little that drivers can do to prevent this "in-cabin" pollution; switching vents on or off has no perceivable effects, air conditioning does not act as a significant filter, and rolling a window up or down causes no significant changes.[35]

Does it make a difference if someone does the driving for you? Not according to research from the Imperial College of London released in January 2006 that found that travel by taxi was more than twice as toxic as travel by private automobile. Researchers believe that because taxis spend so much time stuck in traffic, the average passenger is exposed to far more pollution, especially particulates.[36]

"We would encourage people to walk [to reduce exposure,] and the exercise is good for you," said Dr. Richard Russell of the British

Lung Foundation, who noted that patients who traveled to his clinic by taxi showed higher levels of carbon monoxide and other petroleum air pollutants in their blood samples than those who arrived by other means of transport.[37]

As we grow from children to adults, we face more than the struggle for breath caused by asthma or other respiratory diseases. Our inescapable lifetime exposure to secondhand petroleum smoke may now add up to life-threatening or life-shortening illnesses.

"Of particular concern is human epidemiological evidence linking diesel exhaust to an increased risk of lung cancer," says the USEPA.[38] Of all the threats from petroleum products and their use, diesel exhaust may be the most deadly.

In a comprehensive 1998 report on the health effects of diesel exhaust, the Natural Resources Defense Council (NRDC) explained that diesel exhaust contains hundreds of constituent chemicals, dozens of which are recognized human toxicants, carcinogens, reproductive hazards, or endocrine disruptors. NRDC's research also noted that diesel engines spew out a hundred times more sooty particles than do gasoline engines.[39] These particles, as small as one-tenth of a micron, are so minuscule that they bypass the lung tissue and bloodstream, attacking the very cellular structure of the body and causing a wide variety of additional illnesses, from tissue inflammation to cancer.[40]

As many as 8,800 people die each year in Southern California's South Coast air basin as a result of exposure to this type of particulate air pollution, about four times the number of people killed in automobile accidents each year in the same region.[41] The news is no better in other parts of the United States. Diesel exhaust alone is responsible for causing more than 125,000 cancer cases in the United States each year, and up to 100,000 Americans will die each year from causes attributable to completely preventable smog.[42] Nor, as the evidence shows, is particulate matter the sole cause of cancer from petroleum air pollution.

"Across the state, cancer risk is driven greatly by benzene, and a large source of benzene emissions is automobiles," said Paul Dubenetzky, assistant commissioner for the Indiana Department of Environmental Management's Office of Air Quality, speaking in 2006 after the USEPA revealed that more than 25 percent of the cancer risk in northeast Indiana comes from benzene. The report also noted that the largest contributor of benzene to air pollution is vehicle exhaust, yet USEPA's new proposal to slash those emissions will not be fully implemented until 2030.[43]

Secondhand petroleum smoke is inescapable when we breathe polluted air, but it insinuates its toxins into our bodies in one more unexpected manner. Plants are excellent "scavengers" of pollutants from the air and soil, especially the volatile toxic by-products from burning petroleum.[44] Because of higher petroleum pollution in urban areas, this linkage becomes especially important for foods that are grown in the backyard gardens of smoggy cities. Some 40 percent of U.S. households grow some of their food in a home garden, and approximately one million customers visit local farmers markets each week, buying food grown close to sources of urban pollution. In many cases, we are thereby eating a variety of the 225 toxic substances found in petroleum products.

## Lord, What Fools These Mortals Be: Petroleum Pollutes More Than Air

In *A Midsummer Night's Dream*, Shakespeare's sprite Puck finds human behavior quite foolish and hard to understand. When you consider the many things in our lives that are harmed by petroleum pollution, you may agree.

"Already Independence Hall in Philadelphia, where the Declaration of Independence was signed, is experiencing damage [from air pollution]," explains a 1990 report by the World Watch Institute. "At the Gettysburg Civil War battlefield, every statue or tablet made of bronze, limestone, or sandstone is being slowly, but inexorably, eaten away. Both the Statue of Liberty, made of copper, and the Washington Monument, a granite obelisk faced with marble, are also threatened."[45]

Natural monuments are also affected by air pollution. As a recall of the governor set California politics on fire in October 2003, literal firestorms raced through Southern California, essentially out of control until early rains mercifully gave weary firefighters a reprieve. Why were these fires so epic in scope and so far beyond human control compared with those of previous decades? In a word, ozone, from vehicle exhaust.

Ozone damage to pine trees in the national forests of the San Bernardino Mountains of Southern California has been well understood since at least 1950.[46] Plants use carbohydrates for growth, for maintenance, and for their immune systems. Ozone reduces a plant's ability to produce carbohydrates and triggers its consumption of the carbohydrates it has stored to repair damage caused by that same ozone in the first place. Over a period of years, carbohydrate levels are gradually depleted to the point at which little is available for dealing with exceptional stresses such as drought and insect infestations. This ozone damage then accelerates needle drop in pine trees, triggering a kind of premature aging and causing trees to shed larger amounts of needles than normal.

This sequence of events not only weakened the San Bernardino trees, it also contributed to higher fuel loads on the ground. Bark beetles finished off the vulnerable trees, turning them into standing matchsticks. With this fuel already on the ground, once the fires started, they were virtually impossible to put out. Lives were lost and hundreds of homes were incinerated as entire communities in the foothills and mountains turned to ashes.

If we mortals are fools, as Puck would have us believe, then perhaps the most inexplicable behavior of all is that we know the harms of petroleum pollution, yet we allow the problem to continue, in many regions worse than ever before. Why?

One reason is that science has been slow to reach human health conclusions about smog exposure because some cancers and other diseases are slow to develop and therefore take many years to study for conclusive results. For example, recently published results showing that deaths related to petroleum air pollution may be as much as two times higher than previously thought were based on a study that began more than twenty years earlier, in 1982.[47] Another reason for the lack of effective regulations is that our understanding of the health harms from air pollution is a moving target.

"We [now] know there are serious health effects from low levels of air pollution," says Aaron Cohen of the Health Effects Institute, a joint project of the USEPA and various polluting industries.[48] Cohen was speaking of the steady drumbeat of new studies showing that even tiny amounts of some pollutants, previously assumed to be benign, can cause significant health harms, especially in children, the elderly, and those living in areas with disproportionately high rates of pollution. For example, we have not set stringent standards for manganese in gasoline because it was thought to be relatively harmless. Studies in recent years, however, have discovered that manganese in gasoline may affect the brain, lungs, and testes and can result in a severe degenerative condition similar to Parkinson's disease.[49] Once such problems are diagnosed, regulators struggle to catch up.

The last few residents of Rapa Nui must also have struggled vainly to catch up and trap the last rat or bird for food and to find a way to maintain their lives in what remained of a paradise lost. Their experience warns us that civilizations can falter when people fail to heed the evidence of their effect on the environment that sustains their existence. Those ill-fated islanders might have changed their fate by reallocating crucial resources, but as we have known for decades, the assault of petroleum on our health, at every age of our lives, is inescapable.

Or is it? Where are we most at risk of inhaling or ingesting petroleum toxins? Is there any way to avoid the worst exposure? Is there any hope of escape?

# CHAPTER 2

# A Losing Proposition

WARNING: CHEMICALS KNOWN TO THE STATE TO CAUSE CANCER, BIRTH DEFECTS, OR OTHER REPRODUCTIVE HARM ARE FOUND IN GASOLINE, CRUDE OIL, AND MANY OTHER PETROLEUM PRODUCTS AND THEIR VAPORS, OR RESULTS FROM THEIR USE.

Thus reads the plain language displayed at every gasoline station in California, thanks to Proposition 65, a citizen referendum that mandates warning people when they are being exposed to cancer-causing pollution. As shown in chapter 1, we are under constant threat from petroleum pollution throughout our lives no matter where we live. We can't escape petroleum pollution because the sources of it are all around us. Proposition 65 warns us at one source of potential exposure, but as we'll see, there are dozens more.

## Bad to the Last Drop: Oil Spills, Leaks, and Blowouts

One way to understand the myriad sources of oil pollution is to follow the journey that a drop of oil takes from the moment it is coaxed from its subterranean resting place until the moment it is combusted. Although much of it will be converted into energy, quite a bit will reach very different destinations, such as our water, our food supply, our air, and ultimately our bodies.

### Drilling Rigs

The journey of that drop of oil, and the pollution that comes with it, begins at the moment it reaches daylight. Remember the 1960s TV show with a character named Jed Clampett and a song with the lyric "up through the ground come a bubblin' crude?" Well, because we have already gobbled up much of the oil that once lay near the surface, oil exploration today must plow ever deeper into the earth, generating vast amounts of toxic pollution in the process.

Drilling rigs on land and at sea generate pollution, both permitted and unpermitted, in accidents and in normal operations. Although the George W. Bush administration continues to press for new offshore oil drilling, the U.S. Department of the Interior estimated as long ago as 1990 that a new oil well in U.S. coastal waters carries with it a one in seven risk of a major spill (in excess of 42,000 gallons of oil). Along the California coast, the same Interior Department study estimated that there is a 99 percent chance of one or more major spills before 2030 from existing offshore oil drilling and transportation activities.[1]

If you ask anyone on the street to name an oil spill, chances are they would say the *Exxon Valdez* oil tanker disaster, a devastating spill of some 11 million gallons into the pristine waters of Alaska's Prince William Sound. The world's largest oil spill to date, however, came not from a tanker but from oil wells that spilled 240 million gallons of oil into the waters of the Persian Gulf near Kuwait in 1991. The second-largest spill was another drilling rig, the Ixtoc 1 oil well off the coast of Mexico in 1979, which released 140 million gallons of oil into the Gulf of Mexico.[2] For comparison, the footprint of the *Exxon Valdez* oil spill covered so much area that had it taken place farther south, it would have covered every inch of beach between Oregon and Mexico. The Kuwait spill involved twenty times that much oil, and the Ixtoc 1 spill was more than ten times that amount of oil.

California's offshore oil drilling rigs have been the source of 123 major blowouts (uncontrolled discharges of oil under pressure) since the 1960s, including the 1969 blowout of a Union Oil (now Unocal) rig in the coastal waters of Santa Barbara.[3] The Santa Barbara blowout released nearly 3 million gallons of oil, much of which polluted local beaches and wildlife. It also caused toxic air pollution for residents and workers.[4] That spill, along with infamous pollution incidents elsewhere in the United States around the same time, such as the burning of the polluted waters of the Cuyahoga River in Ohio, is credited with creation of the modern environmental movement. One year later, in 1970, the first Earth Day was celebrated.

Although not all spills are so dramatic, smaller spills add up, too. Oil drilling operations in California reported 38,069 spills for a total of 3,113,880 gallons of accidental discharges in one three-year period alone.[5] Nor does it take a lot to have a significant effect. The single drop of oil whose journey we are tracing can change the taste of up to 14 gallons of water, and just 1 quart of oil can create a mile-long slick on water.[6]

As drilling rigs age, their support network of tanks and pipes begin to leak, creating more toxic pollution. At Guadalupe, California, for example, more than 9 million gallons of oil and toxic solvents leaked over a forty-year period beginning in the 1950s from 158 miles of pipe serving more than 200 offshore oil wells at a Unocal facility, polluting groundwater, surface water, wildlife, land, and air.[7]

Offshore oil drilling also contributes an extremely large amount of heavy-metal toxins to ocean waters and the seafloor. A single exploratory well dumps approximately 25,000 pounds of toxic metals into the ocean from drilling "muds," thick lubricants used to pressure debris out of the well and to cool the path of the drill bit as it rotates.[8] The USEPA and the oil industry agree that more than 1 billion tons of these toxic-laden drilling muds are discharged from offshore drilling operations annually, and they are entirely unregulated.[9] Mercury, cadmium, lead, hexavalent chromium, and barium are common toxics found in muds.[10]

By itself, mercury is known to cause reproductive harms and learning impairment. It is found in increasing concentrations in fish that are routinely eaten by both humans and marine animals. Because small doses build up over time and are stored in the body (bioaccumulation), mercury is one of the more dangerous constituents of drilling muds. In the Santa Barbara Channel, waters that are home to migrating gray whales and hundreds of other species of fish and marine mammals, oil rigs discharge nearly 3 million barrels of drilling fluids and cuttings, including 985 pounds of mercury, every single year.[11] That's the equivalent of 893,520 medical thermometers' worth of mercury discharged annually into the marine environment.

No state or federal agency monitors the effects of this toxic dumping, but analysis of debris mounds in the channel near platforms abandoned by Chevron found mercury, arsenic, PCBs, and a host of other harmful pollutants. The sediment was so toxic that a sample tested on shrimp killed 50 percent of them.[12] Drilling also brings to the surface naturally occurring radioactive materials that can cause cancers and birth defects in fish and humans, even at low levels.[13]

It is important to understand the potential dangers from drilling muds because many new oil discoveries are at great depths, meaning that larger volumes of these contaminated muds will be used and the toxins from them will end up on the ocean floor. In March 2006, for example, President Vicente Fox of Mexico proudly announced that his country's state-run oil company had found a significant deposit in the Gulf of Mexico, under 3,117 feet of water and 13,120 feet of earth, or about 3 miles below the surface.[14]

Finally, drilling rigs onshore and offshore dump tons of nitrogen oxide, carbon monoxide, and sulfur dioxide into the air through the on-site burning of vented gases and waste products. They also add 35 million tons of carbon dioxide and 12 million tons of methane (two primary greenhouse gases) into the atmosphere worldwide every year, along with smoke and soot that cover land and water, contributing to the rising acidity of rainfall.[15]

In California's Santa Barbara County alone, oil rigs also emit more than 2.5 million pounds of sulfur oxide into the air each year, twelve times as much as is released by all the cars in the entire county.[16] Sulfur oxide shortens breath, aggravates asthma, and causes headaches and the burning sensation in your eyes associated with smog. Even abandoned onshore well sites may generate toxic air pollution for decades. In one Southern California example, hundreds of square miles of land were polluted with dangerous hydrogen sulfide fumes from an inactive well, forcing the evacuation of entire neighborhoods.[17]

### Oil Tankers

The *Exxon Valdez* might leap to mind when we think of transporting our drop of oil on its journey from the well to the refinery, but barges, pipelines, tanker trucks, and a host of other conveyances without lofty names on their sterns are also employed to move oil around the planet and into a vehicle near you. Many of them leak.

Much of the world's oil does move to refineries via enormous seagoing tanker vessels. The *Exxon Valdez* measured 300 meters long by more than 50 meters wide and 27 meters deep. That's the size of about three football stadiums welded together with an engine and a rudder. The world's largest oil tanker today measures half again as much. Tankers are some of the least maneuverable vessels at sea, making them especially susceptible to groundings and collisions. Oil tanker disasters have caused eleven of the seventeen largest oil spills in world history, for a total of 648,600,000 gallons, enough oil to produce a slick on the ocean's surface of more than 8.1 million square miles, or more than ten times the size of Alaska.[18]

"Oil was everywhere, and every single day, I would get covered with it," said Randy Lowe, a commercial fisherman from Soldotna, Alaska, who was one of thousands hired to clean up Prince William Sound after the *Exxon Valdez* oil spill in 1989. "When I got done loading a boom, there'd be a foot of oil in the bottom of my boat, and I'd just shovel it out. You'd drink sodas that had oil on it, you'd smoke a cigarette, it had oil on it, if you ate a sandwich, it had oil on it."[19] Hygiene at lunchtime, however, was the least of Lowe's problems.

"When I went out there, I was totally, 100 percent healthy," Lowe continued. "Between 1990 and '97 I've been in the hospital fifty-eight times. I've had pancreatitis, liver problems, spleen problems. I had a pancreas attack in '97, I went into septic shock and finally my body shut down. I was in a coma for fifty-two days, and after that I had to learn all over again how to walk, read and talk. I'm only forty-one years old. I shouldn't be in the shape I'm in."

Lowe's experience was not uncommon among the *Exxon Valdez* oil spill cleanup workers, nor has illness among oil spill workers been limited to Alaska. According to Harvard researcher Paul R. Epstein, cleanup workers have reported similar health problems at every large-scale oil spill (spills of more than 10 million gallons) that has occurred worldwide since the 1960s, the vast majority of which were from oil tankers.[20]

These large spills occur against a backdrop of numerous small spills that, combined, also contribute to environmental damage. In these smaller spill incidents, all seagoing types of petroleum product carriers between 1984 and 1990 spilled an average of 6 million gallons each year, for a total of 96 million gallons over that sixteen-year period.[21] In the sixteen years that followed, more than a billion gallons more were spilled worldwide.[22]

Is keeping the oil genie in the bottle simply impossible? The Geneva Protocol of 1991 acknowledges that the oil industry could equip each method of oil transportation with technologies that would reduce emissions and leaks by 80 percent, noting that doing so would generate significant financial savings that could cover the costs. Yet the oil industry has never been known for long-term thinking.

"Over a five-year period we are going to spend $6 billion picking up oil. I doubt we've spent even $100 million dollars on prevention," admitted Jerry Aspland, the former president of Arco Marine.[23] The result? The U.S. Minerals Management Service calculated that there is a 94 percent likelihood of an *Exxon Valdez*–type spill along the West Coast of the United States by 2020.[24]

The only oil tankers that are now allowed to call on Prince William Sound are those with double-lined hulls, designed to reduce the potential for a spill if punctured by ice or other obstacles. Exxon has petitioned the federal government for permission for one particular single-hulled oil tanker to continue moving oil out of Valdez, Alaska. That ship is the recently refurbished *SeaRiver Mediterranean*. Before it was repaired, it bore the name *Exxon Valdez*.[25]

### Oil Pipelines

Chances are that our drop of oil began its existence in a country other than the United States because 60 percent of the 21 million barrels of oil we consume in the United States each day are imported. Once that drop of crude reaches U.S. shores, it will be transported by an extensive network of pipelines from which it may well escape. From 1990 to 2002, pipeline leaks reported in the United States accounted for an average of 5,274,008 gallons of spilled petroleum products *each year*.[26] Spills from pipelines across every state in the country are blamed on structural damage, equipment failures, and operator errors. Here are just a few examples, along with some of the more serious consequences:

- The U.S. government sued oil pipeline operators in Seattle, Washington, for gross negligence related to the release of 229,000 gallons of petroleum in 1999, which killed a fisherman and two ten-year-old boys, burned 29 acres, and polluted a city creek and a park.[27]

- Near Lake Superior, on January 29, 2003, equipment failure caused a pipeline to release more than 100,000 gallons of oil, much of which spilled into an adjacent river.[28]

- More than 950,000 gallons of diesel fuel spilled into South Carolina's Reedy River in 1996, killing more than 35,000 fish and other wildlife as it dispersed over 34 miles downstream.[29]

- In the largest settlement in USEPA history, Colonial Pipeline Company was found responsible in 2003 for violating the Clean Water Act seven times and spilling 1,450,000 gallons of oil over a period of several years across five states. Colonial blamed pipeline corrosion, mechanical damage, and operator error.[30]

The safe life span of the average oil pipeline is only about fifteen years, but most pipelines are much older, left in place until the cost of repairing leaks exceeds the cost of replacing the pipe.[31] Pipelines, however, are not always trustworthy even within their service life span. For instance, BP's Northstar Oil Field in the Arctic Ocean is served by a subsea pipeline, and the U.S. Army Corps of Engineers estimates a one-in-four chance of significant spills from this brand-new, state-of-the-art pipeline during its service life.[32]

Nor does it take much of a failure in a pipeline to create a major oil spill and impose significant damage on natural resources. In 2001, a bullet hole in the Trans Alaska oil pipeline resulted in a spill of nearly 300,000 gallons. In March 2006, a 34-inch-diameter oil pipeline operated by BP in Alaska sprang a leak from a $^1/_4$-inch hole. Within days, another 300,000 gallons spilled across the wilderness in a region where caribou traditionally traverse the landscape.[33]

Not surprisingly, third world countries are also severely affected by leaking oil pipelines. Both Nigeria's impoverished delta region and the Amazon rainforest of Ecuador suffer from high levels of water pollution caused by thousands of miles of leaking oil pipelines and from damage to once-pristine ecological settings carved up by pipeline service roads. Streams fill with petroleum scum, and in many areas the rain falls black and reeking of oil. Drinking, bathing, and fishing waters routinely exceed by up to a thousand times the USEPA health standard for oil contamination.[34] Along pipelines snaking up the slopes of the Andes, landslides often tear down the mountains, rupturing the steel casing and sending oil gushing in toxic black waves. The Trans-Ecuadorian pipeline alone has suffered more than sixty major ruptures since 1972, spilling 25,788,000 gallons of oil.[35]

Upstream from the Ecuadorian port of Esmeraldas a 1998 landslide broke two major pipelines, sending oil and gas cascading down streets and into rivers. A spark set off an inferno, which devoured cars and homes. People were burned alive; frantic parents put their children in wooden canoes and pushed them into the Esmeraldas River and then watched in horror as fire engulfed the river and the children. Locals now say petroleum is the "excrement of the devil."[36]

The majority of the oil produced in Ecuador is exported to refineries in Los Angeles and San Francisco. Between 1996 and 2002, California ports received 98 million barrels of Ecuadorian oil.[37]

### Refineries
Regardless of its country of origin, our drop of oil must now run the gauntlet of pipes, heaters, pressure cookers, and tanks known as the oil refinery. There are nearly two hundred refineries in the

United States, twenty-one of which are in California.[38] Refineries pollute both air and water, but also discharge toxic wastes, thermal pollution (essentially cooking the water of shallow bays and estuaries where they discharge treated wastewater), and spent catalysts.

Although some pollution discharge from refineries is permitted under the federal Clean Air Act, studies show that legal limits are routinely exceeded. Oil refineries are the largest stationary source of VOCs (the noxious fumes from evaporating petroleum components laden with carcinogenic compounds such as benzene and toluene) in the United States.[39] Illegal discharges of these toxins from refineries are called "fugitive emissions" as if they are somehow beyond the control of facility operators. These fugitives escape regularly from leaky valves and tanks and blow into adjacent neighborhoods, most of which house people of color and low income.[40] As a result, areas surrounding refineries commonly acquire nicknames such as "Cancer Belt" (Northern California's Contra Costa County) and "Cancer Alley" (from Baton Rouge to New Orleans in Louisiana). In Contra Costa County alone, for example, residents are exposed to 60 tons of benzene, 30 tons of formaldehyde, and smaller amounts of other carcinogens each year from the six major refineries in the area.[41]

Even residents who think they live far enough from refineries may need to think again. In 1995, the USEPA's Regulatory Impact Assessment for Petroleum Refineries report concluded that millions of people living within 30 miles of oil refineries around the United States are exposed to benzene concentrations in excess of the Clean Air Act's acceptable risk threshold.[42] The California Air Resources Board confirmed USEPA's concerns, reporting in 2005 that refineries in California are the leading stationary source of toxic pollution from nitrogen oxides ($NO_x$), oxides of sulfur ($SO_x$) and particulate matter (PM 10 and PM 2.5).[43] Industry officials admit that $SO_x$ can cause respiratory problems and routinely warn residents around refineries of unusual SO$_x$ discharges via sirens or automated phone systems, although often too late to be effective.[44]

One congressional study notes that controlling this illegal pollution could be accomplished at minimal cost and that doing so would be the equivalent of removing five million automobiles from the road.[45] Oil companies, however, know that paying fines is cheaper than compliance:

- At the Powerine Refinery in southeast Los Angeles County, more than 400,000 tons of pollutants, such as NO$_x$, SO$_x$, PM, and VOCs, were dumped into the air in excess of permitted levels each year for decades. Powerine received thirty-eight notices of violation, and three officials were personally fined, before operations there ceased in 1995.[46]

- At the Belridge oil field, the California Shell Company paid the USEPA $337,703 to settle charges that it violated limits for venting volatile VOCs for five years.[47]

- At the Unocal Catacarb refinery near Crockett, California, a hole in a major process vessel was allowed to get larger and larger, from August to September 1994, while operations continued and toxic material blew over the nearby town and refinery workers for sixteen days. Approximately fifteen hundred people were sickened by the 125 tons of caustic catalyst. Owners of the refinery paid $80 million in compensation to victims and $3 million in fines, a fraction of the potential lost income had the facility closed for repairs.[48]

- At the Shell Refinery in Norco, Louisiana, twelve major accidents between 1994 and 1999, six in 1997 alone, released 1,316,556 pounds of toxic air pollutants, primarily sulfur dioxide. Shell was fined less than $15,000 by state regulators for the leaks.[49]

Not one of these violations, or thousands more like them, resulted in fines that would have been as costly as compliance. Refineries also routinely spill and dump pollution illegally into coastal waters, as illustrated by these examples:[50]

- Shell, Unocal, and Exxon refineries have polluted San Francisco Bay with toxic levels of selenium, causing the USEPA to label it a "toxic hot spot" and warn consumers against eating fish caught from the bay. This toxic legacy will remain in the bay for decades.[51]

- The ConocoPhillips refinery in Linden, New Jersey, spilled about 1,500 barrels of oil and refinery waste into the Rahway River in December 2005 because of a single leaky valve.[52]

- The dubious honor of "largest underground petroleum spill in world history" goes to the Chevron Refinery at El Segundo, California, which illegally discharged more than 250 million gallons of oil products into groundwater aquifers over several decades, creating a plume of petroleum nearly 20 feet thick. At the current pace of its cleanup plan, Chevron's petroleum pollution will be removed from that groundwater in about a hundred years.

Data from the American Petroleum Institute, a Washington, D.C., lobbying group for the oil industry, reported in 1994 that 85 percent of all member refineries in the United States pollute groundwater in their regions.[53] Many cities pump drinking water from these subterranean aquifers.

### Oil Tanker Trucks
If our drop of oil made it through the refinery without being boiled into the air or spilled into groundwater, it has now been broken down into one of many components. That one drop is now many droplets of gasoline, diesel, naphtha, kerosene, heating oil, lubricating oil, heavy fuel oil, petroleum coke, asphalt, tar, and waxes.

Once refined, these petroleum products are transported not only by tanker ships and pipelines, but also in tanker trucks. Nearly every gasoline station in the United States is supplied by tanker trucks, resulting in millions of such trips annually and innumerable accidents, which spill petroleum products on roadways and pollute air, water, and land. For example, in a six-month period ending in 2000, just three tanker truck accidents on California roads spilled 12,850 gallons of petroleum products into waterways.[54]

These trucks spill more than liquid pollution. They operate on toxic diesel fuel and belch millions of tons of hazardous particulate matter and toxic chemicals into the air each year. To put that in perspective, the average diesel truck emits three times more soot and smog-forming pollutants than a coal-fired power plant for every comparable unit of energy burned.[55]

### LASTs, LUSTs, and RGOs

Thanks to those tanker trucks, our droplets of oil products make their way into storage tanks beneath that ubiquitous icon of the twentieth century, the gas station. Retail gasoline outlets (RGOs) have become such fixtures of our modern landscape, not unlike the moai on Rapa Nui, although when rain washes over the stoic stone visages on a Pacific island, toxic waste doesn't flush into drinking water supplies.

Although the mere act of dispensing fuel at a gas station generates toxic air pollution, most of the toxic story of these facilities is played out beneath the surface. According to data from the USEPA, as long ago as 1992, roughly 25 percent of gas station tanks have leaked their contents into the environment, and according to the American Petroleum Institute, leaking aboveground and leaking underground storage tanks (LASTs and LUSTs, respectively) are responsible for ground or water pollution at a minimum of 35 percent of their members' marketing facilities (distribution centers for refined petroleum products) and 27 percent of transport facilities.[56] These numbers are almost certainly underestimates because not all facilities with petroleum storage tanks—some 1.7 million of them—actually monitor for groundwater contamination. Leaks from LASTs and LUSTs are especially hazardous because, depending on the blend, gasoline contains up to 225 toxic chemicals, some of which are carcinogenic and water soluble, making them particularly difficult to filter from contaminated drinking water supplies.[57]

Ironically, one of those chemicals, MTBE, a suspected cause of leukemia in humans, was added to gasoline to help reduce air pollution. MTBE has already contaminated drinking water supplies in hundreds of communities nationwide. In the most egregious cases, unsuspecting residents were poisoned for years before corrective action was taken because many municipalities did not test for the presence of the chemical in drinking water despite knowledge that storage tanks routinely leak.[58] In my hometown of Santa Monica, California (a city of about 100,000 people), by the time MTBE was discovered in the city's drinking water wells, 70 percent of the supply had been poisoned.

### Combustion

If the progeny of our drop of oil has made it from a LAST or LUST and into a vehicle, it now poses its greatest threat to all creatures that breathe. If oil is the lifeblood of the economy, engine exhaust is its breath, and here the Faustian bargain for our health is most apparent.

The federal Clean Air Act identifies the combustion of automotive fuels as the major source of hazardous air pollutants in the United States, causing or contributing to a wide array of human illnesses, from difficulty breathing and asthma to brain damage and damage to the fetus.[59] Perhaps the greatest threat from our oil addiction, however, is cancer. Of the 225 toxic or carcinogenic chemicals contained in gasoline, three of them—benzene, 1,3-butadiene, and formaldehyde—in the form airborne pollutants, pose the greatest cancer risk to humans. The largest source of these toxins is auto exhaust, and all three chemicals are emitted in excess of federal Clean Air Act health standards.[60]

The U.S. oil and auto industries also produce more greenhouse gases than most other countries produce from all their industries combined, and the source of about half of these gases is vehicles, principally passenger cars.[61] Combining all emissions from every step on the journey of our drop of oil, the U.S. Department of Energy estimates that approximately 25 pounds of greenhouse gases are emitted for every gallon of petroleum fuel consumed. Driving petroleum-powered vehicles in the United States accounts for 20 billion tons of those gases per day.[62] Overall, direct vehicle emissions worldwide are responsible for up to:[63]

- 85 percent of all benzene pollution;
- 80 percent of all CO emissions;
- 60 percent of all $NO_x$ emissions;
- 50 percent of all greenhouse gas emissions; and
- 14 percent of all global particulates.

Ozone is also produced by vehicle exhaust when sunlight reacts with some of these pollutants. As described earlier in chapter 1, ground-level ozone causes both temporary and long-term lung damage, but we now also know that these effects occur as far as 6,000 meters (about sixty football fields) from the source. Remember also that ozone and $SO_x$ directly harm trees, plants, and farm crops by reducing yields and by increasing both dollar and energy costs to replace that lost production elsewhere.[64]

Gasoline engines produce even greater emissions when running cold. Cold vehicle starts account for more than 90 percent of a vehicle's hydrocarbon and carbon monoxide emissions on short trips, mostly because of the inability of cold catalytic converters to work properly.[65]

Finally, automobile and truck emissions are as high as they are because most of today's vehicles are just plain inefficient. Despite more than a century of engineering, the energy produced by 80 percent of the fuel in the average automobile is lost to heat, exhaust, and pollution by-products, and 95 percent of the remaining useful energy output is used to move an unnecessarily heavy vehicle. Only 5 percent actually moves the passenger.[66] One reason for this astounding inefficiency is the significant loss of gasoline to evaporation, which results in more air pollution, whether the engine is operating or not.[67] According to scientists at California's Air Resources Board, vapor leaks from vehicles, running or not, account for 14 tons per day of VOC pollution in the state.[68]

Like the pollution generated by gasoline engines, diesel exhaust, as we've seen, contains hundreds of constituent chemicals, dozens of which are known human toxins, among them carcinogens, reproductive hazards, and endocrine disruptors.[69] Diesel engines account for nearly 20 percent of the total $NO_x$ and much of the toxic particulate matter in outdoor air.[70] And gallon for gallon, burning diesel fuel produces forty times the amount of $NO_x$ as burning gasoline.[71]

### Vehicle Leaks and Discharges

If the fuel products from our original drop of oil had actually been combusted, it might claim to have had a productive, if sometimes polluting, existence. But motor vehicles drip, leak, and discharge petroleum, the equivalent of two *Exxon Valdez* oil spills each year (more than 20 million gallons) onto U.S. roadways, much of this pollution washing via storm water into drinking water supplies and natural habitats.[72] Vehicles also leak coolant, used motor oil, and heavy metals. The United States alone generates 1.3 billion gallons each year of used motor oil, of which less than 60 percent is recycled or otherwise reused. The remainder is dumped illegally into landfills or storm drains. Crankcase oil accounts for more than 40 percent of the total oil pollution in U.S. waterways. This used motor oil is especially harmful to human and animal health if it enters drinking water because it contains heavy metals such as lead, zinc, and cadmium from inside the engine as well as other toxic compounds that are the result of subjecting oil to high temperature.[73]

Another roadside toxic waste generated by vehicles is, ironically, a by-product of an effort to protect the environment. Heavy metals, including platinum, palladium, and rhodium, have built up in soils along roadways from reactions inside catalytic converters, devices that were designed to remove some toxins from vehicle exhaust.[74]

### Big Engines and Little Motors

Thus far we have focused mainly on cars, trucks, and buses that are common to any modern landscape. Their inability to perform their function without inflicting so many harmful side effects might reasonably categorize them as defective. Airplanes, ships, trains, construction equipment, and farm equipment are arguably even more defective, however, because their air pollution discharges remain essentially unregulated and they have therefore been allowed to pollute more than their regulated counterparts (per unit of energy output). Heavy equipment uses vast amounts of petroleum products and often emits much greater volumes of toxins than comparable passenger vehicles or trucks.

For example, airplane fuel contains four times more lead than the gasoline once used by automobiles, despite the less toxic alternative, AGE85, made up of 85 percent ethanol.[75] In this case, the Federal Aviation Administration has bowed to pressure from airline companies that claim engine modifications to use the fuel are too costly.[76]

Ship engines that operate on "bunker fuel"—a toxic mix of petroleum products, including used motor oil—are also far more toxic, horsepower for horsepower, than cars and trucks. The exact

nature of harms emanating from such engines is difficult to quantify because they are completely unregulated and therefore not
widely studied. One estimate puts discharges from vessels at 78 million gallons of petroleum pollution annually worldwide, but the
amount is likely much greater due to the difficulty in measuring this
type of pollution.[77]

Perhaps the most defective of all products that use petroleum
fuels are two-stroke engines, including many boats, recreational
vehicles, personal watercraft, lawn mowers, and small generators.
These super-polluters generate more than 1.1 billion pounds of
hydrocarbon emissions each year, using designs that are essentially
unchanged since the 1940s. Fully 25 percent of the fuel and oil used
in these engines is emitted directly to air and water completely
unburned.[78] Each year, two-stroke boat engines alone dump fifteen
times more oil on U.S. waterways than did the *Exxon Valdez* oil spill.
And according to the California Air Resources Board, the pollution
generated by a two-stroke engine-powered personal watercraft in a
seven-hour period is the equivalent of driving an average automobile for 100,000 miles.[79]

Two-stroke motors are also found on a majority of snowmobiles. Since 1992, well over two million new snowmobiles have been
sold in the United States.[80] So many snowmobiles—an average of
seventy thousand—pass through Yellowstone National Park every
year that repeated efforts have been made to restrict or prohibit
them from the park.[81] Since two-stoke engines can be fitted with
pollution control devices and since there are cleaner four-stroke
alternatives, why not simply mandate one of those solutions?

In a word, the answer is politics. In November 2003 Arnold
Schwarzenegger had been in the California governor's office for less
than twenty-four hours when we got word that Congress was trying to dismantle the state's right to regulate these unbridled sources
of air pollution. Because of having passed its own Clean Air Act
prior to the federal version, California has unique rights under the

federal Clean Air Act, so if California passes a clean air rule, other states can copy it, thus creating de facto national standards. Many pro-oil lobbyists and legislators in Washington have tried to undermine this unique regulatory authority for years.

Missouri Senator Christopher "Kit" Bond authored an amendment to a spending bill that was making its way through Congress in November 2003, just as we in the Schwarzenegger administration were warming our new Sacramento seats. The amendment would strip California of the right to require that two-stroke engines of less than 175 horsepower add catalytic converters to reduce pollution. Not only would the change add 25 tons of pollutants to state skies every day, it would also be the first real abridgement of California's unique regulatory rights and the beginning of a slippery slope toward ending them.

Bond argued that his state would lose a Briggs & Stratton engine factory to China if the pollution control requirement went into effect. He also trotted out the tired, old automaker arguments, used in the fight over catalytic converters for cars, that the requirement was unaffordable, technically infeasible, and unsafe. During several days of debate in various committees, he refused to acknowledge that both Coleman and Honda were already building and marketing these cleaner two-stoke engines in the United States.

Schwarzenegger worked the phones relentlessly for a week, often late into the night, persuading Republicans and Democrats alike that the Bond amendment would be bad for air quality in every state. As secretary of the California Environmental Protection Agency, I was working the phones too, sometimes calling on unusual allies. One such call was to Joe Sparano, president of the Western States Petroleum Association (WSPA). I told him that if California couldn't reduce emissions from small, polluting two-stroke engines but still had to attain federal air quality standards by 2010, additional reductions would have to come from refineries and other sources already being regulated, and these sources were represented by WSPA. Fearing that additional burden on his members, Sparano helped us oppose the Bond amendment.

The amendment was defeated, but it remains a good example of petroleum-powered politics on behalf of defective products. What could be more defective than an engine that spews out more than a quarter of its fuel and oil unburned? And the politics? Briggs & Stratton was a major contributor to Senator Bond's 2002 fundraising campaign.

Why should California fight Missouri over lawn mower engines? Why does it matter to know all the ways we are exposed to petroleum pollution and all the associated health risks? It matters because each day brings new discoveries about how and where we are exposed to petroleum pollution. We are also learning that even tiny amounts of these toxins, including exposures once thought safe, are threatening our health in ways both subtle and profound.

## Living Downwind:
## Why Regulations Alone Can't Protect Us

"The broad public needs to be banged on the head and know that the air you breathe will kill you," declared Constantinos Sioutas, a professor of engineering at the University of Southern California, who has been part of a team studying the effects on human health of simply commuting on the freeway every day.[82]

"It appears that someone driving [40 miles] . . . is getting an enormous exposure to ultra-fine particles," according to John Froines, professor of environmental health at UCLA and head of a research team examining these unavoidable exposures.[83] Froines was one of the Chicago Seven that tried to set off riots at the 1968 Democratic Convention in Chicago. He was the movement's scientist even then, mixing stink bombs and other devices to disrupt the proceedings.

In the ensuing four decades, Froines has devoted his considerable skills to uncovering the profound effects of what happens to our drop of oil after it goes up in smoke. His team found that ultra-fine particles, from petroleum fuel combustion, are at the highest concentrations within 300 feet of freeways and that commuters who spend an hour a day commuting are literally taking years off of their lives.[84] As noted in chapter 1, these particles are so fine that they bypass vehicle air filtration systems and the natural defense mechanisms of the lungs, penetrating right into the bloodstream and ultimately destroying individual human cells.[85]

"This is really important," continued Froines, his hair somewhat grayer than in his rabble-rousing days, but he was still fit and impish. "It has implications for lung cancer, implications for respiratory disease and implications especially for cardiovascular disease." Such discoveries make it difficult for government regulators to agree on pollution controls and standards that will genuinely protect public health because the goal post seems to move farther away with each new discovery and because not everyone's exposure is equal.

Other researchers tell us that people who live near congested freeways are at least twice as likely to develop cancer from breathing vehicle pollution than those who live next to factories.[86] Under current regulations, industrial smokestacks cannot emit pollutants that create a cancer risk greater than twenty-five in one million. Yet those who live near the freeway face a risk up to sixty times greater from inhaling the diesel, benzene, and other toxins found in the vehicle exhaust in their neighborhoods.

"In popular imagination, the smokestack factory, the industrial plant has always been seen as the most toxic threat," said spokesman Sam Atwood of the South Coast Air Quality Management District, the regional air pollution regulatory authority in Southern California. "People don't look at freeways as thousands of tiny smokestacks."[87]

Other researchers put monitoring devices on the clothing of dozens of volunteers to compare the actual exposure to airborne toxins against the levels reported by centralized air-monitoring devices. "Ambient measurements at central sites aren't good predictors of [personal] exposure," says John Adgate of the University of Minnesota in Minneapolis. "Actual exposures are higher."[88] These researchers found, for example, that levels of exposure to the carcinogen benzene measured by the devices on the volunteers' clothing were two and a half times greater than found at the central monitoring stations. The result is a two and a half times greater risk of cancer from this poison.

In 1997, the USEPA established the current standards for reducing particle pollution, estimating that those rules will prevent 15,000 premature deaths, 350,000 cases of asthma, and 1 million cases of lung problems in children by the year 2020. Yet how many more will suffer and die because even those estimates were built on shifting scientific sands? Once regulators learn more about a particular pollutant and its effects on human health, how long does it take to impose new regulations that actually protect us?

## Take a Deep Breath:
## Regulation of Toxins by the Numbers

In 1946, regulators established exposure limits for benzene, one of the most toxic constituents of gasoline fumes, at 100 parts per million (ppm) based on its effects on the central nervous system, including drowsiness, loss of coordination, and even unconsciousness.[89] The postwar boom, though, put more people in cars and more workers in the path of benzene fumes. Remember the days when you didn't pump your own gas, but you could "trust your car to the man who wears the star" in the Texaco commercials? Experience with benzene forced changes to the exposure limit, and by 1956, it was reduced by two-thirds, to just 35 ppm.

Although researchers learned more about the effects of this common pollutant, our understanding of the human body kept getting better too. By 1976, the limit was lowered to 25 ppm based on observed effects to hemoglobin in the bloodstream. Within the next two decades, as scientists learned more about the causes of cancer, benzene was feared to be a carcinogen and the exposure limit lowered again to 10 ppm. Today, we know for a fact that benzene exposure causes cancers of the lung and other organs, so the exposure limit has been lowered to 0.5 ppm, two hundred times lower than was thought safe just three generations ago. It was at a lecture given by an occupational health specialist who works for a federal agency that I first heard this history of benzene regulation.

"Isn't the lesson here that the only safe level of exposure is zero?" I asked. "Every time we set an exposure limit, regulators must have been certain they knew all they had to, that the limit was truly protective of public health. But each time they were wrong. So doesn't that suggest that new science in coming years is likely to show us we're wrong today?"

"Of course not," the lecturer replied dismissively. "The government wouldn't allow these exposures if they weren't safe."

I was stunned by the failure to see past as prologue. The lead that still pollutes us from airplane fuel is another example of regulatory error over time. In the 1960s, visible signs of lead poisoning occurred at blood levels above 600 parts per billion (ppb), including kidney injury and severe brain damage, yet exposure was unregulated.[90] As more about bioaccumulation of lead, especially in children, was learned, the Centers for Disease Control and Prevention continued to reduce the allowable exposure level, first to 300 ppb in 1975, then to 250 ppb in 1985, and then to the current level of 100 ppb in 1991. In 1976, when lead was first removed from automobile gasoline, the average lead level in children was already at 150 ppb. Today, the average found in our kids is about 30 ppb.

"But that's still 10 to 100 times higher than the level in pre-industrial humans," said Dr. Bruce Lanphear of the Cincinnati Children's Hospital Medical Center, a noted lead researcher. "[That level] is low by current standards, but from an evolutionary perspective, it is quite high."[91] Researchers from the USEPA find that, in addition to learning disabilities caused by lead exposure, even very low levels of lead can delay puberty for several months in young girls, especially African Americans and Latinas. This delay may or may not be harmful, but it means that lead is interfering with critical hormonal processes that may have other as yet undetected effects.

"That fits in with the increased interest in general with the idea that environmental chemicals can be endocrine disruptors," said Dr. David Bellinger of Harvard Medical School. "Lead has not been considered as prominently as other chemicals. This suggests that we ought to be looking at it more closely."[92]

That was the point I was trying to make to the lecturer about benzene: every time we have looked more closely, we have learned more. Our growing understanding of the toxicity of oil is a good case in point, and it took the world's most infamous oil spill to provide us with much of that information.

"Oil is much more toxic to coastal fish, birds, and mammals than short-term laboratory bioassay studies used during the 1970s and 1980s [predicted]," explains Dr. Riki Ott, a former commercial fisher and oil researcher, who lives in Alaska and has dedicated her life to uncovering the truth about both the *Exxon Valdez* spill and the chronic effects of petroleum exposure to wildlife and humans. "Concentrations of PAHs [polycyclic aromatic hydrocarbons] causing functional sterility or other maladies in fish, birds, and marine mammals are astonishingly low—1 to 15 parts per billion—or 1,000 times lower than levels previously thought to cause problems."[93]

Even weathered oil contains some hazardous metals and PAHs, a group of more than a hundred compounds, some of which can cause cancer in humans.[94] Comprehensive field and lab studies conducted from 1994 to 2000 in the wake of the *Exxon Valdez* oil spill reveal that oil pollution persists for decades, chronically exposing humans and animals to significant problems. Researchers were astonished to find that some of the oil they were cleaning up in Prince William Sound was from a spill that occurred in the early 1960s, continuing to create toxic effects some four decades later.

Take a deep breath. You may not detect the petroleum-related toxins from our drop of oil that were carried into your lungs and bloodstream, nor will you know for certain what effects that poison will have on your health and well-being. Another equally substantial cost for our Faustian bargain with petroleum, however, can be more easily quantified: the assault on our financial well-being.

---

CHAPTER 3

# Desperate Enterprise

FAUSTUS. Shall I make spirits fetch me what I please,
Perform what desperate enterprise I will?
I'll have them fly to India for gold,
Ransack the ocean for orient pearl . . .

GOOD ANGEL. Sweet Faustus, think of heaven and heavenly things.

EVIL ANGEL. No, Faustus; think of honour and of wealth.

FAUSTUS. Wealth!

(Enter MEPHISTOPHELES)

FAUSTUS. Mephistopheles, how comes it, then, that thou art out of hell?

MEPHISTOPHELES: Why, this is hell . . . [1]

If you were president of the United States, how would you hope to spend a trillion dollars if it suddenly appeared in the nation's annual budget? Free college for everyone, a colony on Mars, the

53

finest health care for anyone who needs it? Closer to home, what would you do with $2,700 if a check appeared in the mail for that amount made out to each member of your family? As we will see, those figures represent an estimate of the actual cost of financial aid given directly or indirectly to the oil and auto industry by each American every year. And based on those figures, we can calculate the true cost of a gallon of gasoline.

Some things cannot be measured: the cost to a family of losing an elder ten years before her time; the lost hours a child spends in bed with an asthma attack; the learning deficits that plague a person throughout a life, caused largely by preventable exposure to petroleum pollution. But even as these threats undermine the foundation of our physical health, how might our Faustian dependence on oil also undermine the bedrock of our economic well-being?

Californians alone bear health-care costs attributable to petroleum that are between $9 billion and $240 billion every year.[2] Such a wide range exemplifies the challenge of estimating these costs, but even using the lowest figure, we're still talking about saddling the area's economic well-being with a cost of billions of dollars each year in just one state. That figure represents the total direct and indirect costs paid by all sources for health care, public and private. What percentage of that burden does the California's taxpayer shoulder?

Although a review of the scientific literature does not uncover any estimates of the state government's specific share of petroleum-related health-care costs, studies on the health costs owing to smoking show that California's Medicaid programs paid for approximately 20 percent of the smoking-attributable medical expenditures in California, the rest coming from private insurance or individual pocketbooks.[3] Applying this percentage to direct health-care costs related to petroleum pollution in California translates to a range of between almost half a billion dollars to as much as $12 billion for annual state medical payments.[4] As a point of comparison, cigarette smoking costs California an average of $8 billion each year in health-care costs.[5]

Thus far, we have seen evidence of numerous toxins from petroleum pollution that harm our health. Among these, the petroleum-related toxin that most harms our lungs also turns out to be the one that presents the greatest threat to our nationwide economic well-being: particulate matter. That alone accounts for more than 90 percent of the health-care costs attributable to motor vehicle pollution.[6]

As mentioned in chapter 2, the fine soot of particulate matter can penetrate deep into the lungs and aggravate respiratory problems. These specks of soot also act as delivery devices for toxins, carrying chemicals and heavy metals deep into the lungs on what are essentially trillions of tiny carbon sponges. A large proportion of petroleum-related health-care costs are due to respiratory illnesses. Such diseases and illnesses are caused or made worse by airborne particulate matter, which in total is responsible for an estimated 9,300 deaths, 16,000 hospital visits, 600,000 asthma attacks, and 5 million lost work days each year in California.[7] These 9,300 deaths are almost four times more than the number of homicide victims annually and well over six times the number of people who die of AIDS each year in California.[8]

Of course, tailpipes are not solely responsible for petroleum-related illness, death, and financial losses. In California alone, hundreds of thousands of people live in the shadow of refineries, transfer terminals, and other oil-processing facilities, inhaling the toxic stew that discharges from these Dickensian industrial behemoths. As noted in chapter 2, the at-risk population numbers in the millions because the evidence shows that cancer rates are elevated as far as 30 miles downwind from these facilities.[9]

Another place where petroleum imposes financial burdens on unsuspecting victims is on the farm. Ozone-related crop damage totals $150 million a year in California's San Joaquin Valley alone. Ozone damage to food crops means less produce sold to markets and less revenue for the farmer, which translates into less income to the state treasury in the form of taxes that would have been col-

lected on that income. Statewide, the loss of farm income is estimated at $300 million, so assuming an average corporate tax rate of
18 percent, that amounts to another $54 million each year of lost
federal tax revenues just from California.[10]

"Ozone is the major air pollutant in the world, it is the most
widespread and does the most damage," said David Grantz, air quality specialist and director of the University of California's Kearney
Agriculture Center, whose research found that ozone damages the
ability of leaves to transport sugars, a key to plant health and productivity. "Some [plants] are adapting and we're selecting varieties
for ozone resistance. Plants can actually adapt faster than humans."[11]
In my role as a government official, I have participated in tough
state budget decisions, allocating limited revenues among competing priorities. This state-sponsored research makes me wonder how
future generations will judge a society that cuts funding for education, for the arts, and for health benefits for our elders, but spends
money to search for plants that can survive in a polluted environment of our own making.

The bottom line is that the true costs of producing, transporting,
marketing, and using petroleum products are not fully borne by the
oil or auto industries. Rather, these "externalities" (costs associated
with a product that are not paid by the manufacturer, but are passed
on indirectly to others, including those who don't even use or consume that product)—including loss of life, health costs, air and water
pollution costs, environmental cleanup expenses, tax subsidies, and
crop losses—are largely subsidized by the American people and by
their state and federal governments. Just how much more than the
price shown at the fuel pump do we spend to support our oil habit?

## Separate Checks, Please:
## A Tally of Who Really Pays for Our Oil Habit

Mark Delucchi and his colleagues at the Institute for Transportation
Studies at the University of California at Davis, probably the

nation's foremost experts in the art and science of calculating the monetary cost of our Faustian bargain for petroleum, put the minimum external cost of air pollution from motor vehicles in the United States at $24.3 billion each year.[12] Such a figure may be barely the down payment, however. Their work and related studies suggest the costs may be far higher when values are added for things like early deaths and lost productivity:

- Direct health-care costs of $54.7 billion to $672.3 billion each year, which includes everything from headaches to hospitalization, asthma attacks to respiratory illness, and chronic illness to mortality. Particulate matter accounted for the vast majority of these costs at $16.7 billion to $432 billion.

- Reduced crop yields of $3 billion to $6 billion each year.

- Damage to materials and buildings of $1 billion to $8 billion each year.

- Damage to forests of $2 million to $2 billion each year.

- Water pollution from leaking tanks, oil spills, and polluted runoff of $4 million to $1.5 billion each year.

These costs are imposed by oil and auto companies on the rest of us, but the picture is incomplete without also looking at the additional financial support we give to these industries. When considering tax breaks and other government subsidies, the Union of Concerned Scientists calculated that the oil industry receives "a multitude of federal corporate income tax credits and deductions, resulting in an effective income tax rate of 11 percent for the oil industry, compared to the non-oil industry average of 18 percent."[13] The result is $2 billion in tax revenues foregone at just the federal level. The oil industry receives even more tax breaks from state and local governments, amounting to another $4.1 billion annually.

Some of these subsidies date back to 1916 and include tax

deductions for "dry hole" costs (wells that ultimately produced no oil), wages, fuel, repairs, hauling, supplies, and drilling site preparation, to name a few. The rationale was that oil was needed to power the growing economy, and finding oil involved a good deal of guesswork. As a result, a lot of dry holes were drilled for every well that became a gusher. The failures of no other industry are subsidized by taxpayers on this scale. Why such special treatment for the oil industry?

According to the nonpartisan Center for Responsive Politics, Congress has been an eager Faust to the oil industry's Mephistopheles. Oil and gas companies have contributed more than $186 million to political campaigns in the United States between 1990 and 2006.[14] Although Big Oil has been generous to all political parties, 75 percent of that has gone to Republicans, who have held the majority in Congress during most of that time and the White House since 2000. Even to oil companies, $186 million is a lot of money, but not when you consider the return on that investment.

When President George W. Bush signed the Energy Policy Act in August 2005, his stroke of the pen added about $60 billion worth of federal subsidies to the oil and gas industry over the next decade.[15] These subsidies include faster equipment write-offs; elimination of numerous royalty payments to the federal treasury for oil taken from federal lands; government payments to oil companies for deepwater drilling; and new exemptions from the Clean Water Act, the Safe Drinking Water Act, and other regulatory requirements.[16] Oil companies that benefit most from this new financial windfall spent $70 million lobbying Congress and donated $15 million to members of Congress in the two years leading up to the passage of these measures.[17]

Add these new giveaways to the various tax breaks and subsidies already in place and the next ten years could deliver well over $160 billion in largess to the world's wealthiest corporate enterprises, a return of almost $1,000 for every $1 invested in campaign contributions. Because many of these subsidies are written into the tax code, they are not subject to annual congressional oversight.

Many of these tax breaks belong in a Monty Python movie or a painting by Salvador Dali. Take the "Depletion Allowance," which gives about $1 billion of tax breaks to oil companies each year based on the decline in their oil reserves. Oil companies didn't create the oil, they didn't plant it or grow it. To be sure, they invested in equipment to drill it out of the ground, but they already receive generous depreciation allowances on their taxes for the declining value of those tangible assets. If giving subsidies for the decline in a natural resource asset is a good idea, why not give the rest of us money for the declining value of things we all share in common, such as clean air and water, the values of which have certainly been eroded by petroleum-related air pollution?

But the mother of all subsidies to the oil industry, and the automakers who depend on it, occurs in the realm of defending the supply of petroleum itself. According to a summary of studies compiled in 2001 by the *New York Times*, the United States had already been spending $25 billion a year on the military defense of oil-exporting countries in the Middle East.[18] The Bush administration will spend $98 million more to protect just one pipeline that delivers oil, bound for the United States, to a transportation terminal on the Colombian border with Venezuela, the Cano Limon oil pipeline, which is owned by Los Angeles–based Occidental Petroleum.[19] Multiple estimates agree that the annual cost to U.S. taxpayers to defend our oil supply around the globe is between $55 billion and nearly $100 billion.[20] This estimate does not include more than $100 billion spent each year in Iraq for the war in that country, at least some of which is attributable to securing oil.

Just how much is this military protection actually worth to the oil companies? In 1997, during a civil war in Afghanistan and well before the Taliban relinquished its control, Unocal began developing plans for two pipelines through that troubled nation. When asked if Unocal was nervous about such an investment, given the risks, the executive in charge of the project replied simply: "With

U.S. government guarantees and the World Bank putting up the money, no. We're not stupid enough to do this on our own."[21] Although the projects have not yet been built, they are still being planned and financed with the help of governments in the United States and Afghanistan.

So taken all together, what is the taxpayer's final tab? Parsing out the most relevant and quantifiable figures, petroleum's ledger book looks like table 3.1.

Monetary estimates of the magnitude shown in table 3.1 deaden the senses, both because of their sheer size and because of the variables involved, but when all is said and done, a fair tally of

### TABLE 3.1. ANNUAL U.S. FEDERAL TAX BREAKS AND OTHER DIRECT SUBSIDIES FOR OIL

| Credit or Subsidy | Estimated Annual Value |
| --- | --- |
| 2005 Energy Policy Act | $6 billion |
| Depletion allowance | $784 million–$1 billion |
| Fuel production tax credit | $769 million–$900 million |
| Enhanced oil recovery tax credit | $26 million–$100 million |
| Foreign tax credit | $1 billion–$3 billion |
| Foreign income "deferral" | $183 million–$318 million |
| Accelerated depreciation allowance | $1 billion–$4.5 billion |
| U.S. Department of the Interior oil resources management programs and federal oil research programs | $153 million–$938 million |
| U.S. Department of Defense programs to protect oil supply (not including wars, such as the Gulf War of 1991 or the Iraq war of 2003 to the present, which costs more than $100 billion per year by itself) | $55 billion–$96 billion |
| State tax subsidies (related to federal tax breaks) | $125 million–$323 million |
| **Total annual U.S. subsidies** | **$65 billion–$113 billion** |

Source: Evan Harrje, *The Real Price of Gasoline* (Washington, DC: International Center for Technology Assessment, 2000); see also citations related to previous text as summarized in this chart.

the total annual federal taxpayer subsidy attributable to our petroleum addiction would run between $65 billion and $113 billion each year. The middle of that range is $89 billion each year. To put that in perspective, $89 billion is more than double the amount spent on homeland security by the United States each year.[22] And, according to the U.S. Government Accounting Office, $89 billion is approximately the total cost to the U.S. economy of the September 11, 2001, terrorist attacks on the World Trade Center.[23]

Moreover, what price do we put on taxpayer losses associated with global warming, water pollution, and the pollution that literally dissolves our national treasures like the Statue of Liberty? We can't quantify many of those costs, but we can summarize what we do know about our Faustian bargain in purely economic terms, including an estimate of how much more we would pay at the pump if those externalities were included in the price of a gallon of gasoline. Although some of the costs are both variable and subject to debate, the sum total of the costs presented in this chapter so far looks something like those presented in table 3.2.

So there it is, the final Devil's invoice, the amount we pay to keep the needle from hitting "empty": well over $100 billion each year and perhaps closer to $1 trillion. That comes to as much as $2,700 for every man, woman, and child in the United States every single year. That works out to $1 per gallon and possibly as much as $6 per gallon added to the actual price of every gallon of petroleum fuel used in the United States for these subsidies, costs, and other externalities.[24] For that kind of money, we could provide health insurance for the forty-five million Americans who have none[25] *and* build fifteen hundred new schools in every state in the union.[26]

Before leaving this topic, it is intriguing to look at the cost of petroleum dependence from the opposite side of the looking glass by examining the financial *benefits* of pollution reduction. Regulations in various parts of the world have reduced air pollution over

TABLE 3.2. ANNUAL COSTS TO U.S. CONSUMERS OF OIL AND AUTO
INDUSTRY SUBSIDIES AND EXTERNALITIES (IN BILLIONS OF U.S. DOLLARS)

| Item | Annual Cost (low estimate) | Annual Cost (high estimate) |
|---|---|---|
| Federal tax breaks and subsidies (see table 3.1) | $65 | $113 |
| Health-care costs | $54.7 | $672.3 |
| Crop losses | $3 | $6 |
| Damage to materials and buildings | $1 | $8 |
| Damage to forests | $0.2 | $2 |
| Water pollution | $0.4 | $1.5 |
| Total of all states' direct subsidies[1] | $4.1 | $4.1 |
| **TOTAL** | **128.4** | **806.9** |

1. According to *The Real Price of Gasoline* (Washington, DC: International Center for Technology Assessment, 2000), these figures do not include other indirect subsidies that governments at all levels provide, including a share of the infrastructure and services that assist more than one industry. Various reports suggest that roads, harbors, and other infrastructure serve the oil and auto industries to the tune of an additional $36 to $112 billion each year. Because we all use those assets, however, parsing out which segment of society benefits proportionally is unreliable, although some dollar figure is certainly appropriate in calculating the total oil subsidy package.

the past three decades, and these reductions have produced some impressive and measurable benefits.

In 1992, one study estimated that the economic value of avoiding air pollution–related health effects was nearly $10 billion annually in the Los Angeles area alone, and the attainment of all air pollution standards existing at the time could have saved sixteen hundred lives a year.[27] A decade later, research showed comparable results when a joint study by the USEPA, the Department of the Interior, and the Department of Agriculture estimated that pollution-reduction strategies would save up to $68 billion nationwide.[28] In September 2003, the White House Office of Management and Budget released a report showing that the benefits from USEPA rules, in all areas of pollution regulation, outweigh the costs imposed on industry and local governments by more than a ten-to-one margin.[29] In short, clean air is a valuable financial investment. Given such positive cost-benefit analyses, what is preventing us from further reducing or even eliminating petroleum air pollution from its biggest source, the vehicle tailpipe?

## Kaizen: Why Can't We Afford Cleaner Cars?

"[Automakers] just lied straight out," recalls former USEPA administrator Bob Fri, speaking of "sky-is-falling" claims by auto companies that they would face bankruptcy if forced to install pollution-reducing catalytic converters on their cars in the early 1970s. "We knew they could comply with what we were asking. They told us they would go bankrupt. This was nonsense."[30]

How did Fri know then, or how would any regulator know today, that these corporations could do better? Perhaps it was because five of the top fifteen companies on the Fortune Global 500 list are automakers and six more are oil companies.[31] Oil companies on the Fortune Global 500 list had total combined revenues in 2005 of nearly $1.3 trillion with profits of $92 billion. As oil gushes past $70 per barrel, the profits of these companies rise to new records quarter after quarter. The automakers on the list had profits of more than $21 billion on revenues of nearly $1 trillion.

Although oil and auto companies refuse to invest in less-polluting products, they seem more than willing to spend lavishly on their corporate leadership, who continue to deliver harmful products to consumers and force the rest of us to pay for their true cost of doing business. Lee R. Raymond, chairman and chief executive officer of ExxonMobil, earned nearly $15 million in compensation for 2001.[32] Just three years later, between his paycheck and cashing out stock options, he collected more than $80 million. And when he retired in 2006, he collected nearly $400 million. James J. Mulva, president and chief executive officer of ConocoPhillips, collected more than $20 million in the same year, but in 2006 he had nearly $100 million in stock options waiting to be cashed out.[33]

Yet as a state government official, almost every time I have asked oil or auto executives why they can't reduce pollution from their facilities or produce products that are less harmful, they use the excuse Bob Fri mentioned and say it isn't affordable. In years past, we heard that installing seat belts or air bags would bankrupt automakers. Today, automakers claim that making the modest technical additions to their vehicles to reduce greenhouse gas emissions will bankrupt them. Providing cleaner burning fuels in California, we were told, was going to bankrupt oil companies. Reducing toxic air and water pollution from their refineries was also just not affordable.

Not everyone in the oil and auto industry uses the "poverty" excuse. John Daum, one of the lawyers who still defends Exxon (now ExxonMobil) from paying court-ordered damages in the *Exxon Valdez* oil spill in Alaska, for example, acknowledged that his client could easily afford to make the payments to sick local residents and unemployed fishers whose livelihoods were destroyed by the spill.

"Why should we pay them?" he asked one night at my dining room table shortly after the tenth anniversary of the infamous spill. "We hired those people to clean up the spill and bought their boats many times over. They don't deserve another penny." Nearly a decade after he threw down that gauntlet, continuing litigation has meant the residents of the Prince William Sound area have yet to collect a penny of the punitive damages they initially won in court.[34]

The ultimate excuse for the continued production of inefficient, polluting products, however, has been to blame the consumer. Providing more fuel-efficient, less-polluting cars is not only unaffordable, we are told, but consumers really want SUVs. Yet the Japanese, German, and Korean manufacturers are kicking American tailpipes by selling something better. Toyota's product line, for example, is notoriously fuel efficient and includes the popular gasoline-electric hybrid Prius model. As the world prepares for China and other emerging economies to gobble up more and more cars, Wall Street has rewarded the world's number two automaker—Toyota—with an extraordinary vote of confidence. By 2003, its stock value had grown to more than that of General Motors (GM), Ford, and DaimlerChrysler combined.[35]

The U.S. auto industry apparently learned nothing from the oil embargo of the 1970s. Japan answered with fuel-efficient cars and dramatically increased its market share, while Detroit kept selling gas guzzlers. Japanese firms not only made their cars more fuel efficient than their U.S. counterparts, but according to consumer satisfaction ratings, doing so has delivered what customers actually wanted.

Toyota has signs throughout their operations that read simply "kaizen," a Japanese concept that as soon as you perfect something, assume that it can still be improved and go back to work. This emphasis on quality and meeting regulatory requirements for seat belts, air bags, fuel economy, and pollution control—compared with Detroit's focus on fighting regulators and stalling on developing fuel and safety product improvements—has helped Toyota gain market share. Those different corporate philosophies may explain why U.S. automobile companies continue to lose market share at an alarming rate, as we will see in chapter 6. Although the Prius may exemplify the approach of Toyota and other foreign automakers, it is the Hummer that best exemplifies Detroit's attitude toward the future: just make it bigger and convince people that their need to carve tracks in pristine wilderness outweighs the added cost of fuel and the wide array of effects on our society.

"A wealthy donor got tired of trying to find a parking spot for this beast, so he donated it to us," recalled Phil Stevens of The Nature Conservancy in California and Nevada, when a donated Hummer H1 appeared at their headquarters. "He thought he was making a charitable donation, but we couldn't afford to feed the thing. I was also astonished when we took delivery of it to find out it only has four seats. Get that—the biggest damn car on the road in the history of cars and it can only carry four people!"

Later models of the Hummer added more seats, but GM made very few other concessions to practicality, quality, or fuel economy. Although Toyota topped the 2002 J. D. Power survey of consumer satisfaction, the Hummer was at the bottom with nearly double the number of consumer complaints.[36] By 2005, J. D. Power reported that the Hummer had improved significantly, but still languished among the makes and models with the least consumer satisfaction.[37] By 2006, not only was the Hummer in the lowest echelons of yet another respected consumer satisfaction list, but *Consumer Reports* noted that for the first time in the nine-year history of their "best" and "worst" lists, the top ten best were all Japanese manufacturers.[38] Not one U.S. automaker cracked the top ten.

Why is this emphasis on "kaizen" important to the discussion of the true cost of our oil addiction? Because Congress provided another massive tax break to the oil and auto industries to help out gas guzzlers instead of rewarding vehicles with lower pollution and better fuel economy. In May 2003, President Bush signed into law a tax deduction of up to $100,000 for buyers of vehicles more than 6,000 pounds, including Hummers.[39] A new Hummer costs around $60,000, so depending on your tax bracket, the U.S. government may effectively slash that price by half. Owners of gasoline-electric hybrids, such as the Toyota Prius, can also claim federal tax credits of up to $2,200, about 10 percent of the car's value, compared to the SUV tax benefits that approach 50 percent.[40]

In reality however, no matter how efficient we make petroleum-powered transportation, it will one day fade into the history books for one simple reason: petroleum is a finite resource. Although much research has been devoted to estimating when oil will run out, such calculations are frequently changed because of our apparently insatiable appetite for it, and even the most reliable estimates are probably wrong. Oil is likely to become a very unreliable energy source much sooner than we imagined.

## A Tide in the Affairs of Men:
## When Will We Run Out of Oil?

About the time I was born, Americans were just beginning to add televisions to their living rooms. Dwight D. Eisenhower was campaigning for what would become his first term as president. My father had been home from the war for six years. On both radio and television, *Your Hit Parade* featured such popular songs as "Unforgettable" by Nat King Cole and "Wheel of Fortune" by Kay Starr, sponsored by Lucky Strike cigarettes.

Marion King Hubbert was a geophysicist for Shell Oil in Houston, Texas, at the time. He probably didn't focus much on the popular culture of the day, being consumed with research that would revolutionize our understanding of oil, although like the theories of Albert Einstein in the same time period, proof would remain elusive for another generation. Hubbert hovered over slide rule and graph paper long into the humid Houston summer nights, perfecting a method of predicting when Industrial Man would run out of the chosen source of energy, oil.

Over the objections of his employer, Hubbert made his findings public in 1956.[41] He developed a deceptively simple bell curve—a graph in the shape of a bell—and theorized that when the rate of increase of oil discovery stopped, the year when we would run out of oil was reliably predictable. His findings showed that we would reach the zenith of that bell curve for oil discovery—and therefore oil production—in the contiguous forty-eight states around 1970, after which production would begin to decline along a predictable trend line until the oil was simply all gone.

In those more naive times, when the postwar economic boom meant that there was no end to prosperity in sight, Hubbert was ridiculed by many and questioned by almost everyone, especially his oil company bosses. But sure enough, in 1970 the United States did hit the peak of oil production in the contiguous states and it has indeed been declining, at the rate Hubbert predicted, ever since. No one dismisses Hubbert's curve any longer.

The oil industry, however, is a worldwide affair, so just what do this Texas oil man's calculations mean for global oil reserves and production? Of the 2 trillion barrels of oil known to exist worldwide, we have now extracted and consumed about half of them, meaning that we may have reached the summit of Hubbert's peak and are now starting down the other side of the mountain, on the same slippery, predictable slope that he showed us for the oil in the contiguous states.

Of course, the "known reserves" is itself an imprecise figure. As the price of oil increases, sources for oil that were previously not counted (because they were uneconomical to exploit) can now be added to the pile. New technology also allows us to squeeze more oil from the existing sponge over time. Nonetheless, a finite volume of recoverable oil—recoverable at any price using any future technology—still exists. We also know that the "proven" oil reserves are at least somewhat exaggerated. Given that Shell employed Hubbert, it is especially ironic that this oil giant was caught lying about its reserves to boost its stock price, but others inflate their estimates of oil available, too.[42] Members of the Organization of Petroleum Exporting Countries (OPEC), for example, are allowed to export oil in relation to their "proven" reserves. During the late 1980s, the majority of OPEC nations inflated their reserve estimates by as much as 200 percent to justify increasing their exports.[43] No actual new discoveries or legitimate recalculation of existing reserves justified those increases.

Beyond these manipulations, we may have even less oil than we currently assume because reserves are estimated based on probabilities rather than actual science. Oil experts use a system in which "P90" reserves are those that are 90 percent probable to exist in a given field, "P10" is a reserve that is no more than 10 percent likely to exist, and so on. Today's assumption that the world still has around

1,000 billion barrels of oil in reserve includes many fields, especially those in Russia, that are no better than P10 estimates. More thoughtful estimates, using P50 as a guideline, conclude that we have no more than around 800 billion barrels, or 20 percent less than today's widely accepted estimates.[44]

Even if we add P10 reserves into Hubbert's global projection just to be on the optimistic side, we are still left with a curve that peaks within this decade. Princeton University geologist Kenneth Deffeyes says the peak has already been reached and that we are now living in a "permanent stage of oil shortage."[45] Houston investment banker Matthew Simmons puts the peak between 2007 and 2009, and California Institute of Technology physicist David Goodstein concurs that the peak will be reached before 2010. Given the emerging demands of countries such as China and India, to name just two, not to mention the increased rate at which Americans are using oil, the slippery slope is likely to be a very fast ride to the bottom of the backside of Hubbert's peak.

Hubbert's research also reveals some other predictive tools. Over the last century, we consumed oil at the same rate we discovered it, although the consumption occurs about a decade after the discovery. Therefore, based on the rate of new discovery, one can reasonably predict how much oil will be available to fight over in coming years. Using that model, both Hubbert and the U.S. Geological Survey predict that we will run out of affordable oil within the next forty years.[46] Between 1980 and 1990, new discoveries added 60 percent to the world's proven reserves. In the following decade, only 4 percent more has was added.[47]

Hubbert is equally pessimistic about our supply of natural gas, which is closely associated with petroleum development, giving it a life span of no more than two decades longer than oil itself.[48] For what it's worth, BP's website agrees with these estimates.[49] Forty years might seem like a relatively long time, but these graphs and calculations assume that we will be able to extract all of the oil we have found, at a price we are willing to pay, whereas the reality is very likely to be something else. Getting the dregs may take more energy and political capital than the resulting products are worth.

"The oil companies . . . know it but are unable to admit it," states an August 1999 Goldman Sachs report. "The great merger mania [among oil companies] is a scaling down of a dying industry in recognition that 90% of global conventional oil has already been found."[50] The real challenge is not only predicting how much oil is left in the ground, but also understanding the pace at which we are sucking the oil reservoir dry and the other forces that are likely to cause future instability of fuel supplies.

"There is a tide in the affairs of men, which, taken at the flood, leads on to fortune," Shakespeare offers. "Omitted—all the voyage of their life is bound in shallows and in miseries."[51]

We are afloat upon such a sea at this moment, and as our dependence on oil steals the breath from our lungs, it also imperils our economic health. The Arab oil embargo of 1973 was a man-made shortage, but the looming shortages of the future are something no government, foreign or domestic, can avoid. As Hubbert has demonstrated, we are in a race with nature. As the "Easter Island Effect" suggests, we are also in a race with human nature.

## The Easter Island Effect:
## When Will We Run Out of Gas?

As experts debate how much useable oil is left in the earth, our economic well-being depends on a realistic assessment of how much refined fuel we can reliably expect to produce over time. Shortages will drive up prices, which make alternative fuels more attractive and affordable. The key to future prosperity is not to wait for those forces to derail economic progress before we develop the alternatives. To be prepared we must understand and try to manage those forces.

Five forces create what I call an Easter Island Effect on petroleum fuels (mostly for transportation) in the United States. First is population growth, which in turn drives an increase in vehicles. The number of cars on U.S. roads is expected to double by the year 2020.[52] There isn't much anyone can do about either trend in the short term.

The second is fuel economy. From 1974 to 1990, the average for cars in the United States climbed from 13.2 miles per gallon (mpg) to 26.9 mpg, but in the years since, U.S. manufacturers have been going backward, largely attributable to the lust for SUVs.[53] The corporate average fuel economy (CAFE) standard for vehicles sold in the United States today is less than it was in 1987.[54] Consumers do want fuel-efficient vehicles, especially since fuel prices soared after the U.S. invasion of Iraq, but many automakers are responding too slowly.

"We can't turn on a dime," said Elizabeth Lowery, GM vice president for Environment and Energy, acknowledging that her company and Ford need more than seven years to take a car from concept to showroom. The National Academy of Sciences reports that fuel economy could be improved 10 percent to 15 percent through the use of existing technologies,[55] such as turbo charging, variable valve timing, continuously variable transmissions, cylinder deactivation (when less power is needed), and electric power steering. Although these off-the-shelf solutions could add as much as $1,500 to a new vehicle, the fuel and maintenance savings could pay that back in as little as three years.

In the meantime, more people driving more cars that are less fuel efficient equals more demand for fuel. Add to this equation the third Easter Island pressure, which comes from our unsustainable land use patterns, or, simply put, sprawl. On average, people live farther from their work, school, and recreation than ever before, driving up the number of vehicle miles traveled per person, which has been doubling every ten to fifteen years.[56] Many state and local governments are working on "smart growth" land use planning and expansion of mass transit, but rebuilding entire communities and adding new subways or light-rail lines takes decades.

The fourth pressure comes from refinery capacity, or more accurately stated, the lack of it. National refineries operate at virtually 100 percent of capacity, and for the past ten years, petroleum consumption has increased two and a half times faster than new refinery capacity.[57] So, let's just build more refineries, but where? No one wants a source of toxic air pollution in his or her neighborhood, especially since we now know that effects of refinery air pollution are significant as far as 30 miles downwind, and even an oil company making billions in annual profits can't afford more coastal real estate simply to build the next Superfund site.

"Refiners told us they no longer see an imperative to supply the market at all costs," a recent RAND report concludes. "Therefore, they no longer build in extra capacity." One refiner was quoted in the report as saying that he would maximize profits by making no more than "cheapskate investments" and relying on the existing overburdened, aging facilities, even if that reduced overall output. "The [oil] industry has learned that it's OK to fall short on product," another oil executive said in the report. "There is no reward for being long on product or production capacity."[58]

Capacity is not only a matter of pipes and cracking towers, it is also a matter of keeping the facilities running. California offers a good case study of this challenge. The ConocoPhillips refinery in Wilmington, built in 1919, and the Chevron refinery, built in El Segundo in 1911—the same one that spilled a quarter of a billion gallons of petroleum products into aquifers beneath the facility undetected over an eighty-year period—are both nearing the century mark. The youngest of the refineries in California is nearly forty years old. Located in Benicia, it suffered five serious breakdowns in the first half of 2003 alone.[59] During the same period, breakdowns at three other California refineries cut gasoline supplies by more than 8 percent.

"It's not a track record that anybody would be proud of," said Bill Buckalew, general manager of the Valero refinery at Benicia.

"There's a misunderstanding about how really complicated these things are. Everything in those pipes is highly flammable, and a lot of it is at high temperature and high pressure. There are thousands of pieces of equipment, and all of them have a finite lifetime and need maintenance."[60] Nationwide, natural disasters can also disrupt fuel supplies and create shortages and price spikes. Hurricane Katrina in late August 2005 resulted in damage to refineries in the Gulf states that sent gasoline prices up by more than 10 percent across the country.[61]

Refineries are not the only weak link in the petroleum production chain: pipes, oil tankers, and every other part of the system are suspect as well. On July 30, 2003, a single 8-inch-diameter petroleum pipeline between Tucson and Phoenix, Arizona, ruptured. Three weeks later, when repairs to the break were still not completed, regional supplies of fuel were so affected that California motorists paid 22 cents more for each gallon of fuel. The pipeline's operator, Kinder Morgan, began trucking gasoline into Arizona from California refineries, but even so, drivers in Phoenix paid $4.50 for a gallon of gasoline. ConocoPhillips ran out of fuel at 180 of its 300 filling stations, and other companies reported similar shortages.[62]

The fifth and final Easter Island pressure on our transportation energy is money. Sixty percent of the 21 million barrels of oil used in the United States each day are imported, sending $612,500 overseas every minute (based on $72 for a barrel of crude in early 2006) and seriously undermining the U.S. balance of trade and economic stability in the process.

There isn't much consumers or governments can do to increase refinery reliability or capacity, short of building publicly owned refineries, nor can we do much in the near term about the money we send overseas for oil. The result of these five Easter Island Effect forces, however, is that the California Energy Commission predicts potential shortages of petroleum fuels before the end of the decade and prices likely to top $5 a gallon.[63] That price may seem cheap in the next few years, if expert predictions about skyrocketing global demand for oil are accurate.

## The Next Cold War? A Global Thirst for Oil

If the United States represents the modern Rapa Nui, we are not alone. Although our Easter Island Effect may drive us to petroleum fuel shortages sooner than we expect, that problem will be exacerbated by the equally voracious appetite for oil around the globe. The U.S. Energy Information Administration forecasts that world demand for oil will increase 60 percent by 2020. Already, energy use in Latin America has increased 30 percent since 1985, in Africa by 40 percent, and in Asia by 50 percent.[64]

To illustrate that point, in 2003 the International Energy Agency revised its global oil demand estimate just six months after it was issued, increasing the expected consumption by 2 million barrels a day.[65] The agency blamed its error on unexpected demand from the United States, Brazil, and India. Three years later, however, in 2006, oil demand was still consistently being underestimated. The U.S. Department of Energy again increased its global oil demand estimate, made just months earlier, by 200,000 barrels a day, to 83.8 million barrels.[66]

China's overall oil demand increased by 9 percent in 2003 and its imported oil increased by a third, making the nation of Mao and the Little Red Book the world's second-largest consumer of oil.[67] This fact should not surprise anyone because China's economy is also growing at about 10 percent each year. China is now competing with the United States for oil in just about every country that produces it. History does not look kindly on this type of competition. As chapter 4 describes Japan started a world war over oil, and China has already supplied Saudi Arabia and others with weapons in exchange for oil.

"[A]rms trafficking to these regimes presents an increasing threat to U.S. security interests in the Middle East,"[68] warns a 2002 report from the United States–China Economic and Security Review Commission, a congressional watchdog agency. "A key driver in China's relations with terrorist-sponsored governments is its dependence on foreign oil to fuel its economic development. This dependency is expected to increase over the coming decade."

Chinese government-controlled corporations recently tried and failed to purchase the U.S. oil giant Unocal, but they were more successful in buying a $2.3 billion stake in a Nigerian oil field, a $4.2 billion oil company in Kazakhstan, a $573 million share of the oil fields in Syria, and a $1.4 billion oil field in Ecuador. These purchases are dwarfed by a $70 billion deal that China signed in 2004 with Iran to develop oil fields and liquefied natural gas projects in Iran.[69]

Japan is another rival to China's oil demands. As output declines from China's own oil fields in places like Daquing, just north of the Korean peninsula, China turns its gaze to a pipeline that would bring oil from Russia, near Lake Baikal, to the north of Mongolia. Japan, however, is competing with China for a rival pipeline that would deliver the oil to a port on the coast and into Japanese industry and automobiles. Both nations have spent money and political capital wooing Russia for its black gold dowry and, as the sale of nuclear weapons technology to the Middle East in exchange for oil suggests, each side is willing to go to great lengths to get what it believes it needs.[70]

"China is power hungry," said Wenran Jiang, a China expert at the University of Alberta. "China without energy cannot deliver on its development plans. If China had the same per-capita consumption as the United States, it would need 85 million barrels per day, as much as the entire world consumes today."[71]

Accelerating the competition over oil supply is China's rapidly growing demand for U.S.-style transportation. China is already the world's third-largest car market, behind the United States and Japan, and will add nearly sixty million more vehicles by 2010.[72] Auto-makers are thrilled with sales growth in the United States each year of 5 percent, but in China in 2003, it was 75 percent. China also seems to be copying the American car culture, falling in love with gas-guzzling SUVs.[73] GM will spend $3 billion expanding its mar-ket share in China by 2007, hoping to sell 1.3 million vehicles each year.[74] Ford, BMW, Jeep, and numerous other familiar brands are already pushing cars in China, especially SUVs.

"Our projection is that over the next five years, the SUV seg-ment will go to 20% [of all cars sold in China]," said Paul Alcala, chief executive officer of Beijing Jeep. He and his competitors are certain because they're driving the market that way, introducing twenty new SUV models in 2003 alone bearing names like "Safe" and "Great Wall," the latter applied to a Hummer-like behemoth that befits its name. Another reason automakers are so sure the SUV market will continue to swell in China is that SUVs can be pro-duced and sold cheaply there, as little as $10,000 for a full-sized SUV with all the bells and whistles that would make any urban American driver proud. Even at that price, profit margins are solid.[75]

Fortunately, when it comes to setting standards for fuel economy to reduce air pollution and conserve scarce gasoline, China's gov-ernment is not as beholden to oil and auto lobbyists as U.S. law-makers appear to be. Vehicle exhaust already accounts for 79 percent of China's air pollution.[76] Regulators have therefore demanded improvements in fuel economy of 15 percent within the next few years, and automakers are willing to comply. Jeep, for instance, plans to improve fuel economy in its models by 20 percent.[77] Why it is that these same companies so vehemently oppose fuel economy standards in the United States?

Using all this new information, we can now recalculate the for-mula for estimating how much longer the petroleum-powered joyride will last. Start with about 800 billion barrels of oil reserves and assume an average consumption over the next twenty years of

40 billion barrels each year. That leaves us with no more than twenty years left at the nipple of Big Oil.

August 20, 2003, I was vacationing on the Kern River in the foothills of the Sierra Nevada. The heat was oppressive at midday, but the river was cold and clear. Arnold Schwarzenegger had recently decided to run for governor in the state's historic recall election of incumbent Gray Davis, and I sat on the veranda of a cabin, high above the river, building a team to advise the new candidate on environmental matters. As I read through the local *Bakersfield Californian* for political news and an update on the Arizona petroleum pipeline break, a section of the paper caught my eye, not for the imposing merit of each story, but because of the drumbeat of frailty it represented for a dying industry:

"A bombing in Baghdad . . . delays restoring the country's oil exports . . . sent prices up 21% since late April."

"Shell . . . has told its staff in the [Nigerian] city of Warri to stay at home until ethnic clashes subside."

"Tropical storm Erika, which blew through the Gulf of Mexico on Friday . . . [caused] offshore oil fields [to] cut production by . . . 9451 barrels."

"Shell and Unocal will invest $1 billion . . . to develop offshore oil and gas fields near Shanghai."

"OPEC . . . forecast predicted daily world oil demand would rise . . . up 1.16 million [barrels a day] from 2003."

Five days later, the papers reported that the national average price for self-serve regular gasoline had risen more than 15 cents per gallon in a two-week period, the largest such increase in history. A power outage on the East Coast and the Arizona pipeline break were blamed. By the end of August, California motorists saw another record spike—18 cents a gallon in a single week—as minor mechanical problems struck four of the state's refineries, causing production to drop temporarily by 10 percent. That relatively small interruption was enough to trigger the price increase, even though the price of crude oil during the month remained steady at around $30 a barrel.[78]

A scan of the news these days from around the world almost every day of the week looks much like that day in August 2003. And still another disturbing trend has emerged that is further reducing the supply of crude oil on the global market. In late 2005, protesters forced the shutdown of a major oil pipeline in Ecuador several times, both with peaceful demonstrations and violent attacks on pumping stations.[79] By 2006, oil company executives were being kidnapped, not for monetary ransom, but with demands that foreign-based oil companies leave the country.

Oil production in Iraq fell 8 percent in 2005 compared with the prior year, despite U.S. efforts to rebuild the petroleum infrastructure there, mainly because of attacks on oil facilities.[80] Production is less than half the volume anticipated by U.S. officials when Iraq was invaded in 2003, when then-Deputy Defense Secretary Paul D. Wolfowitz said that Iraq's oil would defray the costs of rebuilding the country after the invasion.[81]

In early 2006, militants in Nigeria destroyed oil facilities and kidnapped oil company executives, demanding that Shell, Chevron, Total, and Agip leave the country.[82] Production declined by a quarter million barrels a day.

If these recurring events make the collar tighten around your neck, consider one final "pinch point." Today, the United States not only imports 60 percent of its crude oil, it also imports refined fuels to make up for the inability of existing refineries to meet American consumer demands. In California alone, refiners buy about 4.2 million gallons of fuel each day, about 10 percent of total demand, from as far off as Finland. These imports are expected to more than double by 2010, but the existing and planned port and pipeline facilities can't handle that additional volume.[83] Peter Konesky, an energy specialist with Nevada's Office of Energy, suggests a desperate, if only half-joking, way to deal with future shortages.

"We're going to hire the 101st Airborne and send them out there to make sure we get our fuel."[84] As he spoke, the 101st Airborne was busy protecting the oil fields of Iraq.

Instead of funding such Draconian proposals, if all the money poured into subsidies for the oil and auto industries, along with a percentage of these companies' vast wealth, were directed to reducing pollution from their products and improving fuel economy, we would not be facing such extreme threats to our public health and economic well-being. At least one thing is clear from this overview of petroleum dynamics at home and abroad: enough time to fix these problems without more drastic sacrifices is running out.

As we contemplate increasing competition with China over oil, world history is already replete with battles over black gold. Not all these conflicts are wars. Some are oil corporations decimating local tribes in third world countries and some are environmental devastation so vast as to conjure images of great military battles, leaving victims from both gun barrels and drill bits. As we will see in chapter 4, oil is the ultimate fool's gold, hardly worthy of the price that Faust paid for his deal with the Devil, that of human life itself.

# CHAPTER 4

# All That Glitters

All that glitters is not gold;

Often have you heard that told:

Many a man his life hath sold

But my outside to behold.[1]

*Shakespeare,* Merchant of Venice

In Shakespeare's *Merchant of Venice*, a suitor for the hand of Portia fails to solve the riddle of the three caskets. He quickly chooses the golden box, based on its outward appearance, and is sent away empty handed. Oil wealth, as we have seen thus far, is an attractive illusion too, but in fact it is impoverishing us in ways we cannot easily measure.

## Oil War Is Hell:
## A Brief History of Global Conflict about Oil

"War is hell," I suspect most would agree, but wars fought over oil must be a special kind of hell. After all, who wants to lose their life for a commodity? Yet since the beginning of the twentieth century, much of international power and politics has centered on oil.

During the 1930s, for example, Japan's various disagreements with the United States and Great Britain led to an oil boycott. The resulting fuel shortage made Japan conclude that it must fuel its future with further conquest because it had no oil wealth of its own to exploit, leading to the invasion of the oil-rich Dutch East Indies (Indonesia) and the start of war in the Pacific. As World War II came to a close, the U.S. government drew at least one conclusion from the devastation. In December 1944, Secretary of the Navy James Forrestal wrote:

> The prestige and hence the influence of the United States is in part related to the wealth of the Government and its nationals in terms of oil resources, foreign as well as domestic . . . it is patently in the Navy's interest that no part of the national wealth, as represented by the present holdings of foreign oil reserves by U.S. nationals, be lost at this time. Indeed, the active expansion of such holdings is very much to be desired.[2]

In his 1992 Pulitzer Prize–winning book about oil, *The Prize*, Daniel Yergin lays out the twentieth century's dependence on oil, and the perversion of national values that it spawned, far better than can be summarized here. Events since that book was published demonstrate that the dependence has only grown in the intervening years. Conflicts over oil are accelerating in direct proportion to the growing demand for—and access to—declining global oil reserves.

"Though the modern history of oil begins in the latter half of the nineteenth century, it is the twentieth century that has become completely transformed by the advent of petroleum," says Yergin. "Today, we are so dependent on oil, and oil is so embedded in our daily doings, that we hardly stop to comprehend its pervasive significance."[3]

Few would argue that a desire to secure oil supplies didn't play some role in the 2003 U.S. invasion of Iraq. Many would argue it was the prime motivating force, especially when it is recognized that no weapons of mass destruction were found, nor any evidence that Iraq was a party to the terrorist networks that spawned the horrors of September 11, 2001. President George W. Bush seemed to admit as much in a press conference in June 2004 when he explained that when in preparation for the invasion with his military advisors, his top planning priority had been to secure Iraq's oil infrastructure from sabotage.[4] The U.S. supply of oil was more important than the Iraqi supply of food, the second priority on the president's s list, for a nation that we were supposedly there to "liberate."

Of course, neither Yergin nor Bush was the first to recognize the political and military significance of oil. That distinction belongs a century earlier to a young government bureaucrat named Winston Churchill.[5]

In 1899, Shell Oil argued that the British government should convert the Royal Navy from a coal-burning to an oil-burning fleet. Opposition to the concept was stiff. Why would anyone move away from proven, reliable technology and an established mining industry—based on a natural resource that is plentiful in England and its colonies and that can be burned exactly as it comes from the ground—toward an unknown fuel that requires expensive, compli- cated conversion to make it useful? There was certainly no known native supply of oil. Who would pay for exploration, extraction, importation, refining, and storage? The idea was lunacy.

But Shell's founder and president, Marcus Samuel, convinced the British, specifically the young First Lord of the Admiralty, Winston Churchill, that oil would provide numerous advantages over the German coal-burning fleet. The biggest advantage was related to the labor needed to shift and shovel coal compared with that for oil use. Within a decade, Churchill had recruited enough allies within the British government to successfully convert the British fleet. Shell, of course, was eager to have the British Navy as a customer, promising to deliver oil from its worldwide resources. Churchill objected, however, because Shell's oil was in far away Indonesia, beyond the reach of the British Empire.

Instead, in 1909 Churchill helped to form the Anglo-Persian Oil Company, with concessions in Persia (modern-day Iran). Although this region was also outside the British Empire, there was at least a land bridge to a significant British military presence in the colonies of Burma (modern-day Myanmar) and India. Churchill also ensured that Anglo-Persian, later renamed British Petroleum and now called BP, remain under his control by having the British government retain 51 percent of its shares.

The British stranglehold on Persian oil instigated a race among the major industrial countries to obtain their own Middle East oil concessions. Conflicts began immediately. Ironically, although the United States and Great Britain joined forces in the invasion and occupation of Iraq in 2003, in the early twentieth century they nearly went to war against each other over Iraq's oil. Ultimately, the two nations avoided conflict by dividing up the resources and the ruling families that controlled them, ensuring their own de facto political control over what was becoming an increasingly valuable resource.

The United States never abandoned its interest in all of Iraq's oil, however. In 1975, still within the shadow of the Arab oil embargo two years earlier, the U.S. Congressional Research Service prepared a document at the request of Congress entitled "Oil Fields as Military Objectives: A Feasibility Study." The congressional study was based in part on "Oil: The Issue of American Intervention" by Robert W. Tucker. In that article, Tucker lays out the case for U.S. invasion and control of an area very much like Iraq, which might require the use of sixty thousand troops in the Middle East "tied down for a protracted period of time."[6] U.S. troops in Iraq, by the time of that country's first election in January 2005, numbered more than 150,000.

Beyond Iraq, the involvement of the major powers in the Middle East and elsewhere over oil resources has continued unabated. At NATO's fiftieth anniversary summit in Washington in April 1999, a new strategy was adopted. Dedicated to protecting the members' "collective interests," it included prevention of "the disruption of the flow of vital resources." The invasion of Iraq four years later may be the first major exercise of that policy. Energy Secretary Spencer Abraham came right to the point in a meeting of Arab oil producers, U.S. government officials, and chief executives of every major oil company in the world.

"America will . . . continue to be more than just a major consumer of Middle East petroleum," Abraham said during a panel discussion at the 2003 United States–Arab Economic Forum. "We will be both a partner and investor as well."[7]

Some "partnership," but war is one of the major costs for petroleum addiction that is not hard to quantify. The U.S. invasion of Iraq in 2003 has cost U.S. taxpayers at least $100 billion a year ever since. It has also cost the lives of soldiers and Iraqi civilians. It may very well be, however, that the greatest cost, defying almost any measurement, is yet to be paid, for who can accurately estimate the value of our climate?

## Hell on Earth? Petroleum-Powered Global Warming

Melting ice caps. Global warming. Climate change. Sounds like just what Mephistopheles had in mind as part of the bargain with Faust. Carbon dioxide, much of it coming from the combustion of fossil fuels, is trapped in the atmosphere and acts like a heavy comforter on your bed, holding the heat inside and building up the temperature over time. At some point, the temperature in your bed becomes uncomfortable enough that you kick off the covers and go back to sleep. In the case of global warming, we can't kick off the covers, so we will sweat. Like the comforter's use on a bed, the generation of some trapped heat in the atmosphere is good; otherwise, we'd freeze to death on a cold winter's night. But too much trapped heat and we suffer other consequences.

The only real questions are where on Earth will we see the greatest consequences of that global sweating and how severe are those effects likely to be? Since the heavy blanket on Earth's bed will keep trapping heat from the sun each day, we will likely see ice caps melt further and sea levels rise more than they have in recent years, consuming significant chunks of coastal real estate. We will likely see some regions become wetter and others drier. We will likely see changes in ocean currents and temperatures, which, like our body's bloodstream, are the planet's primary heating and cooling systems. Although various governments debate the relative importance of global warming and a host of scientists argue over the fine details of exactly what, when, where, and how much, four key facts are not in dispute.

First, carbon dioxide ($CO_2$) is the primary greenhouse gas. Before the Industrial Age began about 150 years ago, the concentration of $CO_2$ in Earth's atmosphere had remained between 180 and 280 parts per million (ppm) for more than 400,000 years.

Second, there is agreement that the level of $CO_2$ is more than 370 ppm today and climbing annually. These first two points are not subject to debate because they have been measured.[8]

The third area of agreement is that this dramatic increase in $CO_2$ coincides with humans burning fossil fuels at a prodigious rate and therefore that humans have contributed significantly to this intoxication of the atmosphere.

Fourth, if we could turn off the $CO_2$ switch—somehow stop dumping tons of the stuff into the atmosphere every day from our cars, power plants, and the like—we will still suffer serious consequences from global warming over the next half century. That's because the $CO_2$ in the atmosphere can't go anywhere, nor can it be consumed rapidly enough by trees and other plants, which absorb $CO_2$ and emit oxygen (the opposite of animals, which take in oxygen and exhale $CO_2$).

There are two reasons the world's plants can't keep up with consumption of $CO_2$. We're discharging more $CO_2$ than ever before, and, perhaps more to the point, we're cutting down trees and clearing forests at an equally prodigious rate, depleting the very lifeforms that might save us from our stupidity. Adding insult to injury, many countries with rain forests are burning the vegetation to clear the land for agriculture, and the burns simply release more $CO_2$ to the atmosphere. By contrast, other plant life and the ocean are two destinations for $CO_2$. Although the ocean absorbs a large quantity of $CO_2$, it does not do so without paying a price, that of disturbance in critical links in the marine food chain.

"Because carbon dioxide is an acid gas, the surface ocean pH is dropping," said Richard Feely, a marine chemist with the National Oceanic and Atmospheric Administration's Pacific Marine Environmental Laboratory in Seattle.[9] Even a modest increase in acidity in seawater (a falling pH) can dissolve alkaline material, like coral, and make it difficult for mollusks to develop shells.

Just how fast are we adding net $CO_2$ to the atmosphere? It might be useful to do a little simple math before proceeding. Table 4.1 gives some figures to work with.

Three billion net tons every year are added to the growing total

### TABLE 4.1. ANNUAL ATMOSPHERIC CARBON DIOXIDE INCREASE

| Carbon Dioxide Source (worldwide) | Carbon Dioxide Released or Absorbed (in metric tons annually) |
| --- | --- |
| Burning fossil fuels | +5.5 billion |
| Deforestation | +1.5 billion |
| Ocean absorption | −2.0 billion |
| Terrestrial plant life absorption | −2.0 billion |
| **Net annual excess of net $CO_2$** | **3.0 billion tons** |

Paul R. Epstein and Jesse Selber, *Oil: A Life Cycle Analysis of Its Health and Environmental Impacts* (Boston, MA: Center for Health and the Global Environment, Harvard Medical School, March 2002), 43–50.

of $CO_2$ in the atmosphere. The United States is home to about 4 percent of the world's population, but it produces 25 percent of the world's $CO_2$ (and a few other greenhouse gases).[10] The burning of gasoline in the United States alone accounted for 1.1 billion metric tons of $CO_2$ emissions in 2000. Including emissions from refineries and other gasoline infrastructure, that swells gasoline-related $CO_2$ emissions in the United States to about 1.3 billion tons each year. The emissions from passenger vehicles in the United States alone exceed the total national $CO_2$ emissions of all but three countries.[11]

One scientist who spends his days trying to interpret what all this greenhouse gas pollution will mean for life on Earth is Geoff Jenkins, the director of Britain's Hadley Centre, essentially the national meteorologist for the United Kingdom. We met in 2004 in the Foreign Office in London over a cup of tea (what else?) in halls haunted ironically by Churchill and memories of the Empire. The staircases are grand, the high ceilings ornately painted with colorful frescoes, and along the walls stand the marble busts of long-forgotten war marshals and diplomats. One corpulent likeness was carved nearly life-size with the subject dressed as Caesar, perhaps intentionally placed near the down staircase on the way to the exit.

"I was asked to attend a screening of *The Day After Tomorrow* [a disaster film depicting dramatic potential consequences of global warming] so I could tell the press if it was possible," Jenkins said, brushing biscuit crumbs off his laptop computer keyboard. "Well, I couldn't say it was IM-possible."

He clicked through slides on his computer and several captured the issue succinctly. He showed me three different graphs with the same trend line: man-made $CO_2$ emissions, $CO_2$ in the atmosphere, and global temperatures from 1861 to 2003. The correlation is unmistakable, and each one of the trend lines is dramatically up in the last fifty years. He flipped through several other climate models and related trend lines, including a few that showed how the Gulf Stream might "switch off" (albeit very unlikely), but his main point was clear. Our job is to reduce the inputs so that we don't make things worse, but prepare for the inevitable consequences now.

That last part is the trickiest, according to Jenkins and others who work on global warming predictions. They don't disagree on what is likely to occur, but models are only so accurate when it comes to predicting where and precisely when. A safe bet, however, is that effects of global warming are coming to a coastline or river near you within the next generation. The fact that scientists agree that something is coming should concern us; that they can't agree on where, when, or precisely what should horrify us. We should be equally alarmed by the fact that the more we study global warming, the more we discover we didn't know. And this should scare us into action. In Great Britain, it has. I was impressed by Jenkins, but sobered by Margaret Beckett, secretary of state for Environment, Food and Rural Affairs.

"Our climate has warmed by nearly one degree centigrade over the last hundred years or so," she told me matter-of-factly. "Scenarios from our researchers show that we may expect average temperatures [across Great Britain] to increase somewhere between two and three and a half degrees centigrade over the next century."

As we sipped tea in her spacious office, surrounded by spiral-bound studies and thick reports, she described her government's "scenario planning," a deceptively simple term for the planning she and her colleagues have undertaken to deal with what they believe are the inevitable effects of climate change. She showed me maps and contingency plans for the entire country, focused largely on coastal resources and on the most valuable asset on the page, London.

"Our scenarios predict a sea-level rise that could cause flooding along the Thames, increasing the water level there between one and three feet in the next hundred years," she concluded. Her charts and studies showed that the property at risk from tidal flooding within the Thames region is worth about £80 billion. The

British government plans to spend £4 billion over the next forty years just to protect London from rising sea levels caused by climate change.

At the same time I was visiting Secretary Beckett in London in 2003, a number of important new discoveries were being announced about global warming. The National Aeronautics and Space Administration (NASA) determined that particulate matter, mostly from diesel engines, is reducing the ability of snow and ice to reflect sunlight. It may thereby be responsible for up to 25 percent of all measured global warming. If verified, its effect would be twice that of $CO_2$ in terms of actual, measurable global temperature increases.[12] At about the same time in 2003, the University of California Irvine published a study showing that oil- and gas-processing facilities emit far more greenhouse gases than previously thought.[13]

"Based on these findings, it appears that the United States is emitting four to six million tons more methane per year than previously estimated," said F. Sherwood Rowland, a coleader of the study. The same study revealed that rural areas that produce the oil and gas generally have higher levels of petroleum pollution than the urban areas that burn it.

And who would have thought that the Pentagon would be the Paul Revere of change in our global environment? Yet even the brass hats have weighed in. In an October 2003 report commissioned by the Pentagon and ominously entitled "An Abrupt Climate Change Scenario and Its Implications for U.S. National Security," researchers Peter Schwartz and Doug Randall examined the destabilizing effects of large-scale floods, famine, disease, crop failure, and human displacement, among other foreseeable consequences of global warming. That the U.S. military establishment studied the implications of these outcomes, or that they believed the scientists who described the possibilities, is not as remarkable as is their presenting these outcomes as unavoidable.

The Pentagon is not the only high-profile organization that is planning for a changing world. The California Climate Action Registry, for example, is an organization dedicated to measurable reductions in greenhouse gases using market forces to push the envelope, and it includes the likes of BP, US Borax, Qualcomm, and every major power supplier in California.

"Large corporations realize that global warming is a serious, long-term environmental issue, and participation in a registry gives them an opportunity to build the skills and knowledge base they will need in an increasingly carbon-constrained future," Diane Wittenberg, president of the registry, told me one smoggy afternoon in Los Angeles. "Since all emissions are a form of waste, companies want to learn how to measure their emissions and reduce them—both to save money and to lower the carbon content of their products."

Insurance companies have also looked at the data and seen the threat to business interests as very tangible. Swiss Re is the world's second-largest global reinsurer, essentially an insurance company that takes on some of the risks of other insurance companies. Swiss Re produced its first climate change risk publication in the early 1990s to prepare for the inevitable disruptions that will occur.

"This issue cuts across all these major business areas," explains Chris Walker, managing director of Greenhouse Gas Risk Solutions for Swiss Re. "For Swiss Re, climate change is more than a scientific issue. It is a financial issue. The world of finance is traditionally very short-term. But as a reinsurer we have to think about the bigger picture. We realized that climate change would be crucial to our long-term health as a business."[14]

Long-term survival was also on the minds of the 155,000 Inuit people of Canada, the United States, Russia, and Greenland when they accused the U.S. government of violating their human rights by failing to take action to reduce greenhouse gas pollution. In a petition to the Organization of American States in late 2005, the native people known as Eskimos in Alaska asserted that climate change has eroded their shorelines, thinned the ice, and otherwise adversely affected their ability to hunt as they have for thousands of years. They blame this change on the United States, as the source of 25 percent of the world's greenhouse gas emissions and the only major polluter that has failed to take meaningful action to reduce these emissions.

"This is not about money,"[15] declared Sheila Watt-Cloutier, one of the Inuit leaders who filed the petition. "We are not seeking damages. What we want is for the United States to stop violating our rights."

The effect of global warming on polar ecosystems has been documented for years. The causes are equally well publicized. The *Los Angeles Times* ran a story in September 2003 provocatively declaring "Arctic's Biggest Ice Shelf, a Sentinel of Climate Change, Breaks Apart." In the middle of the story was an ad for that icon of poor fuel economy, indeed the poster child for global warming emissions, the Hummer.[16]

A Hummer ad in the middle of an article about global warming should insult us, but it passed without comment. Why? Perhaps because we've already made our Faustian bargain with our petroleum-powered lives and everyone is resigned to the notion that we can't change it. At least most of us in oil-consuming nations seem to act that way. What we fail to address is that oil consumers don't pay all the costs of this bargain. Many oil-producing nations bear costs that are neither easy to quantify nor ever added to the price of a gallon of gas.

## Costs Without Measure:
## The Fate of Oil-Producing Nations

We are so used to hearing about the fabulous wealth that came to some small Middle East nations that it's easy to miss the realities of oil-producing nations elsewhere. As we have seen, whether you are a farmer in California's Central Valley, a property owner along the

Thames River in London, or simply a citizen breathing polluted air in a smoggy metropolis, you are paying a hidden price for our addiction to oil. Yet you may never hear about the many hidden costs that are being paid by our counterparts in third world nations that supply much of the petroleum we consume.

Global Witness, a respected human rights organization, reports that ExxonMobil paid millions of dollars to President José Eduardo dos Santos in the 1990s, allowing him to prolong Angola's civil war.[17] Venezuela has raked in more than $600 billion in oil revenues in the last three decades, but its per capita income fell some 15 percent in the 1970s and 1980s and is once again headed downward in the new millennium.[18] At the height of the Arab oil embargo of the 1970s, when rulers in the Middle East held the health of Western economies by the nose, Juan Pablo Pérez Alfonso of Venezuela, a cofounder of the Organization of Petroleum Exporting Countries (OPEC), called petroleum "the devil's excrement" and complained of the "waste, corruption, consumption, our public services falling apart. And debt, debt we shall have for years."[19]

As I traveled the globe over the past three decades, I have met many amazing people and been witness to the effects that our addiction has wrought on their lives. Here are stories from three continents that best exemplify what a founder of OPEC meant by "devil's excrement."

## An African Petroleum Tale: Nigeria

In the early 1990s, I lived in Lagos, Nigeria. It is an intensely crowded city, and more people live on the street or in cardboard huts than in apartments or homes. Traffic is gridlocked 24-7. Vendors squat alongside every roadway selling bananas and rice, large grilled rodents euphemistically called "bushmeat," and tiny packets of Chiclets gum. Parallel to the roads are open sewers, covered only by wood or steel planks that act as driveways into the ubiquitous walled compounds. Poverty is the norm in a country where a person with clean clothes and a working bicycle is middle class.

Wanle Akinboboye is a proud, regal man, prematurely balding at thirty-eight, the owner of an eclectic recreational services business, married with two kids. His gaze is at once piercing and inquisitive, but boyish and vaguely gullible. Perhaps that last quality is just optimism in a nation that breeds little of it, but needs a lot. Wanle is intensely proud of his country and crusades to bring the Olympics to Nigeria one day, making it the first African nation to host the games, he hopes.

So that I could truly understand the country and its people, Wanle took me neither to a wildlife preserve nor a tourist bazaar but to the funeral of his friend's mother. Vast buffets of exotic meat and drink were laid out, and I tasted my first roasted dog. World-famous musician Sunny Ade and his band played from ten at night until after sunrise without a break. We danced on the outdoor stage with the musicians, honoring them by sticking dollar bills to the sweat on their foreheads. Each guest brought gifts of food and drink. Wanle sent a refrigerated trailer of meat and water.

While the wealthy few live in comfort with satellite dishes and cell phones, even mourning in lavish style, the majority of Nigerians live in unimaginable, hopeless poverty. Graft is rampant, but nowhere more so than in government, especially at the highest levels. Various presidents and military dictators have made themselves rich beyond belief, mostly via profits skimmed directly or indirectly from Nigeria's incredible oil riches.

Wanle showed me the Niger River delta and the postapocalyptic industrial city of Port Harcourt, site of Nigeria's main oil production facilities. All of Nigeria is hot. In summer, it is also humid and intense with tropical decay. In winter, it is hot and dry, covered with red dust from the Harmattan winds that blow in from the Sahara to the north, leaving fine particles on your desk in which you can write your name, wipe it clean, and within an hour scribble again. But in Port Harcourt, as one local resident describes it, the air simply attacks your eyes, your nose, your lungs.

"Open flares of natural gas . . . are burned off daily, emitting a pungent smell that tickles the nostrils," the man from Port Harcourt said. "New galvanized rooftops are caked with rust within two years, thanks to acid rain. And miles of brown, rusting oil pipelines that dot the landscape often leak or burst, sending streams of sticky black liquid into the fields."[20]

Not far from Port Harcourt, an oil pipeline burst in the city of Warri in October 1998. Impoverished local villagers rushed to the growing pool of oil to collect what they could in buckets, hoping to use it for cooking fuel or to sell for cash. Within minutes, thousands had waded ankle deep in a sea of oil that had grown to the size of a football field. Celebration was in the air, the joy of an unexpected windfall, probably similar to my naive joy as a child when a blizzard canceled school for the day.

"It was like a marketplace," recalls Chief John Ogude, a local tribal elder who rejoiced at the unexpected wealth that had fallen into the laps of his friends and neighbors. In the end, though, there is no joy in oil.

"The vast pool of oil . . . accidentally ignited," Chief Ogude said stoically.[21] Within minutes his tribe literally went up in flames. Five hundred people died instantly in the inferno, and two hundred more died of their injuries within days. Where celebrating tribespeople had once danced for joy over their windfall, there now danced fearsome flames more than 60 feet high, consuming man, beast, land, and soul.

Nor was this an isolated incident. Nigerians have filed suit against ChevronTexaco, alleging the oil giant's responsibility for deaths of still other hapless villagers, this time at the hands of armed thugs, who descended on the simple tribesmen protesting against oil exploitation in their country.[22] ChevronTexaco doesn't deny that it hired the Nigerian military and police officers responsible for the killings, but it claims that it did not authorize the use of deadly force. The lawsuit is scheduled to go to trial in late 2006, and a class-action lawsuit will be heard in 2007.[23] Chevron should take note of the fate of its competitor, Shell, who lost a court battle in Nigeria in early 2006 over pollution on the Niger River delta and must pay local tribes $1.5 billion.[24] Shell has indicated that it will appeal, so it may be a long time, if ever, before the villagers see a penny.

In Lagos, I was struck by a popular billboard for Benson and Hedges cigarettes. The ad simply showed the hand of a white man, extended down from the top right corner of the billboard, reaching toward the hand of a black man, reaching up from the lower left. The white man's arm displayed an impeccable suit and a mono-grammed shirt with expensive cuff links. The black man's clothing was more modest business attire. The white man was handing the black man a package of cigarettes. It could just as easily have been a quart of oil or an SUV.

I wonder now if Wanle showed me the destruction wrought by petroleum on his homeland because he hoped that I, as a consumer of the same commodity that had so impoverished his people, would accept a modicum of responsibility. Or, did he do it out of a naive honesty, seeking to portray his country as it is, the astonishing beauty and cultural diversity held up against the bleak waste brought on by greed? When I lived there in the early 1990s, gasoline sold for 15 cents a gallon, a subsidy that officials consider "payment" to the masses for allowing the rape of a nation. In the years since, Nigeria has earned more than $300 billion in oil revenues, but its per capita income is less than $1 a day, still one of the lowest of any nation.[25]

## South American Petroleum Tales: Colombia and Ecuador

In the 1980s, I spent many months in Bogota and other parts of Colombia. In those days, Colombia was already suffering from vio-lent battles over the lucrative drug trade. In the midst of it all lived people like Hector Castro (no relation to any Caribbean dictators) and his family. Hector was a gentle man of quiet integrity who had made a tidy sum buying and selling natural gas, used mostly for the same domestic purposes we use it for in U.S. homes.

Hector's wife, Gloria, set a lovely table, adorned with her grandmother's china and lace tablecloths she had purchased in Spain. Their two teenage children were starched and deferential, fascinated with American pop culture, but firmly rooted in their Colombian heritage of cousins, uncles, aunts, grandparents, and old family retainers. At meals with guests, in their home or at one of Bogota's many pulsating night spots, vast quantities of *aguardiente* (burning water) appeared, a liquor made from sugarcane and flavored with anise that has hundreds of local variations, much like fine wines from Napa Valley.

"To Wednesday," Hector would shout, exercising his privilege as host and patron to offer the first toast. All had to down their glasses, but no one would drink more quickly than the foreign guest.

"To our women on Wednesday," came another toast.

"To our mothers," came another. After the third glass of *aguardiente*, I have no idea what the remaining toasts were about.

The darker side of life, however, lurked right outside the Castros' door. Their comfortable home was ringed with high walls, razor wire, and heavy, metal gates. They owned a Mercedes, but they mostly drove an unremarkable Ford sedan with faded paint to avoid attention. Kidnapping, a cottage industry in Colombia, darkened their otherwise shiny existence.

One summer day, Hector's fourteen-year-old son, Hector Jr., was snatched as he returned from school. Hector received his son's ear after three months of waiting. He waited another two months before the first ransom note came. After several more months, during which money changed hands on several occasions and impotent local officials paraded before the Castros, their son was returned. Hector Jr. survived his ordeal, but kidnapping and the violent murder of judges and high-level politicians remains commonplace. Why? Because of U.S. demand for oil and drugs. Oil is inextricably linked in Colombia to the drug trade, and both are heavily subsidized by U.S. taxpayers.

The United States has long sent money and men to fight alongside Colombians in the attempt to stem the drug supply. In the fall of 2003, for example, the United States and Colombia sent thousands of troops into the tiny village of Arauca to protect the oil there, although the two governments claimed it was done to battle drugs.[26]

Arauca is both a department (province) and a modest town that has grown about sixfold since the discovery of oil. Now a bustling city of 60,000 people, on the border with Venezuela northeast from the capital of Bogota, it is a place of natural drama, with massive rivers flowing from the towering Andes mountains to the west, wetlands and fertile grasslands to the east. Until two decades ago, it was a region of peaceful farmers who grew cacao, banana, rice, fruits, cotton, and sesame and tended lots of cattle fattened on the fertile grasslands, much like our own Great Plains that once sustained vast herds of buffalo. There were few roads and no electricity or modern plumbing.

My flights to Colombia were often populated with oil explorers who went to Arauca and found what they sought, and in 1983 Occidental announced oil discoveries there. The Cuban-inspired leftist rebels, the National Liberation Army, or ELN as they are called based on their name in Spanish, however, demanded payoffs from the oil companies to ensure uninterrupted access to the black gold. As its insurgency grew, ELN rebels needed more money for guns and soldiers. They first turned to bombing the same oil pipeline they were once paid to protect and then extorted protection money from the repair crews that were sent in to deal with the damage.[27]

ELN is not the only insurgency using oil leverage to attempt the overthrow of the government in Bogota. The Revolutionary Armed Forces of Colombia, known by their name in Spanish as FARC, also attack the Arauca oil pipeline. The intention was to destabilize both the federal government and their ELN rivals by robbing both of oil revenues. FARC derives its income from the drug trade, and the last thing it wants is for global oil companies to attract military attention from Bogota and Washington, D.C.[28]

FARC's concerns were warranted, as the United States led an offensive designed to protect the oil pipeline and to secure a chunk of remote jungle real estate near Arauca believed to hold 20 million barrels of oil. "Secure" in this case meant clear-cutting every living thing—including coca plants—for acres around to make the land easier to defend. Colombia admits that revenue from the oil pipeline—some $500 million a year, roughly 5 percent of the country's entire annual budget—is crucial to fighting both drug lords and political insurgents.[29] But even that wealth isn't enough.

"If the Colombian state can't assert itself and take care of its territory, then regional security is undermined," said a State Department official, who spoke anonymously to the *Los Angeles Times*. "A variety of U.S. goals in the region are compromised, and the overall security of the U.S. is undermined."[30]

As with most things on our petroleum-powered planet, however, the story does not stop there. As extortion money from oil companies fades for ELN and drug revenues plummet for FARC, both groups of rebels turn to kidnapping and ransom—of people like Hector Jr.—to pay for soldiers and buy the hearts and minds of Colombians.

Human rights groups in Colombia assert that although U.S.-sponsored offensives in Arauca have resulted in fewer attacks on the oil pipeline, they have come with a price tag of eroded democratic freedoms, something the United States once hoped to export beyond its own borders. There have been widely publicized arrests of political and labor leaders, and in September 2002 Colombian

President Alvaro Uribe suspended constitutional guarantees in the Arauca area.

"Everyone here is terrified," said Martin Sandoval, a former member of local government and now a respected human rights activist. "There is no freedom of expression, no freedom of assembly, no freedom of anything."[31]

The State Department pushed the idea to Congress of U.S. taxpayers funding the pipeline protection, ultimately obtaining $99 million for the project.

"The cost doesn't matter, whether it's blood or money," said Oscar Garcia, a union organizer of petroleum workers in the Arauca region. "The U.S. is not going to allow a shortage of oil."[32]

The FARC and ELN are responding, not only with continued attacks on the pipeline, but by offering a $33,000 reward for each captured U.S. soldier.[33] Amazingly, the U.S. commander in the joint offensive was quoted in the *Los Angeles Times* as saying he has no problem putting his life at risk to protect a pipe full of oil.

"The Colombian government and its infrastructure is very important . . . to the stability of the U.S.," he said dutifully. "Oil or whatever—is important for the United States."[34]

Sadly for those who have lost their lives protecting "whatever is important to the United States" most of the oil fields in Colombia have been exhausted and the country will likely become a net importer of oil before the end of this decade. Twenty years ago, Colombia's papers spoke breathlessly of seemingly inexhaustible oil reserves exceeding a billion barrels. Those original finds are now virtually wiped out, and today the country has nothing to show for it except pollution, crime, and political instability. Arauca has one of the highest homicide rates in the world.[35]

Arauca is not the only land laid waste by oil in South America, leaving no one in particular responsible, but everyone suffering. Remote parts of the rain forest in Ecuador have been the focus of oil development by U.S. companies since the 1960s.

"Before ChevronTexaco came to the Amazon, we had extensive lands, clean air, clean water, and plenty of food," said Cofan tribal elder Toribio Aguinda at the 2004 ChevronTexaco shareholder meeting in San Ramon, California. "The Cofan people are on the verge of extinction. . . . I would like to ask you: Do you want the Cofan people to disappear?"[36]

The Cofan people inspired a shareholder resolution to persuade ChevronTexaco to invest a tiny amount of its 2003 net income of $7.2 billion in a cleanup of its former oil fields in the Amazon. Corporate management responded that it was a minority partner in the oil field with the Ecuadorian government and that it had spent some $40 million to clean up its share of the pollution before pulling out a decade ago. Regardless of who is responsible, however, the job is apparently not finished.

"We have witnessed the suffering," said Reverend Steve Harms of Peace Lutheran Church in Danville, California, after taking a trip to the Cofan's homeland. "There is no clean water [and] everyone is dying slowly of stomach cancer and there is no medicine."[37] ChevronTexaco admits that vast pollution remains and that human health effects from 18 million gallons of toxic oil waste has fouled the land and rivers for more than 100 square miles.

"Any further liability is the responsibility of PetroEcuador," said ChevronTexaco chairman David J. O'Reilly to his shareholders and the Cofan tribal elder. "The environmental damage is not our responsibility."[38]

Ecuador's undersecretary for the environment, Jorge Alban, disagrees. His government acknowledges that ChevronTexaco has cleaned up more than two hundred of the waste pits it created in the region, but two years before that shareholder meeting, Ecuador petitioned the oil giant for $5 billion to clean up more than four hundred more that it left behind.[39] O'Reilly was apparently more persuasive than Undersecretary Alban, Chief Aquinda, and the Reverend Harms combined. The shareholder resolution was voted down by 91 percent of the shareholder votes. Proponents have also turned to the courts and have filed lawsuits against the California oil giant.

"We've lived there for thousands of years, and we've never had diseases like this before," said Humberto Piaguaje, a leader of Ecuador's Secoya tribe. "We want Chevron to do a true cleanup of the areas they contaminated."[40] The case languished in U.S. courts for years before being transferred to courts in Ecuador. The trial finally began there in 2004 and has proceeded slowly because the judge wants to inspect more than 120 of ChevronTexaco's dump sites.

"This is rainforest Chernobyl," said Leila Salazar-Lopez of San Francisco–based Amazon Watch. "Before Texaco arrived, this was pristine Amazon rainforest where five indigenous tribes depended on a clean, healthy environment to survive. Now they're basically living in a giant Superfund site."[41]

Like the oil fields of Arauca, those around the Cofan tribal homelands are now exhausted and abandoned, another tribal homeland laid waste. To put it all in perspective, consider that when all is said and done in Arauca, the resources so vigorously protected by the U.S. and Colombian militaries at so great a human cost might secure a grand total of 20 million barrels of oil, about the volume consumed by the United States in just one day.

## An Asian Petroleum Tale: Kazakhstan

Nigeria, Colombia, and Ecuador: each of these countries was thought to be the next savior of the industrialized world, offering plentiful, cheap oil teased from the planet by a willing, inexpensive, local labor force. Now some see the lands of the former Soviet Union as the next great petroleum hope, containing vast untapped reserves that will guarantee our business–as–usual consumption for several more decades. The Kazakh region is preeminent among the latest oil-fired dreams.

In fact, the most hopeful estimate of Kazakh oil production is 3 million barrels a day, or 10 percent of U.S. daily use by the time such results might be manifest. What have we done to secure such a sultan's ransom? For starters, the United States propped up Kazakh president Nursultan Nazarbayev, a notorious strongman accused of silencing domestic opponents and rigging elections.[42]

"Nazarbayev came to realize that there would be no serious consequences for his antidemocratic actions," said Martha Brill Olcott, a consultant to ChevronTexaco and an expert on regional affairs at the Carnegie Endowment for International Peace.[43]

Like most leaders of third world republics with oil, Nazarbayev has used his U.S. support to feed at the petroleum trough. His daughter owns the construction company that has built much of the housing and office space for oil workers. His other daughter controls the Kazakh national media. U.S. consultants, with close ties to high government officials, have been indicted for bribing Nazarbayev and other Kazakh officials on behalf of their oil company clients.[44]

"In my experience, there was an unprecedented level of input [in local politics] from oil companies," notes Robert Baer, a former CIA analyst and author of *Sleeping with the Devil*. "We considered it to be in our national interest for oil companies to invest there, and we didn't want anything to get in the way."[45]

In March 2002, the Heritage Foundation, known for its conservative views, ranked Kazakhstan 131st of 161 countries in terms of its commitment to free market capitalism, calling the country "mostly unfree." Yet two months later, Commerce Secretary Donald L. Evans, after heavy lobbying from the U.S. oil industry, dropped Kazakhstan from the U.S. list of "nonmarket economies."[46] This change was an important distinction because having that label would impose tougher sanctions in the event of trade disputes.

The U.S. State Department issued a scathing report in 2003 on human rights and democratic conditions in Kazakhstan, but after a

month of intense lobbying from oil companies, the Bush administration certified that the Nazarbayev regime had shown "significant
improvement" in human rights and sent $51 million taxpayer dol-
lars in U.S. aid that year to Kazakhstan. Senators John McCain (R-
Arizona) and Patrick Leahy (D-Vermont) strongly disagreed with
the release of aid money, but they eventually lost to the influence of
six highly paid lobbyists employed by ChevronTexaco to win the
funding.[47]

In *Sleeping with the Devil*, Baer argues that oil led to our support
for oppressive regimes like Saudi Arabia, which in turn led to the
hatred of the United States that spawned the September 11, 2001,
attacks. The 9/11 hijackers, he shows, were given special treatment
for a type of visa that is generally afforded to Saudis, but no one else
on Earth, all to facilitate the trade of oil.[48]

Ironically, on September 11, 2001, I was in an Exxon station in
Santa Monica, pumping $1.25 a gallon gasoline into my car, when I
heard over the radio that the second plane had hit the World Trade
Center. As the source of funding for the hijackers emerged in the
following months, I thought about buying a car powered by batteries or compressed natural gas. On the second anniversary of that
attack, though, I was back in the same Exxon station at exactly the
same hour, filling the gasoline tank at $2.40 a gallon and listening to
9/11 memorials on the car radio.

If my friends in Nigeria and South America were trying to tell
me something about the true price of our own addiction to oil, the
cure has been too slow in coming, both for their countrymen and
mine. Many costs of our oil dependence are easily quantifiable, but
wars, erosion of our humanity and political integrity, a changing climate, and destruction of native civilizations that have survived in
peace with the planet for untold millennia are costs that cannot fully
be measured, especially if we refuse to confront them, if we refuse
to see beyond the glitter of the false gold.

How did we come to this place? How could we have given up

so much for so little in return? As chapter 5 describes, that false gold buys conspiracies, deceptions, and frauds that have kept us in the dark for decades, covered in oil. It is that false gold that has corrupted our political leaders, our corporate leaders, and many of us who consume petroleum products and fail to demand something better.

# CHAPTER 5

# Wealth Seems Rather to Possess Them

The lust of avarice has so totally seized upon mankind
that their wealth seems rather to possess them than they
possess their wealth.

*Pliny*

D o the business practices of oil and auto companies explain
how they have been so successful in heaping the true
costs of their products on the backs of consumers, taxpayers, and innocent bystanders in third world countries? Deceiv-
ing the public and government regulators about products that are
known to be harmful is not a tactic taught in business schools, but
it is remarkable to see in court records and other government documents how similar practices were employed by oil companies,
automakers, and their tobacco company brethren over the same
time span. As noted in previous chapters, many of the toxins and
related harms of petroleum pollution are identical to those of

tobacco products, so perhaps this comparable corporate approach shouldn't be surprising.

## A Tale of Two "Franks":
## The Twin Deceptions of Tobacco and Oil

As the United States reached the midpoint of the twentieth century, emerging from the shadow of war in Europe and the Pacific, teachers in U.S. schools reported that the top three problems facing them in their classrooms were students talking out of turn, running in the hall, and littering.[1] We might find that quaint today, but it was certainly a sign of those times, the world into which I was born in 1952. People, at least in public, valued honesty and believed that fairness and hard work were the best policy, be it in the classroom or the boardroom.

That belief, however, turns out to be a naive view compared to the gritty dramas that were unfolding behind boardroom doors at the time. Before I blew out three candles on a birthday cake, tobacco companies, under growing pressure from regulators and after years of denial, jointly issued a "Frank Statement," admitting that their products might create toxic smoke and thereby cause lung damage. The companies pledged to work together, to check their competition at the door on this one issue, and to draw on the best science to make products that were safe when used as directed. The record shows, however, that they formed the Tobacco Institute to do just the opposite, to hide the harms of their products, to lie to the public and regulators, and to continue manufacturing products that were killing millions of their best customers.[2] The companies claimed that cigarettes were not addictive and that the amount of nicotine in them was not manipulated; they claimed they did not intentionally market to children with promotions like the once-ubiquitous Joe Camel ads; they claimed they did not have evidence that smoking caused lung cancer. Thanks to former tobacco company executives such as whistle blower Dr. Jeffrey Wigand (the central figure portrayed in the

1999 film *The Insider*), we now know that none of these assertions were true.[3]

"For more than 300 years, tobacco has given solace, relaxation, and enjoyment to mankind," the tobacco industry's Frank Statement read in part. "We accept an interest in people's health as a basic responsibility, paramount to every other consideration in our business."

Also in the mid-1950s, auto companies, under growing pressure from regulators and after years of denial, took a page from the tobacco playbook and jointly issued what could be called their own "frank statement," admitting that their products might create toxic exhaust and thereby cause lung damage. The companies pledged to work together, to check their competition at the door on this one issue, and to combine the best science to make products that were safe when used as directed. The record shows that they formed the American Automobile Manufacturers Association (AAMA) to do the exact opposite.

"[T]he automobile manufacturers, through AAMA, conspired not to compete in [the] research, development, manufacture, and installation of [pollution] control devices," reveals the U.S. Department of Justice in a 1968 memo, "[but] collectively did all in their power to delay such research, development, manufacturing, and installation."[4]

Actually, Big Auto, along with Big Oil and Big Tires, had been caught with its big hands in the cookie jar long before tobacco companies faced the legal hickory stick. The clearest and earliest evidence of this tobacco-like corporate philosophy was embodied in the infamous National City Lines conspiracy.

In 1922, Warren G. Harding presided over a United States where the price of a three-bedroom home was $4,125 and a loaf of bread was 9 cents. Americans were humming "Way Down Yonder in New Orleans" and flocked to see *Orphans of the Storm*. The product of film master D. W. Griffith, *Orphans* portrayed two sisters, one blind and the other duped by a wicked aristocrat.

Also in 1922, Niels Bohr won the Nobel Prize in Physics "for his services in the investigation of the structure of atoms and of the radiation emanating from them," an indication that we were just beginning to understand how things in our universe work at the atomic level. On another continent, conspirators were just beginning to understand how the marketplace works at a new level, using that knowledge to make themselves rich at others' expense. We too in a way were blind "orphans," being led to a kind of doom as surely as those who faced the guillotine in Griffith's epic film.

It was that same year, 1922, when GM's Alfred P. Sloan Jr. secretly hatched a plan to replace the nation's clean, electric mass-transit railcars with dirty diesel buses and petroleum-powered automobiles. Faced with record red ink the year before, Sloan knew he would need to expand the market for his company's products. Nine of ten vehicular trips in the United States were made on mass transit at the time, and nine of ten Americans did not even own a car. Sloan connected the dots and aimed his sights at a large, but obvious target: kill the urban rail systems and essentially force people to buy cars and force cities to buy buses.[5]

Like a good military general, Sloan knew that he needed allies. GM, Standard Oil, Phillips Petroleum, Firestone Tire & Rubber, and Mack Truck all made a profit from selling buses, trucks, and cars, not from selling electric-rail mass-transit trains. Sloan and his allies created a shell company, National City Lines, to quietly buy up the nation's mass-transit agencies and scrap the electric trains they operated. National City Lines could then replace the trains with buses made and fueled by the conspirators. In the process, it could reduce overall mass-transit service and promote automobile sales as a more convenient option to millions of consumers.

Between 1920 and 1955, a nation came of age as its stock market crashed and rebounded, its sons and daughters joined the world at war for the second time in a generation, and women won voting rights and a share of jobs previously reserved for men. As the nation grew, and grew up, the conspirators methodically bought electric-rail mass-transit systems in forty-five U.S. cities, including New York, Philadelphia, St. Louis, and Los Angeles. With warlike precision, they converted each system from electric rail to diesel-powered buses, which were less efficient, dirtier, and more expensive to operate.

Nor were the conspirators content with expanding market share for their products; rather, they were determined to permanently crush their competition. In Los Angeles, for example, they doused the famous Red Cars with kerosene as they were retired and set them ablaze. (The 1988 movie *Who Framed Roger Rabbit* was loosely based on the scandal and depicts that fateful scene.) A few of the railcars were sent to museums; a few others were dumped in the Santa Monica Bay to attract game fish for local anglers.

Fortunately for the United States, government regulators were watching. In 1947, the administration of Harry Truman filed antitrust lawsuits against the companies; in 1949, those companies were found guilty in federal court of violating federal antitrust laws and conspiring to monopolize the sale of buses and force their sale to the public transit agencies. The companies were, in effect, eliminating clean, electric-rail mass-transit and replacing it with their products. Unfortunately for the United States, government regulators acted too late. Although the conspiracy was proven in court and later upheld by appellate courts, the corporations involved were fined only $5,000 and the executives were fined just $1 apiece because the judge determined that there wasn't much anyone could do about the lost mass transit and the now-ubiquitous diesel buses and gasoline cars on dozens of American Main Streets.

With the demise of the Red Cars, the City of Angels was one of the big losers. Before the conversion, greater Los Angeles was served by one thousand electric trains a day. In 1961, as the last electric train carried Angelenos to work and school, scientists identified the components of smog for the first time. And since the Red Cars were scrapped, there has been a dramatic and steady increase in the percentage of Los Angeles residents who suffer from asthma, and asthma-related deaths.[6]

Sloan's strategy to rescue his ailing company seems to have worked. GM is now the world's largest automaker and one of the Fortune Global 500 top ten corporations on the planet, with annual revenues nearing $200 billion in 2005.[7] The other conspirators also became dominant in their industries, especially Standard Oil, which subsequently morphed into a little company called ExxonMobil. Now the most profitable corporation in the world, ExxonMobil had revenues in 2005 of more than a quarter of a trillion dollars and profits of $25 billion.[8]

The exclamation point on this sad history of the genesis of smog in the United States is that the new owners of the mass-transit systems ordered the tracks ripped up so that no one would be tempted to return to cleaner, more affordable transportation in the future. Once the rail lines were gone, the streets were repaved, largely at taxpayer expense, using asphalt, a by-product of the oil-refining industry. As incredible as this tale of corporate greed and conspiracy may seem, there is abundant evidence and a host of fascinating details that read like a pulp fiction novel. A more complete account can be found in Jack Doyle's excellent 2000 book, *Taken for a Ride*.

## The Avarice of Oil: Injured Workers, High-Octane Lies, and Creative Accounting

Although the National City Lines conspiracy involved varied corporate interests, oil companies have engaged in duplicity on their own to protect and promote their products. One example can be found in the world's most infamous oil spill, another at just about every gas station in the United States, and still another in the ledgers of oil companies and many oil-producing nations.

In the aftermath of the *Exxon Valdez* oil spill, Exxon (now ExxonMobil) repeatedly misled its cleanup crews about their exposure to petroleum toxins and withheld information from the federal government about illnesses that, by law, they were required to report, according to evidence compiled by Dr. Riki Ott, author of *Sound Truth and Corporate Myths*.

"Exxon told the workers that the oil was safe," explains Ott. "Just wear the right protective clothing."[9] But the high-pressure hot-water wash used in the cleanup actually created a toxic petroleum aerosol, scattering oil from the rocks and driving it deep into workers' lungs. Some respirators were provided, but only to the cleanup workers actually applying the dispersants. Exxon found concentrations of oil in the air that exceeded federal standards by up to four-hundred-fold, but failed to report a single occurrence.

Exxon also apparently failed to report, in direct violation of federal law, 6,722 cases of upper respiratory "infections," injuries from what Ott calls "a mass epidemic of chemical poisoning."[10] The results of the exposures were respiratory ailments, headaches, nose-bleeds, dysfunction of the immune system and nervous system, and blood disorders.[11] Exxon lobbied successfully to avoid having the spill designated as a cleanup of hazardous waste because if it had been, they would have been required to pay workers for forty hours of hazardous materials training. That, in turn, would have forced Exxon to acknowledge the toxins to which their workers were being exposed.[12]

Oil companies deceive more than their workers when they sell consumers millions of dollars of petroleum products every year that they don't need. Did you ever wonder why just about every pump at a gasoline station has three grades of gasoline even though the vast majority of cars on the road today are designed to use only the lowest—and cheapest—grade?

The lowest grade is called "regular" and is typically labeled with dull colors and symbols, while the higher—more costly—grades are labeled with bright, eye-catching colors and starbursts and given names like "premium" and "super." And because we read left to right, you might assume grades of fuel would be set out on a pump as low to medium to high, from left to right, but many pumps actually put the highest octane—and most expensive—gasoline on the left, where your hand might naturally go first.

You may not have noticed these marketing ploys, and oil companies hope you never will. But make no mistake: many people unnecessarily fill their cars with higher-octane fuels every day because for years they have been misled about the utility of those fuels by deceptive ads and misleading marketing at the pump. The Federal Trade Commission has taken action against Exxon and other gasoline retailers for making false claims about the benefits of using high-octane fuels in average cars, but marketing tactics at the pump and in the media suggests that the practice continues today.[13]

Octane is a measure of a fuel's ability to resist premature detonation, a condition that may cause an engine to "knock" or "ping." For cars, it is expressed as a number, typically between 87 and 94. Engines knock or ping when the fuel-to-air mixture is ignited prematurely, causing the pistons to operate out of order. More than 90 percent of all cars on the road in the United States today are designed to use fuels with an octane rating of less than 87, which is "regular" fuel at most gas stations.[14]

"In most cases, I view buying premium fuel as throwing money away," said David E. Cole, chairman of the Center for Automotive Research in Ann Arbor, Michigan. "I buy regular fuel. I think it's the best deal, and it's not going to hurt your car."[15] As Cole and others have explained for years, unless you drive a high-compression luxury vehicle or a sports car, it's likely that your vehicle came from the factory designed to operate on gasoline rated around 80. As engines age, deposits are left in combustion chambers and slightly higher octane may then be needed for smooth performance, but typically not more than an additional two to four points. Modern cars don't even need that; computer-controlled engines adjust for these elements and keep the car running smoothly at all times, regardless of fuel.

In other words, despite the proliferation of premium and super gasoline pumps, 90 percent of the cars on the road today don't need gasoline with an octane rating greater than 87, yet 40 percent of the fuel sold to U.S. consumers is rated and priced much higher than that. Other than paying for something you don't need, this high-octane deception harms us in other ways because higher-octane fuels require more energy to produce and thereby generate more toxic air emissions.

"Making a higher octane product can entail a crude run [through the refining process] twice that for a suboctane product," explains the *Oil & Gas Journal*.[16] It takes so much unnecessary energy to produce high-octane fuels that the federal government considered taking steps to end the practice as a matter of national security. Within two months after the 1990 invasion of Kuwait by Iraq, Energy Secretary James Watkins proposed a plan to curtail the sale of unnecessary high-octane fuel as a way to save 80,000 barrels of crude oil a day, the amount of extra energy wasted in making high-octane fuels.[17] Let me repeat that: tens of thousands of barrels of oil are wasted each and every day making harmful products we don't need.

"Octane demand is a situation forced on customers," notes the *Oil & Gas Journal*. The health effects of this marketing ploy are also forced upon noncustomers and any other living organisms that breathe the dirty air because higher-octane fuels, compared with lower-octane ones, contain more "aromatics" (the lighter components whose fumes are highly toxic, potentially carcinogenic, and easily evaporate).

For decades, lead was added to gasoline to increase octane. When it was phased out of most fuels beginning in the 1970s, however, the oil industry came up with an even better plan for manipulating octane levels. Petroleum naturally contains benzene, toluene,

ethylbenzene, and xylene ("BTEX" compounds), and refiners discovered that by increasing the levels of these highly toxic compounds, you could increase the octane. In other words, you could
make and sell these unnecessary high-octane products from additives that were already present in your refinery.

As it comes out of the ground, oil contains less than 2 percent
of these BTEX aromatics, but to replace lead and to continue selling high-octane fuels, oil companies boosted the BTEX compounds
to as much as 45 percent. In short, oil companies replaced one
highly toxic additive with even greater volumes of another, a move
reminiscent of the manipulation of nicotine levels in cigarettes by
tobacco companies.

There were other choices. Oil companies knew that they could
add cleaner octane boosters, such as alcohol and ethers, but those
are made from organic substances (such as wood and corn) that
were outside the control of refiners.[18] In later years, when regulators required refiners to "oxygenate" gasolines to make them burn
cleaner, oil companies repeated this pattern, selecting MTBE
instead of ethanol (again, made from corn) because they controlled
production of the former and had no way to make money from
the latter. As described previously, gasoline with this additive, suspected of causing leukemia in humans, escaped from leaking storage tanks and, because of its ability to mix easily with water, contaminated the drinking water supplies of millions of unsuspecting
Americans.

As BTEX compounds increased in gasoline during the 1980s, so
did measurable air pollution. The USEPA found benzene concentrations in air increasing by as much as fourteen times the level
detected before BTEX compounds were added.[19] During the same
period, fuel injection became ubiquitous in new car engines. Fuel
injectors are easily clogged with the constituents in high-octane
gasoline, which results in deposits that further decrease engine performance.[20] The ultimate irony is that engine performance can only

be restored by burning a higher-octane fuel to compensate for the reduction in performance caused by a clogged engine. "Detergent" gasolines are sometimes erroneously assumed to clean deposits from your engine, but the federal Clean Air Act requires detergent additives to help *prevent* deposits from building up in the engine, a problem that is often caused in the first place by use of gasoline with unnecessarily high-octane ratings.[21]

"Reduced aromatic (BTEX) content [in gasoline] could provide ... less engine deposit formation," admitted GM's director of research, Joseph M. Colucci.[22]

Oil companies mislead consumers and government regulators about other things, too. One of a petroleum company's primary financial assets is the amount of oil reserves it controls. Share prices of a company are based in large part on this estimate, and as noted previously, several oil giants have come under fire for overstating their reserves to prop up share prices, a blatant securities fraud.

"I'm sick and tired about lying," wrote Shell executive Walter van de Vijver in a November 2003 e-mail to other company executives about the issue. Still, investigations reveal that for at least two years, Shell continued to misstate its estimates of reserves.[23] Shareholders are put at financial risk from these and other illegal oil industry practices, such as the millions in bribes paid to political leaders of oil-rich third world nations, including Kazakhstan and Angola as described in chapter 4. Bribes are so commonplace that large institutional investors fear the potential effect on stock prices when such news becomes public. The issue came to a head in May 2003 when ten investment funds representing $600 billion in assets demanded disclosure of such payments, calling it "a significant business risk ... possibly compromising their long-term commercial prospects."[24] No oil company has yet complied with such demands.

Oil graft works a lot like oil spills: it spreads in all directions. A year later, in 2004, investigations by the new government in Iraq discovered that former Iraqi dictator Saddam Hussein had skimmed funds for himself from the sale of oil under the United Nations "food for oil" program. He also sold oil at heavily discounted prices to French and Russian oil companies in an effort to get those nations to oppose U.N. sanctions against his regime. The oil companies and traders subsequently sold the oil at full market value, pocketing the difference or using it to bribe government officials around the world in exchange for additional support of Hussein's government. Hussein also bribed journalists and U.N. officials with his illegal oil profits.[25]

## Avarice and Autos:
## Fake Pollution Control, Real Consequences

"Some advocates for the automobile industry seem to have learned their science from the tobacco industry," wrote conservative *Washington Post* columnist George Will in 1977. "They argue that there is little 'scientific proof' of the connection between automobile pollution and particular diseases. Such arguments deny the undeniable: statistical patterns that demonstrate a correlation between high pollution and high disease rates."[26]

Like their counterparts in the oil industry, automakers have also engaged in duplicity to protect and promote their products. As we will see, some of the most egregious examples include the way they stalled the adoption of catalytic converters, and, once forced to do so, the ways they installed secret devices on engines to prevent them from operating.

"GM has been cognizant of the exhaust gas problem for many years and the research laboratories of GM have been responsible for the discovery of much of the basic information on exhaust gas that is available today on this subject," wrote GM executives in a 1953 letter to Los Angeles county supervisor Ken Hahn. "Carbon monoxide has generally been considered the principal component of exhaust gas that is injurious to health."[27]

That was the same year that the American Automobile Manufacturers Association agreed to create a committee to investigate and analyze air pollution and its effects.[28] Yet, as Jack Doyle explains in his book *Taken for a Ride*, not GM, Ford, or anyone else in the auto industry did much to actually address these problems.

"The Ford Engineering staff . . . feels that these vapors are dissipated in the atmosphere quickly and do not present an air pollution problem," wrote Ford public relations executives on behalf of Henry Ford II in response to demands for information from Hahn.[29]

Since 1953, Hahn had been pressing GM and Ford for information about what the manufacturers knew about problems with auto emissions and what they intended to do about them. He ultimately received assurances that the problem was not only being diligently investigated, but that it would be resolved within one model year. Extensive documents described by Doyle show that it wasn't until 1966 that auto companies installed pollution control devices on cars, and only after being forced to do so by law.

Like the tobacco industry, automakers relied on slick advertising to convince the public that their products were safe and reliable, or at least irresistible. "Buy me the new Pontiac Tempest; the new '63 Pontiac Tempest . . . and I'll kiss you tempest-u-ously!" claimed one popular ad.

All these years later, I still remember how a seductive woman beckoned drivers into the latest GM products. At the age of eleven, I may not have fully appreciated the sexy model, but I was being hooked with the rest of the United States by the alliance of Detroit and Madison Avenue. My favorite design of the era was the 1964 Thunderbird, the sleek bullet-nosed convertible that I glued together and painted as a plastic model. Selling cars with slick commercials and plastic models is one thing; using sophisticated ad campaigns to mislead the public for decades is another.

In 1970, GM ran full-page ads in newspapers nationwide, pledging "to solve the problem of vehicle emissions in the shortest possible time."[30] Their "solution" appeared in October 1972, when GM published a paper entitled "Study on the Environment," which concluded that the best way to curb air pollution from cars was to make one model for clean air regions and a cleaner one for parts of the nation with dirty air.[31] There was quite a bit of tortured logic that tried to make this proposal sound serious and plausible, but one must wonder if anyone at GM saw the absurdity of proposing to sell dirtier cars in clean air markets, thus transforming those areas into dirty air regions and forcing the sale of the cleaner cars there in the future.

Fortunately, at least some of the misleading ads were noticed by government officials. For example, a GM ad in the *New York Times* in 1973 urged the public to oppose legislation that would limit vehicle emissions, claiming that *relaxed* emission standards would produce greater air quality benefits. The USEPA and the Federal Trade Commission called the ads "false and misleading."[32] By April of 1973, GM steered away from questionable environmental claims and pointed instead at the nation's economy.

"If GM is forced to introduce catalytic converter systems across the board on 1975 models, the prospect of an unreasonable risk of business catastrophe and massive difficulties with these vehicles in the hands of the public must be faced," declared Ernest Starkman, GM vice president for environmental affairs. "It is conceivable that complete stoppage of the entire production could occur, with the obvious tremendous loss to the company, shareholders, employees, suppliers, and communities."[33] Catalytic converters work by "grabbing" carbon monoxide, hydrocarbons, and nitrogen from engine exhaust, further oxidizing them and reducing the amount of pollution emitted at the tailpipe. When regulators didn't budge, GM announced in mid-1973 that it would install catalytic converters on all 1975 model cars, but evidence shows that even this move was misleading. The automaker again turned to newspaper ads.

"General Motors believes it has an answer to the automotive air pollution problem . . . and the catalytic converter has enabled GM engineers to improve performance and to increase miles per gallon," read one ad.[34] When GM published that ad, the entire auto industry already knew that the benefits from these early models of catalytic converter would be temporary at best. As Doyle explains, California air quality experts testified to Congress as early as 1967 that "many cars carrying the [catalytic converter] devices were beginning to emit pollution exceeding legally permissible levels after only 5,000 miles of driving."[35]

Having stalled regulators for years, GM ran another ad in 1975 admitting that smog was a serious problem and that they were still working on resolving that problem.[36] GM and the other automakers also ran ads during the same period to convince consumers that further air pollution regulations would drastically elevate the cost of gasoline, while providing "only marginal improvement to air quality."[37]

Chrysler also used the media to fight clean air, taking out full-page newspaper ads to oppose catalytic converters and the 1975 federal air emissions standards. Two years later, Chrysler turned to direct mail, sending thousands of letters to suppliers, warning them of dire consequences from pending clean air legislation and urging their opposition to any future regulations.[38]

Although this litany of stalling and scare tactics ultimately failed and automakers installed catalytic converters on cars and light-duty trucks, it raises the question of how much unnecessary pollution was thrust upon unsuspecting Americans for years. How many cases of asthma or early deaths could have been avoided if automakers had kept their promise to work together to address tailpipe emissions in the 1950s?

Do automakers continue to make promises they don't keep with respect to reducing emissions from their vehicles?

In January 2003, Beth Lowery, GM vice president for environment and energy, told me that GM was planning a major promotion of gasoline-electric hybrids, like the technology used in the popular Toyota Prius, in the spring, backed up with a massive ad campaign.[39]

"OK, Beth," I said with some skepticism, "but will you spend as much money pushing hybrids as you do pushing Hummers?" She just laughed. The snows melted and the spring thaw crept over the High Sierras. Water filled California reservoirs and before long it was Coppertone time. In August 2003, Lowery got on the phone again.[40]

"I just want to let you know that we will have hybrid options on commercial trucks this year and the Saturn Vue in late 2004," she gushed.

"What about the hybrid option you told me eight months ago would be rolled out into numerous vehicles by last spring?" I asked. She just laughed. By 2006, GM had offered partial hybrid technology in only two of its light trucks and now claims that more models are coming in 2007. Toyota, Honda, and Ford have hybrid sedans and SUVs in their showrooms, and the Prius hybrid has been one of Toyota's most popular cars since 2002.[41]

In June 2004, Lowery again gave California air quality officials more GM-speak.[42] Addressing California's landmark greenhouse gas law, which would limit $CO_2$ emissions from 2009 model cars, Lowery called the law a "state fuel standard," not simply a limit on greenhouse gas emissions, and voiced GM's strong opposition to it.

"We can't make fifty different cars, one for each state," she complained.

That turns the argument upside down. Why wouldn't you make the safest, cleanest car possible, in *all* states, no matter which state asks for it first, assuming that you actually care about your customers? Recall that GM is the company in 1972 that proposed selling a "clean" car in states with dirty air and different versions in states with clean air.

In this half a century of misinformation about air quality technology, the "Cadillac" of all lies was about, well, Cadillacs. In

November 1995, GM paid nearly $20 million in fines for installing a device on 1991- to 1995-model Caddies that would defeat the air pollution control system, thereby emitting significantly more pollution than USEPA standards allowed. Between 1973 and 2000, GM recalled more than 13 million of its vehicles across several product lines for violation of emission standards.[43]

To be sure, GM has not been alone in misleading regulators and the public about pollution control technology, according to the U.S. Department of Justice. As described earlier, federal government levied charges in 1968 alleging that the auto industry conspired as a group, under the Automobile Manufacturers Association, to withhold cleaner technologies for the sixteen years prior.[44] The Justice Department filed a massive antitrust lawsuit, which it later settled. And three decades later, in June 1998, the Justice Department and the USEPA reached a $267 million settlement with Honda over allegations that it intentionally hid pollution problems in its automobiles.[45]

The award for the biggest pollution control deception of them all, however, belongs to the diesel engine manufacturers. In the 1990s, environmental advocacy organizations, including the Natural Resources Defense Council (NRDC), joined the USEPA and air quality regulators from California to establish increasingly tough standards for emissions of nitrogen and particulate matter from new diesel engines. As trucks with cleaner engines rolled into service, results of lab testing by USEPA showed far better emissions reductions than did testing of these vehicles in the real world.[46]

NRDC wrote to President Bill Clinton and demanded that more testing be done. The results of digging deeper uncovered a plot by six engine manufacturers to install "defeat devices" on their engines, essentially an electronic on-off switch that would turn the emissions-control equipment off when vehicles were under way in the belief that they would obtain more power from the engine.

Evenutally, six companies admitted to installing the defeat

devices over a decade's time on more than a million engines. Caterpillar (320,000 engines from 1988 to 1998), Cummins (400,000 engines from 1991 to 1998), Detroit Diesel (430,000 engines from 1988 to 1998), Mack Trucks/Renault (90,000 engines from 1990 to 1998), Navistar/International (78,000 engines from 1994 to 1998), and Volvo (10,000 engines from 1994 to 1998) settled claims with USEPA, agreeing to retrofit the affected engines during scheduled maintenance and to stop making the defeat devices.

Tons of pollution were pumped into our skies as a result of this plot, causing innumerable asthma cases and premature deaths. Those victims were never identified or compensated, and the engine manufacturers, along with lobbyists for truckers, stalled implementation of the agreement.

"What happens when you put more costs on people than they can bear? They go out of business," said Stephanie Williams, senior vice president of the California Trucking Association, referring to the prospect of fees on her members that would be used to mitigate the pollution created by their trucks, including those with the illegal defeat devices. Williams fought California legislation in 2003 that would have required trucks and off-road vehicles to retrofit engines to cleaner models over time. She also threatened me on my first week on the job as the secretary of the California Environmental Protection Agency (CalEPA), when we scheduled a hearing to consider a mandatory timetable to reprogram those pollution control defeat devices on diesel truck engines. The "chip reflash," as it is called, is a procedure that takes less than thirty minutes at a cost of no more than $200 per engine.

"If you let them go ahead with this agenda," Williams told me in a late-night phone call, "I will ring the capital with trucks in protest." I thanked Williams for the "courtesy" call and assured her that we would proceed with the agenda item. I also offered her some advice.

"As a former activist myself, Stephanie, let me compliment you on your tactics," I replied. "But based on lots of experience at this, let me point out that the news cameras will not only be aimed at your aggrieved truck drivers, they will also aim at the black soot belching from the smokestacks of each truck." I also reminded her that it only takes a few minutes to reprogram the defeat device computer chip on each truck and suggested that we could ask each protester to stop at a roadside "reflash" unit that CalEPA would be pleased to set up. Her planned protest never took place and she ultimately worked out a compromise with us on the reprogramming of her members' trucks.

Two years later, the engine manufacturers and California Trucking Association members had completed a small fraction of the promised reflash procedures, forcing the state Air Resources Board to again consider mandatory enforcement. Williams and the engine makers have pledged to fight the State of California yet again.

## Of Lies and Lead

Another petroleum-powered deception that continues to cause illness and death around the globe is the introduction of lead into fuels. The elimination of lead in gasoline began in the United States in 1973, but as we have seen, there is still lead in aviation and other specialty fuels.[47] Lead also remains a component of gasoline in dozens of countries, mostly poor third world nations, and has only recently been removed from fuel in places like Venezuela. More than 90 percent of the gasoline sold throughout Africa still contains lead.[48]

We have already examined some of the health effects on humans from ingestion of lead, much of which was deposited on soils along roadways for decades and still becomes airborne, where we inhale it or where it washes into rivers and the ocean. Lead also has many of the same effects on animals, attacking the nervous system and impairing cognitive abilities and causing weakness in extremities, anemia, and, at prolonged high levels, severe kidney and brain damage, palsies, seizures, and death.[49] Lead exposure to birds is especially devastating, leading to an inability to fly, or, in more extreme cases, total paralysis and death. A study done in Cairo, Egypt, a country that still uses leaded gasoline, looked at cattle egrets that nested in the city center and determined the amount of lead in their feathers was the highest of any bird species examined worldwide.[50] Farm animals, just as humans, store lead in their bones. Animal bones are often ground up and added to feed for other animals, thus exposing them to additional harm and further bioaccumulation.[51]

Leaded gasoline was introduced in the 1920s as an additive to reduce knocking in engines. As we've seen, auto manufacturers and oil companies ignored safer alternatives in favor of the cheaper additive, lead, despite knowing the health risks.[52] In "The Secret History of Lead," Jamie Lincoln Kitman describes how DuPont, Standard Oil, and GM decided to use tetraethyl lead (TEL) in gasoline, even though it was known at the time to be harmful and even deadly:

> In March 1922, Pierre du Pont wrote to his brother Irénée du Pont, Du Pont company chairman, that TEL is a colorless liquid of sweetish odor, very poisonous if absorbed through the skin, resulting in lead poisoning almost immediately. This statement of early factual knowledge of TEL's supreme deadliness is noteworthy, for it is knowledge that will be denied repeatedly by the principals in subsequent years as well as in the Ethyl Corporation's [the company that produced and sold TEL, later renamed the Octel Company] authorized history, released almost sixty years later. Underscoring the deep and implicit coziness between GM and Du Pont at this time, Pierre informed Irénée about TEL before GM had even filed its patent application for it.[53]

In 1973, the USEPA imposed the first regulation on lead

usage, one that would set the strategy for total lead phaseout over the next decade.[54] The agency determined that allowing development of a system of lead trading, and later lead banking, would result in a faster, more efficient, cost-effective phaseout, although it meant that larger amounts of lead would continue to exist in gasoline for years. With trading, companies unable to meet the lead reduction standard were able to purchase the credits of those refineries that were able to meet or exceed current standards (and "bank" the credits for later sale or trade). So, although some companies were producing gasoline with less lead content than specified by the USEPA and some were still producing gasoline with more, there was a cap on the total amount of lead allowed in all fuels combined. USEPA allowed this trading system to continue until 1986.

From 1976 to 1990, sales of leaded gasoline decreased by 99.8 percent around the nation, and blood-lead levels also plunged.[55] According to the U.S. Centers for Disease Control, between 1978 and 1991, Americans between the ages of one and seventy-four had decreased blood-lead levels of 78 percent. Even one-year-olds tested had so much lead in their bloodstreams that it decreased measurably when lead was taken out of gasoline. Of 100,000 children studied prior to the removal of lead from gasoline, 30,000 had dangerous blood-lead levels. After the phaseout, only 1,500 did.[56]

Just how high did lead levels grow in our bodies before we took action? The *New England Journal of Medicine* published an article in 1992 observing that pre-Columbian peoples, living in what is now North America, had blood-lead levels 625 times less than is currently considered "safe."[57]

The phaseout of leaded gasoline occurred more than sixty years after it was first used as an additive. During those years, vehicles burned approximately 70 million tons of lead, sending most of it into our atmosphere.[58] As noted, although unleaded gasoline has been the standard U.S. automotive fuel for nearly three decades, significant lingering environmental and health effects from decades of lead pollution continue. Lead still remains in soils along roadsides.

Despite all the knowledge about the dangers of lead, the Octel Company still manufactures and supplies lead additives for gasoline in third world countries. Commercial airliners continue to use leaded aviation gas, which contains four times more lead content than the gasoline once used by automobiles.[59] And millions of fans who attend car racing events each year under the NASCAR banner are inhaling lead, thanks to a decades-long exemption for the sport from the Clean Air Act.

The USEPA, the agency that grants the exemption, said in December 2005 that leaded fuel "may pose a serious health risk to some subpopulations such as residents living in the vicinity of racetracks, fuel attendants, racing crew and staff, and spectators."[60] A study by doctors at Indiana University School of Medicine confirmed that USEPA conclusion, finding that lead levels in the blood of NASCAR crew members was 40 percent higher than the level considered safe by the U.S. Centers for Disease Control.[61] After years of criticism by public health activists, NASCAR finally agreed to eliminate leaded fuel from their race cars in 2008.

## Why Can't We All Just Adapt?

To be fair, oil and auto companies have admitted over the years that their products are harmful to some degree. When they do, however, their suggested remedies fall somewhere between callous and insulting. For example, when USEPA administrator Carol Browner tightened the limits on ozone and particulate matter from vehicle exhaust in 1996, industry opposition was predictably strident.

"Given the tremendous progress America has made in cleaning the air it is incomprehensible why the USEPA is seeking to tighten the standards for ozone and particulate matter," said Andrew Card (who served as President George W. Bush's chief of staff from 2000 to 2006), speaking for the American Automobile Manufacturers Association.[62] There seems nothing "incomprehensible" in the facts Browner presented in her announcement that implementation of these new rules "would prevent 20,000 premature deaths, 9,000 hospital admissions, 60,000 cases of bronchitis and 250,000 asthma cases–every year."[63]

The reaction of the American Petroleum Industry (API) was similar to that of the auto industry. Paul Bailey, API's director of health and environmental affairs, believed that ozone shouldn't be regulated because its detrimental effects were inconsequential and said, "It is clear to us that the ozone standard doesn't need to be changed—no ifs, ands, or buts. The effects that are typically seen are very short-term and very reversible and people exposed to ozone actually adapt to it."[64]

Twenty thousand premature deaths are a rather extreme form of "adaptation." As we have seen, ozone acts like an acid on the lungs, causing and aggravating asthma and other respiratory ailments, impairing lung function, harming the immune system, aggravating heart disease and emphysema, and potentially causing fetal heart malfunctions.

Richard Klimisch, another auto industry representative, seems to accept the evidence, but doesn't find it alarming. He said, "The effects of ozone are not that serious. I hate to say that. But what we're talking about is a temporary loss in lung function of 20 to 30 percent. That's not really a health effect."[65]

Another industry representative tried to sound more reasonable, proposing alternatives to pollution exposure. His suggestion was, well, to stop breathing. His comment? "People can protect themselves. They can avoid jogging. Asthmatic kids need not go out and ride their bikes."[66]

Yet another lobbyist cut right to the chase. He said that statistics of elderly deaths, related to air pollution, should not be counted because the subjects were going to die anyway.[67]

These are but a few examples of the oil and auto industry priority of profit over the health and well-being of their customers. If it sounds familiar, it is essentially the same corporate behavior displayed by tobacco companies for decades. Such callous corporate behavior isn't limited to selling us harmful products we don't need or misleading ad campaigns or violating the law by disabling pollution control devices. As the evidence in the next chapter shows, oil and auto companies have gone to extraordinary lengths to undermine even the most basic efforts to curtail the harmful effects of their products, determined to keep us addicted to oil in one way or another.

# CHAPTER 6

# Worse Poison to Men's Souls

There is thy gold—worse poison to men's souls,
Doing more murders in this loathsome world,
Than these poor compounds that thou mayst not sell.
I give thee poison; thou hast sold me none.

*Shakespeare, Romeo and Juliet,* act V, scene 1

The products of oil and auto companies have poisoned our bodies and their vast wealth has been used to tarnish some of our most cherished values. To be sure, every one of us who uses petroleum products and motorized transportation is an essential member of the cast in this epic tragedy, but our addiction is partly the direct result of corporate practices that prioritize profits over the health and well-being of consumers.

As a former government regulator, I know that it is the job of laws and regulations to attempt to level the playing field, to protect consumers from this type of corporate predation. But as a government official who has witnessed oil and auto industry duplicity and lobbying firsthand, I can testify that it is nearly impossible to perform that function sitting on the other side of the petroleum-powered smoke screen. Both the oil industry and auto industry have acted again and again to deceive regulators about the hazards of their products and have used their wealth to hamstring attempts by state and federal legislators to make laws that address such threats.

The result of such corporate tactics is not just continued pollution, illness, and other consequences, but missed opportunities for the world economy. The corporate philosophy of these industries has prevented consumers from buying safer, cleaner, more sustainable transportation choices. That, in turn, has stunted the potential growth of technology industries that could have provided stable, high-paying jobs for decades to come. As we will see, there have been many conflicts with government regulators who are trying to protect public health and the economy, fights that are far from over.

## We Can Be Seen to Be Very Busy: Regulators Wrestling with Pollution

A 2003 survey revealed that automotive consumers believe that if major corporations market a product and the government allows them to do so, the product is likely to be safe.[1] Between railroad barons in the nineteenth century, tobacco companies in the twentieth century, and Enron and Haliburton in the first few years of the twenty-first century, our faith in corporate citizenship should long ago have been shattered. Blind faith in government should also have evaporated by now, given the all-too-frequent failure of our elected officials and regulatory agencies to protect us in a timely manner. But for generations, not much has changed with that rose-colored faith in corporations and government, on either side of the Atlantic.

"I am not satisfied that . . . legislation is necessary at present," Harold Macmillan, Britain's minister of housing, said in Parliament in response to the idea that regulation of air pollution might be needed in 1952. "We do what we can. Today, everybody expects the government to solve every problem. Smog has captured the imagination of the press and people . . . I suggest we form a committee. We cannot do very much, but we can be seen to be very busy."[2]

Macmillian, who became prime minister of England five years later, did offer one concrete solution at the time. He suggested handing out masks to the population. Ironically, U.S. tobacco companies offered to pay for the masks, providing they could emblazon them with their logos.[3]

Of course, the growing problem of smog in urban centers was not limited to the United Kingdom. In Los Angeles in December 1969, the air so filled with carbon monoxide, sulfides, and particulate matter, mainly from vehicle exhaust, that thousands of people were sickened and hundreds died.[4]

In response to incidents like that, President Richard Nixon signed the federal Clean Air Act into law in 1970, modeled after California's own state law, and created the Environmental Protection Agency.[5] Nixon may have been responding to polls and the overwhelming outpouring of concern witnessed on April 22 that year, the first Earth Day, rather than to any genuine intent to clean up air pollution. Why should one be so skeptical? Perhaps the answer is because Nixon agreed to his environmental agenda that year from the same oval office where he kept the air conditioner running cold enough at all times to offset the fire that burned in White House fireplaces, a practice he continued during the energy crisis three years later.[6] But the real reason to question his motives are found in his own words, speaking about the advocates who pushed for those laws in the first place.

"You better watch out for those crazy enviros, Bill," Nixon sternly warned William Ruckelshaus, the first administrator of the USEPA. "They're a bunch of commie pinko queers."[7]

The Clean Air Act has accomplished a great deal, but it has also made us keenly aware of how much has yet to be done and its proudest moments were painfully slow in coming. To his credit, Ruckelshaus used the authority of the act to remove lead from gasoline beginning in 1973, based on overwhelming evidence of the harm to the brains of children.[8] Still, more than two decades passed before the retail sale of leaded gasoline stopped entirely, and it has still not been removed from airplanes or NASCAR racing cars.

Whether it is the long-known health effects of lead or the newly emerging science around the harms of particulate matter, our policy makers have often been slow to protect public health. Consider the case of butadiene, a toxic chemical found in gasoline and that has been used in the making of synthetic rubber since World War II. The American Council of Government and Industrial Hygienists established an inhalation exposure limit for workers at 1,000 ppm in the early 1980s, with no recommended limit to the length of exposure. By 1985, a convincing series of studies showed that repeated exposure at that level over a two-year period caused cancer in mice. (When exposed to butadiene as low as 6.25 ppm, mice developed rare lung and heart tumors, even when that exposure was as brief as thirteen weeks.)

Still, not until 1996 did the federal government lower the permissible exposure limit from the 1983 standard of 1,000 ppm of open-ended exposure to 1 ppm over no more than an eight-hour period. And not until 2001 did the federal government formally label butadiene a known carcinogen. By that time, more than 18 billion pounds of butadiene had been produced and were in use worldwide.[9]

Ozone offers another example of how regulatory action lags far behind the health sciences. In 2004, California's Office of Environmental Health Hazard Assessment said that "the numerous . . . studies of ozone-related [deaths] indicate that . . . there is no . . . concentration below which health effects would not occur in at least some individuals."[10] That sober assessment makes it abundantly clear that any ozone standard above zero will harm someone, yet no federal or state government regulator has advocated for an exposure limit of zero.

Nor is there much consistency among government regulators when they do act. Consider limits on particulate matter. California regulators admit that the exposure limits on particulate matter set by the state won't protect the health of everyone, while federal limits allow concentrations that are 300 percent higher than that. Such inadequate standards remain unchanged despite mounting evidence that inhaling these particles is responsible for an increasing number of illnesses.[11] This federal foot-dragging is especially problematic because some sources of these pollutants remain under the sole jurisdiction of the federal government. Ships, trains, construction equipment, farm machines, and other nonroad engines have been exempted from any emission standards at the federal level for decades, and federal law prohibits states from imposing limits of their own.

That federal roadblock to cleaner air hasn't stopped some progressive officials from using health data and public opinion to obtain voluntary concessions when they can. For example, health risks posed by diesel exhaust from construction equipment at the World Trade Center reconstruction site prompted concerns from area residents, so New York City and state officials have demanded that contractors use ultra-low sulfur fuel and the cleanest equipment available.[12] Other communities have not been as successful in securing voluntary pollution reductions. For instance, the ships in Los Angeles and Long Beach in California, where almost half of all the goods imported into the United States are handled, are another source of pollution where only the federal government can act. Oceangoing ships spew 52 tons per day of smog into skies around those massive port complexes, and polluters have not stepped forward to regulate themselves.[13]

"Yes, [companies] care about the environment, but the bottom line is they can't adopt a technology that will make it difficult to [compete]," said T. L. Garrett, marine environmental supervisor at the Port of Los Angeles. "We certainly don't want to put our customers at a competitive disadvantage within the industry."[14] Apparently, the disease and death of local residents and port workers does not constitute a "competitive disadvantage." A 1999 international treaty allows a nation to require cleaner fuels on ships that call at their ports, but the United States is one of only three nations that has yet to ratify it.[15]

Great caravans of trains roll into and out of those same port cities, producing 36 tons of air pollution each day, more than the 100 largest oil refiners, chemical plants, and industrial plants in the region combined.[16] These sources of pollution are also under the sole jurisdiction of the federal government, which has done little about them. Frustrated California legislators, who represent the neighborhoods along train tracks, offered legislation in 2004 requiring a retrofit of locomotive engines or payment of a pollution fee. It was defeated by the railroad industry.

In the final analysis, government regulators could have done much more over the years to protect public health from harmful petroleum pollution. Yet it is extremely difficult for government officials to fight wealthy corporations determined to use almost any means to stall or stop meaningful regulation. Two classic examples of this challenge are the battles over fuel economy and zero emissions vehicles.

## That's Mad, That's Crazy: The Fight to Kill CAFE

Perhaps the most important regulatory program that remains entirely within the jurisdiction of the federal government, and that has the greatest potential to ease out oil addiction, is the fuel economy standards for passenger vehicles and light trucks. A poll released in 2002 found that voters in Michigan, the birthplace of the U.S. auto industry, support increasing these fuel economy standards.

Surprisingly, the poll also showed that United Auto Workers members are even more likely than other voters to favor tougher fuel economy standards. When the auto industry has repeatedly said that such regulation will kill U.S. jobs and force plant closures, why would autoworkers favor such measures? The poll found that autoworkers and other Michigan residents don't believe the corporate scare tactics, but rather believe that improving fuel economy will help U.S. automakers sell more cars, thereby securing jobs and helping the local economy.[17] Given the evidence of health harms and economic costs related to burning petroleum products in vehicles and given that their workers support an increase in fuel economy standards, wouldn't the oil companies and automakers also support it? Not exactly.

When Saudi Arabia led an OPEC boycott of petroleum sales to the United States in 1973, I owned a 1963 Ford Galaxy with broken windows and dashboard wiring that overheated and smoked. I had bought this jalopy for $200 from the cashier at the Sheraton Universal hotel, where I worked nights to make my way through college by day. Like everyone else in the Golden State, we sat in our gas-guzzling cars in lines that snaked around several city blocks, hoping for our turn to worship at the altar of the gasoline pump. Prices rapidly doubled at gas stations that still had any part of the nation's evaporating fuel supply.

One of the few responses to the embargo (which ended when the Saudis grew more fearful of shortages in their bank accounts than we were fearful of lines at the gas pump) was an effort to increase the fuel economy of the cars sold in the United States. It was assumed that no company would make more fuel-efficient cars on its own, but if the law required all automakers to improve fuel economy at the same time, no company would be disadvantaged and all could easily comply.

It was also argued that individual car models shouldn't be regulated; rather, a limit should be set on the average fuel economy of all cars sold by each company. Thus, a company like GM, for example, could sell gas-guzzling Cadillacs, as long as they sold enough fuel-efficient Chevies that the average of all cars sold by that automaker reached a certain target. It seems to be a fair and market-based system, right? Not to the automakers, who launched their trade group, the Alliance of Automobile Manufacturers, to fight this simple concept, corporate average fuel economy, or CAFE.[18]

In 1974, auto executives began their attack on CAFE by telling Congress that such regulations would "outlaw" large engines and reduce all vehicles on the road to *subcompact-sized cars or even smaller.* Ford said CAFE would "possibly result in a Ford product line consisting either of all sub-Pinto-sized vehicles or some mix of vehicles ranging from sub-sub-compact to perhaps a Maverick."[19] Similarly, Alan Loofburrow, Chrysler vice president, told a U.S. Senate subcommittee in the same year that CAFE might "outlaw a number of engine lines and car models including most full-size sedans and station wagons. It would restrict the industry to producing subcompact size cars—or even smaller ones—within five years." Not to be outdone, the last of Detroit's Big Three automakers at the time chimed in too. GM president E. M. Estes argued that "absent a significant technological breakthrough . . . the largest car the industry will be selling in any volume at all will probably be smaller, lighter and less powerful than today's compact Chevy Nova."

Despite the opposition, long lines at the pump were too powerful an image for lawmakers to ignore, so the CAFE law was passed in 1975, giving automakers ten years to plan and comply. At least some automakers took the law seriously. The Japanese already made more fuel-efficient cars and began to eat Detroit's market share for lunch. Did the U.S. companies fight back with equally fuel-efficient models to compete with the foreign makes? No, they began to fight lawmakers and then fed on one another.

According to CAFE rules, by 1985 automakers' fleets would have to reach an average fuel economy of 27.5 mpg. GM and Ford did not comply, relying instead on their application to the National Highway Traffic Safety Administration (NHTSA) for relief from the standard. Back in Detroit, though, the smallest of the Big Three, Chrysler, was actually preparing to meet its CAFE target.

"Chrysler will meet the standard because, even when we were going broke a few years back, we invested heavily in a corporate strategy geared to satisfying the market while meeting the fuel-economy law," said the president of Chrysler, Harold R. Sperlich, when testifying to a U.S. congressional subcommittee in September 1985. "Our compliance with the Corporate Average Fuel Economy (CAFE) standard is proof that the 27.5 mpg standard is technologically feasible and that other manufacturers could have met the law as well."[20] Chrysler had invested $5 billion to meet its CAFE obligation and Sperlich was blunt in his assessment of his U.S. rivals.

"[It is] not about saving jobs or saving factories," he said. "It's about maximizing profits, pure and simple. Those who want the standard dialed back have forgone the investments necessary to move their CAFE to the statutory level of 27.5 mpg; now they want an administrative ruling to forgo paying the fines that Congress intended as the penalty for noncompliance. . . . [It is] unfair that GM, Ford, and several low-volume luxury importers are flunking the standard, and Chrysler is paying the penalty."

GM and Ford knew how to play political hardball, though, and they went on the attack. In the summer of 1985, Ford told the Reagan administration that it would connect layoffs to the CAFE standard and blame the administration for the loss of U.S. jobs. Among other tactics, Ford threatened to move some of its assembly lines overseas to take advantage of a CAFE loophole that excluded "imports" from compliance with the standard.

"I would not [shift production abroad] except for the CAFE law," proclaimed Louis Ross, Ford vice chairman, to the press, hinting that now a rollback of the 1985 standard would not be enough to keep jobs in the United States. Instead, he implied, multiple years of relief from the CAFE would be needed to keep Ford on U.S. soil.

The Reagan administration blinked and rolled back the CAFE standard from 27.5 mpg to 26 mpg for model year 1986 cars. Then GM and Ford pressed for more rollbacks through their lobbyist Jeffrey Conley, executive director of AutoChoice. He told the *Washington Post* that the rollback allowed his clients to "breathe a sigh of relief," but added that the "same kind of adjustment is necessary for future years to avoid economic hardship to the domestic auto industry. One year of relief is not enough."

"I'm a little more than unhappy about it," snapped Chrysler chairman Lee Iacocca, upon learning of the 1986 rollback. "We spent millions to meet the law when we were hanging on by our fingers. It's damn stupid to be penalized for obeying the law. It's a shot in the head. . . . GM and Ford said if they couldn't sell big cars in order to meet CAFE they would have to shut their plants and lay off people. Would GM shut a plant because instead of making $5,000 profit on a car they had to pay a CAFE fine and only make $4,500? That's mad; that's crazy."

Iacocca seemed prescient when he predicted America's future. "We are about to put up a tombstone," Iacocca mused. "Here lies America's energy policy." He then paid for ads exposing the CAFE rollback for exactly what it was then and remains today, a threat to U.S. national security.

"[D]ialing back fuel standards on cars will set up the American people to be energy hostages again and again," the ads read in part. It is worth reading that line again. This ad wasn't placed by an environmental organization. Iacocca made that statement two decades ago, and it is certainly fair to say that subsequent events have borne out his warning.

Nonetheless, GM and Ford kept up their threats of layoffs in the auto industry, and within months, the Reagan administration rolled back the CAFE standard to 26 mpg for three more model years,

1987 through 1989. With four years of rollbacks, and considering that at least one of the Big Three and several Japanese automakers were meeting the 1986 CAFE standard, now GM and Ford would do their duty and start making their own CAFE improvements, right?

Nope. When U.S. secretary of transportation Samuel Skinner announced in May 1989 the resumption of the original 27.5 mpg CAFE target, GM chairman Roger Smith, the elusive subject of Michael Moore's 1989 documentary film *Roger and Me*, told reporters that the world's largest automaker was incapable of complying.

"[W]ith the CAFE running on up, we could close some plants," Smith told reporters imperiously. "There's no question about it."

Ford was marching in lockstep, telling the *Washington Post* that "its only other options were to discontinue or restrict production of the two cars [that were the worst gas guzzlers in their fleet, holding their CAFE standards below the target], either of which would cause a greater job loss in the United States, where the parts are now made, and in Canada, where the cars are actually assembled." In an *Alice in Wonderland* perversion, Ford also made statements through an executive who held the rather disingenuous title "Manager of Fuel Economy and Compliance."

"If we don't supply those cars, somebody else would supply them," said David Kulp, Ford's executive with that perverse appellation. "And if we restricted their production, we would be facing the same issue of losing sales because of a lack of product to meet buyer demand." History shows that Ford had used these tactics before. In 1966, Henry Ford II argued that implementation of federal safety requirements for seat belts would force his company to "close down."[21] History also shows that when they want to fight something, oil and auto companies keep using the same tactics again and again.

"We view some of the [CAFE] laws in Congress as real threats to GM's franchise," blustered GM executive Robert C. Lange as recently as 2001. "We would either have to cut production at those plants or downsize our entire fleet of vehicles."[22]

Studies show that improvements in CAFE standards would actually create jobs, especially in high-tech components and engine controls. The Union of Concerned Scientists estimated in its comments to NHTSA that "achieving a fuel economy standard of 40 mpg by 2012 would create 182,700 new jobs—with 41,000 in the automotive sector alone."[23]

Claiming job losses, plant closings, and outright bankruptcy are only three of the tactics used by automakers to scare the public and lawmakers. In the early 1990s, when CAFE again became a topic for congressional attention, Ford chairman Harold Poling began to shift the blame to consumers. This tactic remains the salvo of choice for automakers to this day when they reload their cannons and aim at CAFE each time it is revived on the national agenda. Blame—and scare—the consumer.

"Some of the most popular and versatile vehicles on the road today also are among the least fuel efficient," said Walter E. Huizenga, president of the American International Automobile Dealers Association. "If Congress mandates an increase in fuel economy, certain models of pickups, minivans and sport-utility vehicles could potentially be eliminated from the market. Customers who want and need these products would be deprived of the choice of owning them." Not to be left out of the consumer blame game, GM vice chairman of product development Robert Lutz suggested making drivers pay more as the best way to use less oil.

"If we're really serious about fuel economy and cleaner emissions, the only way we're going to get there is to use the tax mechanism to curb demand," he pontificated. "If your kids are eating too much candy, you take their allowance away. If you want people to eat less, you raise the price of food. Instead, what the government is trying to do with CAFE is fight national obesity by making the clothing industry manufacture only small sizes."

One final automaker smokescreen is to "volunteer" to improve products and assert that there is no need for government regulation. In 2000, Ford was one of the few companies to offer voluntary improvements, of 25 percent within five years in the fuel economy of its SUVs and light trucks. "We fundamentally believe this is what customers want," said Jacques Nasser, Ford president and chief executive officer, in a speech to the National Press Club. Voluntary measures were more likely to bear fruit than mandates, he assured his audience. "You're better off letting the competitive forces in technology address the issue of improved fuel economy," Nasser went on to say. By 2006, Ford had achieved none of its own voluntary goal.

Perhaps the most graphic example of how the fight against CAFE is as "mad" and "crazy" as Lee Iacocca thought was the oil and auto industries' response in the wake of the September 11, 2001, attacks. In 1996, the U.S. House of Representatives had frozen CAFE standards at essentially their 1985 levels and prohibited the federal government from even studying the potential benefits of higher mileage standards. This federal freeze lasted until 2001. It was the attack in September of that year that got the government thinking again about fuel economy.

Since 9/11, gasoline prices in the United States have spiked to more than $3 a gallon and many have suggested that the money we spend on oil has financed terrorism around the world, including on that fateful day in 2001. In response, NHTSA announced in early 2002 that it was once again considering a modest increase in CAFE standards. Instead of finding a way to help, to respond to what many were calling a patriotic duty, the oil and auto lobbyists held NHTSA off for more than a year. Then, in April 2003, NHTSA tried a fresh approach. Automakers had objected to standards that covered their entire fleet of vehicles, but what about tackling the worst offender and leaving the bulk of each company's fleet alone? Assuming that even the petroleum-powered lobbyists had heard the growing chorus of criticism and scorn for gas-guzzling SUVs, the agency proposed CAFE standards for only light trucks and SUVs, calling for just 1.5 mpg fuel economy improvements by 2007. Folding this change into the existing fleet would mean that the new overall CAFE target would actually drop from the 1985 level of 26 mpg to just 22.2 mpg. Even President Bush supported the proposal, but the automaker tribe banded together to fight again. Josephine Cooper, president of the Alliance of Automobile Manufacturers, quickly summoned old demons.

"This proposal threatens jobs, the economy, and family vehicles such as SUVs and minivans, and it represents a ban on light trucks," she said.[24] The alliance has made no estimates of the U.S. jobs lost to Japanese automakers since the mid-1970s when fuel-efficient cars came from Tokyo and not Detroit. Ironically, in the same month as automakers took potshots at the NHTSA proposal, the United States invaded Iraq, the price of gasoline again shot up to more than $3 a gallon, and even battery-electric cars flew out of dealer showrooms.

Moreover, a 2002 report by the National Academy of Sciences (NAS) estimated that off-the-shelf technologies could justify an increase in CAFE standards of as much as 12 to 14 mpg in cars and 11 to 13 mpg in SUVs and light trucks. Among the technologies that NAS recommends, you will not find anything about making cars any smaller or lighter than they are today. But like the red herring that the automakers used to argue against CAFE improvements from the beginning, Detroit returned to claim that higher-mileage cars can only be delivered by smaller, lighter models that will be inherently unsafe. As we have seen, many SUVs are designed to weigh in at a massive 6,000 pounds just to qualify for federal tax credits that were designed to help small businesses purchase delivery vans. The problems related to SUV rollovers are well documented, demonstrating that simply making cars heavier or larger does not make them safer. Dr. Jeffrey Runge, NHTSA administrator and former emergency room doctor, said that he wouldn't let his children drive an SUV "even if it was the last [vehicle] on Earth," because of their high propensity to roll over.[25]

In the end, after intense lobbying by the oil and auto industries the 9/11-inspired improvements to CAFE were defeated by Congress in July 2003. Eighteen Democrats, all from auto manufacturing states, joined Senate Republicans in defeating the proposed standards.[26] The Senate not only voted the CAFE measure down, it also approved an industry-backed measure to set any future CAFE standards based solely on economic and some safety concerns.

"I don't want to tell parents . . . they cannot get the SUV or minivan they wanted for their family or business because Congress decided it would be a bad choice," said Republican Senator Christopher "Kit" Bond of Missouri during the debate, in the course of trotting out the tired lie that improvements in fuel economy inevitably result in the production of unsafe cars.[27] If that name sounds familiar, it's because he is the same U.S. senator who tried unsuccessfully to strip California of its right to regulate highly polluting two-stroke engines during the first days of the Schwarzenegger administration.

In truth, the decades-long fight against improving fuel economy, led mostly by U.S. automakers, has not served their financial interests any more than it has served our energy independence interests or our public health. In 1970, domestic automakers commanded 86 percent of the U.S. market for cars and light trucks, compared with just 11 percent for Japan and Europe. Today, domestic automakers account for 51 percent of those sales, while Japan and Europe combine for 49 percent.[28] In early 2006, the U.S. government again introduced modest proposals to improve fuel economy standards for SUVs and light trucks, which automakers again say they oppose.[29]

## Clearing the Air: The Fight to Kill ZEV

Stalling CAFE is not the only way in which oil and auto companies sidetrack meaningful government regulation of their business interests. Forced to deal with the worst air quality in the nation and a federal government that can't provide tools like CAFE standards, the California Air Resources Board came up with a simple plan: demand that all automakers produce a number of zero emission vehicles (ZEVs) by a certain date, thus leveling the playing field for all competitors and jumpstarting a new automotive product technology. ZEVs include vehicles powered by batteries, electricity, hydrogen, and even conventional biofuels and petroleum fuels, as long as no harmful emissions are discharged from the tailpipe.

In late 1990, the California Air Resources Board passed the ZEV regulations, which said that 2 percent of all vehicles sold in the state must be ZEVs by 1998, 5 percent by 2001, and 10 percent by 2003. That's a goal of 10 percent of the new car fleet within thirteen years. For a nation that can put a man on the moon and sell consumers millions of gallons of premium fuel they don't need, achieving this goal should be a no-brainer for the auto and oil giants, the descendants of Fords and Rockefellers, right?

It wasn't just California that thought so. A group of northeastern governments, including New York and Washington, D.C., also adopted California's ZEV plan, thus dramatically expanding the market for ZEVs and making it even more attractive for inventive automakers around the world to deliver these smog-busters to showrooms. In the shadow of the Arab oil embargo and the first Gulf War, anything that reduced the need to import more oil would seem a desirable goal.

When the ZEV mandate was unveiled, the auto industry had learned at least one thing: they knew that they had to appear to play along. Taking a page from their 1950s playbook on smog, the Big Three (GM, Ford, and Chrysler) formed the U.S. Advanced Battery Consortium (USABC) in 1991 to join forces, to check their competition at the door on this one issue, to ensure that within a few years every car company would have advanced batteries that could power vehicles to meet consumer demands. The record shows that, like the tobacco, oil, and auto industry collaboratives of the 1950s, the USABC was actually formed to thwart progress on ZEVs and create a place, in plain sight of the public and regulators, where they could join forces with like-minded business interests to kill the ZEV mandate entirely. Don't take my word for it, though. Ask an auto company executive who worked on ZEVs, John Dabels.

"The automakers formed USABC to hinder rather than to enhance [ZEV] product development," admitted this former GM executive flatly.[30] The collaborators also shrewdly recruited financial partners, so the arrangement would cost very little of their own money. Most of the funding for the USABC was provided by you and me, the taxpayers, via the U.S. Department of Energy.

Like Britain's Harold Macmillan several decades earlier, Dabels explained that the strategy agreed upon was to look very busy. USABC would look for a battery technology that could propel a typical sedan at least 200 miles on a single charge, believing that it was technically and financially infeasible. Within three years, however, battery makers Ovonic and Electrosource were close to perfecting the very batteries that the automakers wanted to claim could not be made. Both GM and Chrysler used confidentiality agreements to prohibit the battery companies from publicizing their progress, however. Ovonic had an ad ready for placement in major newspapers, touting "batteries that make electric vehicles practical and fun to drive," but was not permitted to publish it.[31]

Knowing that the "impossible" battery was actually possible, the conspirators began to worry more about one another than about state regulators. Like the ill-fated tribe members of Easter Island who turned to cannibalism when the going got tough, they turned on one another. Fearing that GM might actually use the battery technology to be the first to bring an affordable ZEV to market,

Chrysler and Ford threatened to use their membership in USABC to pull Ovonic's research grants if GM proceeded with using the new batteries.[32] In response, GM threatened to dismantle the USABC altogether. A stalemate was the result and everyone stayed silent and kept their products off of the market.

Even the Big Three realized, however, that you couldn't keep the technology a total secret, so they returned to the bargaining table of USABC in 1994 to devise a new stalling tactic. GM would make a ZEV car, Ford a ZEV pickup, and Chrysler a ZEV minivan, but that wouldn't stop any of them from continuing their joint and several efforts to terminate the ZEV program altogether. Chrysler got a brilliant idea on that front and attacked first.

"Chrysler will impose a surcharge of up to $2,000 on gasoline-powered automobiles in . . . California and other states with . . . ZEV requirements in 1999," announced Chrysler Chairman Robert Eaton on October 10, 1994.[33] His simple plan was to threaten his own customers and hope regulators or lawmakers would intervene. Meanwhile, Eaton's USABC partners were recruiting new allies. The Western States Petroleum Association (WSPA), the California Manufacturers Association, and that 1950s veteran, the American Automobile Manufacturers Association (AAMA), were all enlisted to lobby California policy makers. The automakers lobbied the California Air Resources Board to slow the ZEV mandate timeline and sued the State of New York to block implementation of the mandate there, while WSPA began running a public media campaign and lobbying the utility industry.[34]

The utility industry? Sure. It would be necessary for all the new electric car owners to develop a network of recharging stations and, of course, to provide the electricity to recharge all those high-tech batteries that USABC was planning to put into vehicles. Oil companies reasoned that they could convince utilities that good existing customers—like refineries and gasoline stations—were worth more than prospective ZEV customers.

Evidence presented to the Antitrust Division of the U.S. Department of Justice by the Sierra Club Legal Defense Fund on January 17, 1996, showed that oil companies threatened utilities, saying that they would buy natural gas and electricity from other sources, even develop their own generating capabilities, if the utilities didn't cooperate.[35] To ensure that the point was driven home, when the California Public Utilities Commission held hearings on the viability of the ZEV mandate, WSPA made its first-ever appearance before the regulatory body to lobby against it. One estimate placed their expenditures on just this part of the campaign at $20 million. It was apparently money well spent. Among other victories, WSPA was successful in lobbying the commission to exclude testimony from the proceedings related to air quality benefits from the ZEV mandate, persuading the commission to deem such information as "irrelevant."[36]

An intensive ad campaign was launched by Mobil Oil at about the same time, excoriating the electric battery as both technologically and economically infeasible.[37] With a touch of George Orwell, Mobil launched a campaign called "Clearing the Air," running frequent, large ads in national publications. Some tried to get consumers to believe that they'd have to pay for this mandate through hidden costs such as utility price hikes and taxes, and other ads painted gasoline as the only feasible method of vehicle propulsion.

"We have no problem competing with electric powered cars," said Mobil's executive vice president Bob McCool in 1995. "But we do object to the government . . . subsidizing our competition."[38] This statement came from an industry that is directly subsidized by U.S. taxpayers, using even the most modest estimates, to the tune of $128 billion each year in tax breaks, health-care costs for victims of air pollution, and military expenses associated with defending the supply of crude oil around the globe, to name just a few of the many handouts described in previous chapters.

With their oil company colleagues attacking the ZEV mandate

in paid media and the regulatory arena, the auto industry launched its own effort at the grassroots level. In 1995, the AAMA sent out a request for proposals from public relations firms seeking "a qualified contractor to manage a statewide grassroots . . . campaign in California to create a climate in which the state's [ZEV] mandate can be repealed." What is even more noteworthy about this document is its acknowledgment of the potential success of ZEVs, stating that "recent surveys indicate a majority of Californians believe ZEVs are a 'workable and practical' means of reducing air pollution. This . . . may indicate greater consumer acceptance of electric vehicles."[39]

To give themselves ammunition in the halls of Sacramento and the pages of news media, the oil and auto corporations funded "studies" asking skewed questions and using other questionable methodology in trying to show that ZEVs were impractical and unacceptable to consumers. Each study was quickly refuted by a host of experts, but the bogus science hung in the air like the bad smell 30 miles downwind of an oil refinery, always threatening and hard to eliminate completely. The companies began using the questionable studies in their ads.[40]

To reinforce the notion that ZEVs were too expensive to mass produce, the automakers decided to use only the most costly technologies in each of their ZEV programs, including the most expensive chargers.[41] Moreover, each of the Big Three set up its accounting system to make its ZEV programs appear even more financially impractical. Dabels revealed that GM manipulated its ZEV accounting records to make the vehicles appear significantly more expensive than they really were.[42] Ford engaged in similar practices with its electric version of the Ranger pickup truck.[43] Entire factories, research and development costs, and other overhead that served numerous product lines were attributed to the ZEV programs alone, making each car produced appear to be unreasonably expensive.[44]

Suspecting that automakers' claims about cost were exaggerated, the California Air Resources Board held hearings to get the facts. While auto executives testified against the program, Ovonic was finally ready to begin mass producing its battery technology that would accomplish precisely what automakers told regulators was impossible.[45] This battery was said to be the big breakthrough, a rechargeable, environmentally friendly battery that could produce more than 200 miles of travel on a single charge. Yet, in the automakers' testimony to the board, the feasibility of an electric battery was questioned and the mandate opposed.[46]

Ironically, all this behind-the-scenes effort took place amidst a backdrop of internal support for both the mandate and ZEVs themselves. Jim Ellis, GM's chief of engineering, and Dabels, GM's marketing executive for ZEVs, both believed that the mandate was achievable and that their company could make products that would meet consumers' needs and make a profit for their shareholders.[47]

By late 1995, however, the California Air Resources Board began to wilt under the unrelenting pressure from the oil and auto industry attacks and deceptions. Deadlines were extended, ZEV numbers were eased. Still, after several more years of foot dragging and intense lobbying, the auto companies took off the gloves and simply sued the California Air Resources Board in 2001 to derail the ZEV mandate completely. In court pleadings, automakers complained that the ZEV rules failed to consider the "jalopy effect," which might increase air pollution if people kept their older cars on the road longer rather than paying higher prices for new cars, higher prices that were the direct result of the ZEV mandate. The automakers also argued that the nation would see more fatalities as more people took to the streets in neighborhood electric cars, essentially street-legal golf carts.[48]

In the end, in a 2003 settlement designed to salvage at least some progress, the California Air Resources Board agreed to a longer timetable for the introduction of ZEVs and "credits" for ZEV-like activity, including production of hydrogen fuel cell vehicles.

Although a ghost of its former self, ZEV rules still live in California and several northeastern states.

*Ghost* may be the applicable word. In light of their victory, the car companies took their toys and went home. To be sure, several of the automakers did actually introduce and lease battery-electric ZEVs into the marketplace. GM produced 1,100 of their EV1 model alone. Once relieved of the bulk of the mandate, though, GM not only halted production but made one more move, reminiscent of burning the Red Cars and ripping up the light-rail lines: they ordered all the leased ZEVs to be returned to the dealers so they could be crushed, shredded, and sold for scrap. ZEV lease holders were outraged and begged to buy the vehicles rather than allow them to disappear forever. GM wouldn't budge. To show their displeasure, EV1 owners held a mock funeral in July of 2003 before their beloved ZEVs could be laid to rest by GM and its USABC collaborators.[49]

"The detractors of electric vehicles are right," proclaimed actor Ed Begley Jr. in his eulogy at the Hollywood Forever Cemetery where the event was staged, wreath-draped EV1s in the background. "Given their limited range, they can only meet the needs of 90 percent of the population," he added sarcastically.[50] Loyal drivers, some with license plates reading "NOT OPEC" and "REVOLTS," gave similar testimony to the value and practicality of the commuter car that gave them more than 100 miles of silent, clean driving on a single charge. Eric Garcetti, a Los Angeles City councilman, vowed to drive his EV1 until GM could "pry it out of my charger's cold, dead hands."[51]

GM made good on its threat. Seeing the consumer anger, Toyota decided to sell its leased RAV4 battery-electric models to interested lessees. DaimlerChrysler quickly followed suit, but with a twist. The German–U.S. automaker had produced "city cars," which were like golf carts on steroids. These street-legal, egg-shaped cars had a range of 35 miles and a top speed of about 30 mph, but many were in service as "errand" cars in city use. To meet its ZEV targets, DaimlerChrysler donated hundreds of these ZEVs to charities. In early 2003, they had promised hundreds more to the California Association of Non-Profits, which in turn donated them to member charities, including the foundation I managed at the time, Environment Now.

As the day for delivery of our ZEV neared, we began planning the local trips we could take to the office supply store, local meetings, favorite lunch spots, even commuting from our homes a few miles away. In April, though, the United States invaded Iraq and the price of gasoline soared to more than $3 a gallon. DaimlerChrysler withdrew the offer and instead sold its ZEVs through its dealers. At least one dealer, in a television interview in Santa Barbara, bemoaned the lack of inventory, having sold his last six ZEVs for the full $8,000 asking price. We never got our "free" ZEV and neither did any of the other charities, but automakers continue to insist there is no market for electric cars.

## Politics as Usual

As the CAFE and ZEV fights demonstrate, it is not only particulate matter and ozone that are stealing the breath from our lungs and pushing us to economic and environmental crises; politics also continues to poison the air. In his landmark 1994 study of the oil industry, *Crude Awakening*, Jack Doyle lists a dozen major federal environmental laws that partially or entirely exempt petroleum companies, along with automakers and related industries. Victims include the Clean Air Act, the Clean Water Act, the Safe Drinking Water Act, and, astonishingly, the Oil Pollution Control Act of 1990.[52]

Exemptions in these laws read like cut-and-paste pages from oil and auto industry lobbyists' playbooks. One law says that the oil industry should be free from "needless interference with oil and gas production." Another allows polluted oil drilling wastes to be dumped into navigable waters or areas used by wildlife. Used motor oil is classified as nonhazardous under another law, and petroleum and natural gas is classified as nonhazardous under yet another.[53] Recognizing that such exemptions do not pass the smell test, Congress has occasionally tried to change them. In 1991, for example, Representative Cardiss Collins (D-Illinois) authored a bill to amend the Resource Conservation and Recovery Act to define used motor oil as hazardous based on its high lead content.

"We prohibit lead from being added to gasoline and paint, we no longer accept its use in water pipes," Collins noted. "Yet the federal government has virtually ignored the problem of lead in used oil."[54] Oil companies contributed more than $3 million to congressional election campaigns the year before Collins's legislation was introduced.[55] The bill was defeated and the federal government still considers used motor oil nonhazardous.

"Poison to men's souls."[56] Like the elixir that Romeo bought from the apothecary, petroleum, the internal combustion engine, and tobacco are not inherently evil. Like the corrupting influence of money that Romeo describes, it is the vast wealth that the oil, auto, and tobacco industries have amassed, and now spend on lobbying and deceit, that has fouled our health, economy, and political life. What if we could harness the creativity and capital that the oil companies and automakers have to transport us toward a future that is both environmentally and economically sustainable? Could we civilize that corporate energy and direct it to fuels that neither pollute nor come from economic and political terrorists? Could we modernize the genius that once put an affordable horseless carriage in every barn thanks to an innovation called the assembly line?

Are we intelligent enough to evolve, to bring our thinking—in business, government, and society—into the twenty-first century before we find ourselves emulating the islanders in the final days of the great civilization of Rapa Nui?

# CHAPTER 7

# Postcards from the Year 2025

Our most basic common link is that we all inhabit this small planet. We all breathe the same air. We all cherish our children's futures. And we are all mortal. And is not peace the right to live out our lives without fear of devastation—the right to breathe air as nature provided it—the right of future generations to a healthy existence?

*President John F. Kennedy,*
*Commencement Address, American University,*
*Washington, D.C., June 10, 1963*

Given the harm already done by our addiction to oil and dependence on outdated vehicles from the big automakers, is it realistic to hope that these industries will deliver us from the threat of even more damage to our economy, society, and public health? Are there viable alternatives to their products that can be rapidly commercialized, before petroleum fuels become too unstable to support our economy?

## Two Very Different Views from the Year 2025

Think ahead to 2025. There are many variables in the shaping of tomorrow and therefore many possible outcomes, but here are two very different visions for our future. In the first "postcard" from the future, we see peoples of the world on New Year's day 2025, looking back over a recent past marked by shattered dreams:

*In just the first decade of the twenty-first century, the stability of the foreign oil supply was disrupted by a coup and strike in Venezuela, a civil war in Nigeria, the U.S. war in Iraq, and rebellions and social unrest in Colombia, Russia, Saudi Arabia, and Mexico. People in these countries, who benefit little from their nation's oil resources, have continued to attack oil pipelines to siphon off their share and to interrupt others from getting theirs. Oil tankers and refineries have also become frequent terrorist targets.*

*China and India have added much strain on world oil supplies, and the Easter Island Effect (described in chapter 3) in the United States has created shortages and long lines at gas stations across the country. Gasoline and diesel prices double every twenty-four months. Black marketeers hijack fuel trucks and people siphon supplies from cars in parking lots, selling gasoline for five times the price at the pump, reminiscent of events during the crisis brought on by the Arab oil embargo of 1973. The United States begins to resemble a third world country, with periodic power outages and clogged roads littered with vehicles that ran out of fuel.*

*U.S. troops are protecting U.S. oil interests in so many places around the globe that taxes soar to unprecedented levels to support a continually growing military. The draft was reinstated in 2010 for all American men and women on their eighteenth birthday.*

*Seventy-five percent of Americans drive cars made by Japanese, Korean, or Chinese companies, all of which moved rapidly to produce fuel-efficient hybrids early in the twenty-first century. Ford and GM reorganized under bankruptcy laws after decades of producing gas-guzzling vehicles that no one wanted. Neither company manufactures vehicles of its own; now both sell cars and trucks made by Chinese companies and adorned with their once-proud American nameplates.*

*Pollution has grown beyond the ability of government regulators to moderate it because baseline sources of pollution, both air and water, are now joined by petroleum fires and spills from aging infrastructure and increased dependence on coal-fired power plants. As a result, two million Americans died prematurely from completely preventable air pollution in the first quarter of the twenty-first century and ten million more were hospitalized. The cost for health care and solving other oil-related problems tops the $20 trillion mark, draining money from other needed services. Because of the great number of retiring baby boomers, the Social Security Administration declared bankruptcy in 2015 and now only pays 30 cents on the dollar in promised benefits.*

Is this vision of 2025 too apocalyptic to be credible? "They" won't let this happen, right? In May 2004, business columnist James Flanigan wrote in the *Los Angeles Times*:

> SunCor [a Canadian oil company] President Rick George notes that the use of oil energy will grow more in the next 25 years than it has in the last quarter-century. Car culture is just coming to China. The pressures on the resource base, on the capital markets to fund the development of more oil and on the environment to tolerate the burning of more hydrocarbons will expand geometrically.[1]

Of course, that need not be our fate. An alternative vision for 2025 is equally plausible:

*Half the vehicles in the United States are powered by hydrogen or bio-fuels (gasoline and diesel made from crops or waste materials), and*

*California becomes the first state to ban the sale of any new vehicle that burns petroleum. China, India, and several other emerging economies have leap-frogged into a biofuels and hydrogen economy, much as have nations that jumped right to cell phones instead of first building massive hard-wire communications systems. As a result, three-quarters of the vehicles in those nations are clean, efficient, and running on domestic energy.*

*U.S. automakers are in solid fiscal health. Ford burst into the future first with internal combustion hybrid hydrogen cars, making them the market leader in the eyes of consumers. GM took a few years longer, but grabbed market share with high-tech products using fuel cells and drive-by-wire technology. Both companies also built millions of vehicles in the past twenty years that run on batteries, natural gas, and biofuels as a transition to hydrogen-powered vehicles. Foreign automakers remain a dominant force, though, offering consumers home hydrogen and natural gas fueling appliances along with their cars, making a growing number of consumers truly energy independent.*

*Since the U.S. invasion of Iraq in 2003 and the lengthy military aftermath, no further wars were fought over oil, saving thousands of lives and billions of dollars. As a result of these changes, the U.S. economy is strong, the deficit erased, few terrorist actions have taken place, and the global fleet of oil tankers is systematically being converted to move scarce supplies of fresh water around the globe. Although these tankers still routinely leak, because it's only water, no one objects. The sky is bluer again and the water is cleaner, with the end of human-made pollution from petroleum products not many years in the future.*

Is this scenario unlikely? Perhaps it is, unless we commit ourselves now to a vision of making this brighter future a reality. We need not wait for oil to run out.

"The Stone Age did not end for lack of stone and the Oil Age will end long before the world runs out of oil," observed Sheikh Zaki Yamani, Saudi Arabia's oil minister for some three decades. If the name is vaguely familiar, you may recall that Sheikh Yamani was the architect of the Arab oil embargo of 1973.[2]

What if the United States had responded to the September 11, 2001, attacks by directing the $100 billion that was spent during the first year on war in Iraq on a crash program to build alternative-fuel vehicles and fueling stations, launching a new economy, phasing out our use of oil, and underwriting well-paying U.S. jobs and exports in alternative energy production for decades to come? What if we were to take a page from our forebearers and declare our *energy* independence now? The steps in that direction are easy to comprehend and not as hard as one might think to implement. Here are three steps to energy independence.

## Energy Independence Step One: Conserve

First, we must immediately squeeze more out of the energy resources we already have. In a word, conservation. In April 2001 at a speech to the Associated Press in Toronto, Vice President Dick Cheney infamously derided conservation as a mere "personal virtue" that produced few results, but his opinion assumes that conservation alone will solve our energy problems. Of course, it won't, but it is a critical first step and an indispensable part of a comprehensive energy strategy.

Conservation can have dramatic effects in a short time. Los Angeles County in the late 1980s and early 1990s endured a gripping drought that threatened day-to-day lives in the region. Californians launched an aggressive campaign to avoid overwatering lawns, passed laws to mandate installation of low-flow toilets and showers when buildings were sold, and encouraged farmers to shift to drip irrigation and other water-saving techniques. Over time, people began to see water not as an endless, mindless commodity that originates in a faucet and ends up in a toilet, but as liquid gold. The result? By the turn of the twenty-first century, Los Angeles County used no more water than it did in 1990, despite a 15 percent increase in population, thanks to conservation.

In the first years of the new century, all of California faced another type of shortage, this time electricity. Facing probable rolling blackouts, the state launched "Flex Your Power," a campaign to educate consumers about using less electricity during peak hours, distributed a million compact florescent lightbulbs to replace inefficient incandescent bulbs, provided monetary incentives for energy efficient appliances, and expanded energy efficiency standards in building and appliance codes.

The result? Needing to conserve 11 percent to avoid blackouts, Californians reduced peak loads by 14 percent and avoided most of the pain.[3] The state is growing by half a million people every year, and although new power plants are being built, they cannot possibly be built fast enough to meet growing demand. Still, California has not suffered major blackouts since the crisis, thanks largely to conservation.

Perhaps the most impressive "green" savings from conservation are in the form of money. In Dearborn, Michigan, Ford Motor Company turned to the visionary designer William McDonough to remodel its nearly hundred-year-old landmark vehicle manufacturing facility with an eye toward improving their environmental footprint, but also hoping to improve Ford's profitability. Bill Ford Jr. took me on a tour of Ford's new campus in 2004, justifiably bragging that what was good for the environment was also good for his company's bottom line.

"You won't believe how cool this stuff is," he beamed, pointing out many of the conservation features from a special observation tower high above the 1,100-acre River Rouge complex. Trees and grass that now line roadways cleanse polluted storm water, saving $35 million in treatment costs.[4] The roof of the main assembly building is covered with living grasses, an approach that costs about the same as a conventional roof but that lasts up to twice as long because the roof doesn't expand and contract as much under extreme temperatures. The "living roof" also stores millions of gallons of storm water for use in the plant, measurably improves air quality, and provides such good insulation that 40 percent of the heating and cooling ducts were eliminated, all of which saved even more money. In addition, something as simple as introducing more natural lighting through skylights saves Ford $50,000 each year on its electricity bill.

Squeezing more from existing energy resources is relatively easy and usually profitable. It's about personal choices, but it's also about providing products to match those consumer needs. Automakers tell me again and again that they only make the vehicles consumers demand. That is akin to McDonald's saying that it only introduced "supersizing" in response to customer demand. In fact, McDonald's taught its counter staff to push larger-sized portions to make money, not because anyone was still hungry after consuming the "normal"-sized meals.[5] It is also morally bankrupt for the oil and auto industries to hide behind "consumer demand" as the dictator of actual practice. If that were the primary driving force in our commerce and society, we would long ago have institutionalized drugs, prostitution, gambling, and the three-day work week.

We can dramatically decrease our gasoline consumption without waiting for the auto companies to develop more efficient vehicles. Regardless of the vehicle, drivers can conserve up to 20 percent of their fuel budgets, literally overnight, with a few simple tactics (see the tips for reducing fuel consumption on the next page). If everyone began to adopt even a few of these strategies, we could quickly lower dependence on oil.

## Tips to Reduce Your Fuel Consumption by 20 Percent or More[1]

- Driving at the posted speed limit is probably the single-most effective strategy to conserve fuel. It may now be legal to drive 75 mph on some open roads, but it costs about 15 percent more fuel than if you were to stick to around 60 mph.

- You can save another 2 to 3 percent of your fuel by properly inflating your tires. Think about it. Underinflated tires are flatter and therefore present a greater surface area against the road. That creates more friction, which creates more drag, which requires more energy to overcome the drag. Added friction also wears tires out faster, giving off toxic tire dust and resulting in more frequent tire replacement. This tip helps even more on large commercial vehicles. One study showed that a farm tractor using correctly inflated tires required 20 percent less diesel fuel than one with improperly inflated tires.[2]

- In hot weather, it's tempting to keep your air conditioner running at its maximum much of the time, especially when you first get into the hot car. The higher settings on the air conditioner demand much more energy than the lower settings, so to save another 2 to 3 percent of your fuel, simply open the windows to get the bulk of the hot air out of the car before turning on the air conditioner.

- Jackrabbit starts—racing to beat the other guy when the light turns green—may cost another few percent, depending on how much city driving you do.

- Motor oils that have the "Energy Conserving II" label contain friction-reducing additives and can save another 1 to 2 percent of your fuel.

- Fuel needs space at the top of the tank to expand as it warms during the day. If there's no space, it will discharge through vents, so don't "top off" the gas tank and do make sure the gas cap is tight after refueling.

- Travel light. A loaded roof rack or carrier increases aerodynamic drag, which can cut mileage efficiency by 5 percent, and an extra hundred pounds in the trunk cuts a typical car's fuel economy 1 to 2 percent.

- A lot of gas is wasted when your car is idling. Try parking instead of using the drive-through at the fast-food place, and shut off the engine when you're waiting at the curb to pick someone up at the airport.

- Telecommute to work or take public transit. Using mass transit even one day each month will save 5 percent of the fuel you use for commuting. Of course, we could do much more. The American Public Transportation Association tells us that if Americans used public transportation at the same rate Europeans do, for just 10 percent of their daily travel needs, we would save more energy every year than all the energy used annually by the U.S. petrochemical industry and nearly equal to the energy used to produce food in the United States.

- Don't waste your money buying high-octane gasoline, which also wastes the extra energy needed to make such fuels. Stick with regular octane unless your owner's manual requires (not just "recommends") the use of a higher-octane fuel.

1. Data for these tips and even more fuel-saving information can be found at http://www.fypower.org/save_gasoline/.

2. *Overinflated Tractor Tires Waste Fuel, Reduce Productivity* (Oakland, CA: California Agriculture, University of California, Division of Agriculture and Natural Resources, March–April 1996). Available online at http://californiaagriculture.ucop.edu/9602MA/toc.html#tires.

### Energy Independence Step Two: Fuel Efficiency

The second part of energy independence is a midterm strategy, designed for the next decade. Simply put, we must buy the most fuel-efficient vehicles available, such as the popular gasoline-electric hybrid Toyota Prius and comparable models from Honda (and other automakers as they introduce them, too). These cars can get as much as 60 miles on a gallon of gasoline thanks to the electric motor that does the work at slow speeds and assists the small gasoline engine at higher speeds.

Energy independence also means buying the most fuel-efficient vehicle in whatever size and class we need. An SUV may be perfectly appropriate if you have a large family or carry bulky loads. Energy independence means sending every signal we can to Detroit, Tokyo, Munich, and Seoul that we want the most fuel-efficient cars in every size and class.

Hybrids are not the only fuel-efficient vehicles we can drive. Although the major automakers have come and gone from the electric vehicle (EV) marketplace, many smaller firms are providing great choices of battery-electric commuter cars and trucks that can be recharged on household current or at the large network of EV charging stations that have been built around the country in the past decade. Vehicles powered by natural gas, serviced by a growing network of fueling stations nationwide, provide another practical alternative. Like petroleum, most natural gas is a nonrenewable fossil fuel, but it's far cleaner at every stage of extraction, preparation, delivery, and use than petroleum fuels. Some renewable natural gas (methane) is being harvested from landfills and decomposing waste materials, including sources such as dairies and urban green waste.

Biofuels, like ethanol (the gasoline alternative typically made from corn), are also cleaner than petroleum and are domestically produced from crops and organic waste materials. Most gasoline in the United States already contains some ethanol, and a growing number of vehicles are designed to use fuels that contain up to 85 percent ethanol. The major limitation for this option is finding enough biomass to displace a significant volume of petroleum. To put it in perspective, we would need to have an area roughly fifty times the size of the arable land in the entire United States to grow enough soybeans to make biofuels that could displace the total volume of petroleum fuels used in this country every year.[6] Biofuels can also be made from waste materials, but that will not add enough raw material to displace all the petroleum fuels used today. That said, biofuels, like conservation, are an important component of the energy independence strategy and are available today.

Because these midterm alternatives are steps in the right direction but can't supply all our transportation fuel needs, we need one more step to secure genuine energy independence. We must evolve from petroleum fuels or their alternative counterparts, and the vehicles that combust them, to something that can power our entire transportation needs, our imaginations, and our future.

## Energy Independence Step Three: Evolve to Hydrogen Fuel

If you are a fan of *Star Trek*—and who isn't hopeful that the future portrayed in that TV show is indeed our own?—you probably appreciate NASA's plans to build a colony on Mars. If given such a blank canvas to develop for human use, how would you begin?

Would you build residences in the middle of the most fragile natural resources and then build the workplaces 50 kilometers away? Would you connect the two with costly ribbons of steel and concrete, scars across the virgin territory you just adopted? To get from one point to another, would you put people in 3-ton steel and plastic containers, propelled by a highly flammable substance that could only be found in sufficient quantity on the opposite side of the globe, a substance that could only be made useful by drilling thousands of meters into the planet and then filtering the stuff in factories built on vast, industrial wastelands?

Imagine what you have wrought for energy production on your newly found paradise. Your raw material would be transported thousands of kilometers back to the other side of the planet in vessels the size of the Empire State Building, occasionally spilling large volumes along the way like a drunken waiter in a cocktail lounge. Back at the colony, an industrial landscape of pumps, pipes, towers, compressors, valves, furnaces, heat exchangers, and other components produces your fuel by running the raw materials you just sucked from the planet's bowels through a distillation tower and a monstrous pressure cooker that uses heat to separate liquid and vapor. Another leviathan mixes a powdery catalyst with the heavier liquids at 1,300 degrees Fahrenheit to "crack" larger molecules apart and create the fuel and a host of toxic by-products.

Would you then encourage your colonists to waste as much of this hard-won energy resource as possible, fouling what atmosphere and water supplies you've been able to generate for yourselves? Would their vehicles be so impractical that only 5 percent of the energy in this newly made fuel was used to move the colonists or other cargo, while the remainder was wasted as heat energy and toxic emissions?

Instead, you might set up your colony with homes near the workplaces and power your transportation fleet with the most plentiful substance on the planet, indeed in the entire universe, a substance that you could make in a variety of simple, nonpolluting ways from a wide variety of raw materials that were all close at hand: hydrogen, or $H_2$. Your vehicles would be efficient, converting the majority of the fuel supplied to them into useful energy.

Because the technology already exists to make that brighter vision a reality in outer space, why not take advantage of it today right here on planet Earth? Much has already been written about the transition to a hydrogen economy and the barriers to practical, sustainable deployment related to that energy strategy. Take a look at Peter Hoffmann's *Tomorrow's Energy—Hydrogen, Fuel Cells and the*

*Prospects for a Cleaner Planet*, or *Out of Gas* by David Goodstein, or any of the articles and books written on the subject by Jeremy Rifkin, including *The Hydrogen Economy*. There are also many challenges to using hydrogen for a transportation fuel or to power our electrical needs. This chapter will examine some of those challenges, but the best book to raise those concerns in depth is *The Hype about Hydrogen* by Joe Romm.

These books all describe the technology of hydrogen and its history, current state, and its future. Probably the single easiest "read" for the time-challenged is *Twenty Hydrogen Myths* by noted scientist and futurist Amory B. Lovins of the Rocky Mountain Institute (RMI), published in June 2003 and available on the RMI website for free. In addition, because commercialization of hydrogen technology is rapidly evolving, a good source of current information that is updated regularly can be found at Energy Independence Now's website, www.energyindependencenow.org.

Just how close do these books, and all the other hydrogen research and development done especially in the past decade, predict we are to a hydrogen-powered economy? What do they say stands between us and that cleaner, more sustainable future?

"[T]he first car driven by a child born today could be powered by hydrogen, and pollution-free," offered President Bush in his January 2003 State of the Union address, suggesting that the federal government sees commercialization of hydrogen for transportation by 2020.[7] A look at some of the basics of hydrogen, including a journey along the "hydrogen highways" of Canada, several states in the United States, Iceland, China, and many others, however, suggests that a hydrogen economy could be a reality on our planet long before 2025.

## What about Hydrogen?

Hydrogen is the most abundant element in nature, making up some 75 percent of all mass in the universe. Hydrogen atoms fuse into helium in the sun to create the energy that radiates to our planet.[8] Unlike natural gas or oil, though, very little hydrogen exists on Earth by itself. The largest sources of hydrogen are water, where hydrogen is combined with oxygen ($H_2O$), and fossil fuels, where hydrogen is combined with carbon.

Therefore, to use hydrogen as a fuel, we must first separate it from these other elements. As such, hydrogen is often called an energy "carrier" rather than a stand-alone energy "source." To illustrate that point, consider that electricity cannot easily be stored in a vehicle, but can be used to make hydrogen, which can then be used as a vehicle fuel. By running electricity through water, hydrogen can be separated from oxygen in a process called "electrolysis." The resulting hydrogen is then used for fuel, but it was the original energy source for the electricity that is actually powering the vehicle. The original energy source may have been sunlight, wind, natural gas, coal, or any number of other primary energy sources. Therefore, both the hydrogen and the electricity are carriers for that primary energy source.

Hydrogen as an energy carrier is an important tool for maximizing the use of clean, renewable energy sources. For example, wind and solar are intermittent energy sources that may not always produce power when it's needed most. Using the electricity from those clean energy sources to make hydrogen as described above, however, gives us a practical way to store the energy until it's needed. As early as 1995, the Xerox Corporation opened a solar-powered hydrogen fueling station on its campus in Torrance, California, to power a small fleet of hydrogen-powered pickup trucks.[9]

Hydrogen can be burned in a standard internal combustion engine (ICE), like the millions of vehicles on the roads today, although that is extremely inefficient, mostly because of wasted heat energy. By combining a small ICE motor with an electric motor, however, hybrid engines make it much more practical to use hydrogen in technologies that are readily available today. The most likely form of a hydrogen-based vehicle fleet, though, will be cars and trucks powered by fuel cells. Fuel cells convert hydrogen into electricity, leaving as by-products only heat (which is captured and used in most fuel cell applications), oxygen, and a small amount of water. The electrical energy is used to power electric motors for the vehicle, so the car of the twenty-first century will actually be an electric vehicle. Unlike storing electrical energy in special batteries, fuel cells do not require heavy weights to be lugged around, therefore reducing vehicle range and efficiency, nor are there long recharging times. Refueling with $H_2$ takes no longer than the same process with petroleum fuels.

Hydrogen fuel cells are already powering transportation around the world. The first commercial demonstration of a hydrogen-fueled bus fleet was in 1993 in Canada, and hydrogen-powered buses shuttled tourists around the Commonwealth Games in Vancouver in 1994. Chicago, Amsterdam, Barcelona, Hamburg, London, Luxembourg, Singapore, Stockholm, Reykjavik, and more than a dozen other cities followed suit over the next decade, and now hundreds of hydrogen-powered buses are in operation around the world.[10] Even oil companies are getting into the game. In March 2006, Chevron, AC Transit, and other partners opened a fueling station in Oakland, California, for a fleet of hydrogen-powered buses and passenger vehicles.[11]

Every major automaker in the United States, Asia, and Europe already has hydrogen-powered fuel cell cars in demonstrations around the world, many at the California Fuel Cell Partnership in Sacramento, California. The hurdles to mass marketing these vehicles are safety, price, range, temperature, durability, and adequate fueling infrastructure. Let's take a look at each.

### Safety

GM engineers assert that a hydrogen vehicle is safer than today's petroleum counterpart. Hydrogen is fourteen times lighter than air, so it dissipates quickly if it leaks. One dramatic study compared two identical sedans—one hydrogen powered and one gasoline powered—whose fuel tanks were ignited.[12] The hydrogen in the first vehicle burns clean, in less than a minute, harming nothing. Compared to petroleum flames, $H_2$ radiates less heat and contains no soot, which is what sticks to the skin and causes horrific burns in petroleum fires.[13] The gasoline vehicle in the test burned for several minutes, incinerating the entire vehicle and anyone who had been unlucky enough to sit inside.

Does that mean that $H_2$ is significantly safer than petroleum fuels? A former manager of Lockheed's hydrogen programs, G. Daniel Brewer, has long voiced his belief that fewer people would die in fiery runway collisions of aircraft if those planes were fueled by liquid $H_2$ rather than petroleum products.[14] Many people, however, cite the fire on the German airship *Hindenburg* in 1936 when talking about hydrogen and safety. The *Hindenburg* was covered with a highly flammable skin material that was used against the better judgment of several engineers at the time. Lightning or static electricity is thought to have ignited it. The $H_2$ combusted almost instantly, but the skin of the vessel and the diesel fuel that powered the engines burned for an hour as the entire airship crashed to the ground. No one died from burning hydrogen; they died when they jumped from the vessel while it was still several hundred feet above the ground or in the flames of the diesel fuel. The majority of passengers survived when the vessel came to rest and were able to run free.[15]

To be sure, $H_2$ is a combustible fuel, in liquid or gaseous forms, and therefore must be treated with respect. Extensive experimentation with $H_2$ over a century and a half however, has led experts to conclude that $H_2$ presents no greater danger—and in many ways less danger—than any conventional fuels on the market today, especially those made from petroleum or natural gas.[16]

## Price

Like anything else, higher costs for a hydrogen vehicle will ultimately be addressed by mass production and advancements in technology. Today's fuel cell "stack" costs about ten times that of a comparable petroleum internal combustion engine, down from a multiplier of fifty since 1998. The 2005 Honda fuel cell vehicle, for example, uses 50 percent fewer parts and materials than Honda's model of just two years earlier, drastically lowering the price.[17] Moreover, fuel cells, like batteries in your iPod, are scalable. Do you need more power? Then add more cells. The cells for a truck, though, are the same as those for a Mini-Cooper, making mass production much easier and more profitable than the innumerable engine and transmission variations found on today's petroleum-powered vehicles.

"We can get the cost curve down," says GM's Larry Burns, who directs that automaker's $H_2$ development program. "Look, the cost of a gigabyte of computer memory in 1988 was about $17,000, but now it's down to $6, a reduction of more than 99 percent in 14 years. We can do the same [when] mass production kicks in."[18] That prediction from an automaker is echoed by a manufacturer of fuel cells and other hydrogen power components.

"We will have the technology for full mass production of a unit by 2010," says Firoz Rasul, chairman of Ballard Power Systems, the world's leading manufacturer of $H_2$ fuel cells. "At which point it will be totally price competitive with the gasoline internal combustion engine."[19]

Yet don't forget the solutions that may be right in front of us. During the 1960s, NASA needed a ballpoint pen for writing in space. After many months of work and more than a million dollars of research and development, they developed the "Space Pen," which not only worked in outer space, but can still be purchased today by earthbound mortals as a novelty item. The Soviet Union, faced with the same problem in their space program, gave their cosmonauts a pencil.

So it is with hydrogen-powered vehicles. As German engineer Rudolf Erren demonstrated in the 1920s by converting more than a thousand ordinary cars, buses, and trucks to run on hydrogen, any existing ICE can be tuned to run on hydrogen.[20] As noted previously, the efficiencies of fuel cells can be nearly achieved in an ICE, if that engine is coupled with a small electric booster motor (the now-famous hybrid technology). In other words, the near-term solution to making $H_2$ practical is already rolling down every street and highway in the world.

Having addressed the cost of the vehicles, what about the cost of hydrogen as a fuel? Like many aspects of this debate, the answer has several parts. Because a hydrogen fuel cell vehicle is two to three times as efficient at the task of converting fuel into usable energy as one powered by a petroleum internal combustion engine, the cost per mile driven for $H_2$ fuel is likely to be equal to or less than the cost of gasoline. That calculation is especially true as the price of gasoline skyrockets and as mass production lowers the cost of $H_2$ fuel and vehicles.

"Since you buy automotive fuel to get miles, not energy, ignoring such differences in end-use efficiency is a serious distortion," notes Amory Lovins of the Rocky Mountain Institute, one of the world's leading authorities on hydrogen fuel and energy efficiency. "[This] accounts for much of the misinformation being published about hydrogen's high cost."[21] Using the cost per mile evaluation, the U.S. Department of Energy estimates that $H_2$ fuel, made on-site by passing steam through natural gas to separate out the $H_2$, would cost as little as 24 cents per "gallon of gasoline equivalent" (the amount of hydrogen that would power a vehicle the same distance it travels on a gallon of gasoline).[22] Of course, if you put hydrogen into an ICE, which is not as efficient as a fuel cell system, the true cost is higher. [23]

## Range

How far can you go on a tank of gasoline? If you could go 200 miles before refueling instead of, say, 300 miles, would it matter that much as long as there were enough gas stations around? Range is only limited by access to a fueling station, but automakers assert that $H_2$ fuel cell cars, some of which today can go up to 200 miles before refueling, won't be marketable until they deliver 300 miles between stops at the pump. Yet many petroleum-powered vehicles get far less than 300 miles on a tank of gas, so this factor is apparently not a limiting one to consumers. The reality is that if you take a long drive, say from Los Angeles to Sacramento, a distance of about 380 miles, you will have to stop to fill up once no matter what type of vehicle you drive. Range has been a bigger issue with battery-electric cars because no matter what the range, when the batteries are discharged, the time needed to recharge is up to eight hours.

Fuel cells in automotive uses are also becoming more efficient over time, which improves the miles-per-gallon equivalents at a rate of about 20 percent each year. Another way to increase range is to carry more fuel in the vehicle, either by making larger tanks or by squeezing more hydrogen gas into a tank by increasing the pressure. It does take more energy to fill a tank at higher pressures, so there is a practical limit to that latter approach. GM is experimenting with increasing the tank capacity by deploying several small tanks connected together that are built into otherwise wasted space in the vehicle. Methods using liquid $H_2$ and impregnating graphite or other fibers with gaseous $H_2$ are also being studied as means to add more fuel to a smaller tank.

## Temperature

Fuel cells don't work very well in extremely cold weather, but research is being done to fix that. Diesels didn't start in extremely cold conditions either and catalytic converters still don't, but we have managed to overcome those limitations. In July 2004, Honda demonstrated a hydrogen fuel cell product that operates seamlessly at below-freezing temperatures.[24] Moreover, millions of U.S. consumers live in temperate climates, so for many people, temperature won't be much of an issue in the first place.

### Durability

Automakers have recently put consumer-ready fuel cell cars in the hands of average drivers to get more data on durability, which will affect decisions on warranties and resale value. Test fleets on the road today will answer those questions. One disarmingly simple solution to the durability question, indeed to all these questions—safety, price, range, temperature, and durability—is to mass produce $H_2$ vehicles using familiar ICEs, something that both Ford and BMW are doing in demonstration models. Rather than wait for further improvements to fuel cells, these automakers are betting on a near-term demand for $H_2$ and using ICEs as a transition to get consumers familiar with the fuel. As noted earlier, the latest ICE-hybrid technology gets very near the efficiency of fuel cells, and BMW has announced the sale of ICE cars that operate on either gasoline or liquid hydrogen beginning in 2008.[25]

In fact, the only real impediment to full commercialization of hydrogen-powered vehicles is mass production of both the fuel and the vehicles. That's what brings down the price of anything, making it available to the widest spectrum of consumers, but that's where someone needs to break the chicken-or-egg cycle.

## California's Hydrogen Highway Network

Actor and environmental activist Ed Begley Jr. once said to me that if we leave $H_2$ fuel and vehicle commercialization up to the oil and auto companies, "they are the cars of the future . . . and always will be." No car company will mass produce cars without fuel infrastructure, and no energy company will install significant numbers of hydrogen fueling stations until there are vehicles to use the fuel on a regular basis. Chicken or egg? There is a great deal of agreement among automakers, energy companies, academics, government officials, and independent experts that $H_2$ is coming to a fueling station near you in the not-too-distant future, but everyone wants someone else to go first. There's the rub.

If you want to commercialize something, you put it in the easy grasp of as many people as possible as soon as you can. The U.S. interstate highway system was designed to be within easy reach of most Americans, and, in California, these highways are within a few miles of the vast majority of Californians. So, wouldn't it make sense to spread out a network of $H_2$ fueling stations along this already ubiquitous transportation system?

Let's say that a consumer should not have to travel more than 10 miles to the nearest station. That would mean putting one $H_2$ station about every 20 miles along each of the interstate highways. In California, that translates to just about two hundred total stations, a small number compared with the 10,000 retail gasoline outlets in the state or the 2,500 diesel stations. So, with no more than two hundred stations, spaced every 20 miles along each major highway in the state, you can put $H_2$ fuel within easy reach of most Californians.

With this in mind, Governor Arnold Schwarzenegger signed an executive order on April 20, 2004, creating the California Hydrogen Highway Network and today the basic network of two hundred stations is being built in California in partnership with a variety of stakeholders.[26] By the beginning of 2006, more than two dozen stations were operating in California, most dedicated to specific demonstration projects, but all prepared for public use. Just a few miles from the famous Los Angeles City Hall that Superman flew from in the 1950s TV series, I actually became the first retail $H_2$ fuel customer in the United States.

On August 13, 2004, in Diamond Bar, California, the South Coast Air Quality Management District cut the ribbon on the nation's first truly public H$_2$ filling station, built by Stuart Energy to convert water and electricity into clean H$_2$. I was driving a Honda FCX fuel cell vehicle loaned to me by the City of Los Angeles from its demonstration fleet. Three colleagues were with me in this very comfortable, familiar-looking car, traveling at speeds of 75 mph along Southern California freeways to arrive at the new fueling station.

The simple attachment of the fuel hose to the car was akin to the snap connector I have at home on my propane barbeque. I hit the on switch, and H$_2$ filled the tank at the same pace as filling a gasoline tank in a conventional car. When I had finished, the display on the pump showed I had pumped about 1 gallon of gasoline equivalent into the car for a grand total of 5 cents. I pulled a $1 bill from my wallet and presented it to Cynthia Verdugo-Peralta, the visionary board member of the district who was our host that day. That tank of H$_2$ then powered my car another 100 miles around the region, and I returned the car to the city garage with half a tank to spare.

"We are talking just hundreds of hydrogen-powered vehicles on the roads now," notes Mark Mehall, Ford's fuel cell vehicle program manager. "But by 2008 it will be thousands and by 2012, tens of thousands."[27] California is not alone in expanding the nascent network of H$_2$ stations. BP's general manager for hydrogen, Michael Jones, notes that his company is already the world's leading supplier of H$_2$ for vehicles, operating stations in Singapore, Barcelona, Berlin, Hamburg, London, Munich, Porto, Stuttgart, and other locations in Australia, the United States, and China.[28]

"We produce enough hydrogen at our oil refineries to refuel 10 million vehicles. And the cost is the same as petrol before taxes," said Jones, speaking in 2004 in Singapore at the opening of the second hydrogen fueling station there, which powers a fleet of buses.[29]

Not all hydrogen technology deployment is in vehicles. In July 2005, the Sierra Nevada Brewing Company in Chico, California, unveiled a 1-megawatt $H_2$ fuel cell (enough power for up to a thousand homes) that powers its entire brewery. Waste heat from the fuel cells will be captured to create steam for the brewing process, and any extra electricity generated will be sold back to the grid, lowering Sierra Nevada's energy cost and eliminating air pollution equivalent to taking five hundred gasoline-powered cars off the road.[30] In Carson, California, BP unveiled plans in 2006 to use $H_2$ in another creative way. A 500-megawatt power plant will burn $H_2$ that is stripped from natural gas. The $CO_2$, a greenhouse gas, that results from this reformation of the natural gas will be injected into nearby oil formations to repressurize them and return them to productivity, thereby capturing and permanently storing the $CO_2$ in this "sequestration" process.

In sum, hydrogen commercialization projects around the globe are showing that there is a path to energy independence. But there is, of course, no free lunch. Converting energy from raw natural resources (oil, biomass, sunlight, etc.) into something useful (gasoline, methane, hydrogen, etc.) takes technology, money, and other resources. Moreover, if cleaner fuels such as hydrogen are made from unsustainable sources, especially fossil fuels, we are neither independent nor building for the future. So, is there a way to ensure that hydrogen puts us on a highway to genuine energy independence?

## Getting the Hydrogen and Making it Green

At least thirty-six states—most notably Arizona, Florida, Hawaii, Illinois, Massachusetts, New York, and even the home of our petroleum-powered past, Michigan—now have major research, development, and commercialization programs for $H_2$, using it for both electricity and transportation energy.[31] In Las Vegas, a major $H_2$ energy station produces both electricity and vehicle fuel.

What is noteworthy about many of these efforts is the focus on producing $H_2$ from renewable resources, such as biomass, or from solar-powered electrolysis of water. Three multistate collaboratives are also experimenting with $H_2$ fueling networks, including a hydrogen highway from Boston to Washington, D.C. These regional efforts produce and share hydrogen from the most abundant renewable resource in each region, mostly biomass, solar, wind, and geothermal resources. Other collaboratives are using nonrenewable energy sources that are abundant in their regions, such as coal, but experimenting with ways to permanently sequester the $CO_2$, a by-product when $H_2$ is extracted from the coal.

For now, much of the $H_2$ fuel will be extracted from natural gas, which is still relatively plentiful. To be sure, that is only a transition energy source because no one wants to switch from dependence on one fossil fuel to another. Yet one of the many benefits of $H_2$ as a fuel is that it can be made from a variety of sources using a variety of technologies. Below are discussed some of the methods for producing $H_2$ that are both sustainable and provide a net benefit to the environment.

### Hydrogen from Wastewater and Stranded Electricity

One of the most efficient ways to make hydrogen is by electrolysis of water, using excess electricity generation capacity. "Off-peak" power is electricity that is generated during times of the day or night when demands for power are lowest. The unused capacity of the generators may therefore be said to be "stranded."

The water for this process can come from another "stranded" asset, in fact, from one that is otherwise being thrown away: treated wastewater. Every gallon of water contains enough $H_2$ to power a car about the same distance it now travels on a gallon of gasoline. Studies by Joan Ogden at the University of California Davis Institute of Transportation Studies show that by using water and off-peak electricity from existing power plants in the territory of Southern California Edison, enough $H_2$ can be created to power up to six million cars.[32]

Wouldn't we run out of water at some point, though? No, we

won't; there is enough hydrogen in the water discharged just from the sewage treatment plants in Los Angeles—about 700 million gallons each day—to power the entire U.S. fleet of cars and trucks on a daily basis. When all the stranded electricity is consumed, however, added generation would be needed to obtain all transportation fuel hydrogen made from electrolysis of water. Some fear that making such demands on the nation's electrical grid will promote the expansion of nuclear power, but growing fights over disposal of nuclear waste are likely to severely limit any expansion of that energy source.

Instead, the growing demand for electricity is already increasingly being supplied by renewable energy sources, such as wind, solar, biomass, and geothermal energy. Many states have "renewable portfolio standards" that require utilities to obtain a certain percentage of their power sources from renewable energy by specific dates. In California, for example, the law requires that 20 percent of the state's power come from renewable sources by 2017. Schwarzenegger has introduced legislation to achieve that goal by 2010 and a full 33 percent by 2020. If the electricity comes from these renewable energy sources, hydrogen made from electrolysis of water will also be renewable and "green."

### Hydrogen from Organic Waste

In Chino, California, not far from downtown Los Angeles, tens of thousands of dairy cows convert tons of feed into milk and, of course, tons of manure. The Inland Empire Utilities Agency built an anaerobic digester, essentially a giant mechanical stomach, using nature's refining process to turn the waste via natural decomposition into methane and hydrogen. Using the waste also reduces disposal costs and protects air and water quality.

Fifty miles north, in a suburb of Los Angeles, tons of urban green waste will soon be converted into methane using a similar digester. The BioConverter Company will use the methane to power a fleet of vehicles. A by-product of the process is organic liquid fertilizer, a valuable soil amendment in high demand, and some of the energy in each project will also be used to make $H_2$.

Progress is also being made in the science of conversion technologies, the process of converting waste materials such as old tires, plastics, and medical waste into $H_2$. Numerous processes can accomplish this conversion, including one in which waste is run through what amounts to a giant microwave oven and the heating process converts solids into $H_2$ and other useful gases.[33] In California, these various methods of converting waste products into useable fuels, especially $H_2$, have the potential to displace as much as 25 percent of the state's energy needs by 2025.[34]

### Hydrogen from the Wind and Sun

Sunline Transit in Palm Springs produces the $H_2$ for their fleet of fuel cell buses using solar- and wind-powered electrolysis of water. At Honda's North American headquarters in Torrance, California, an array of solar panels does similar duty to generate $H_2$ for the company's growing fleet of fuel cell cars.

Converting wind energy into $H_2$ makes a lot of sense because wind blows at the times of the day when the electricity generated from it isn't particularly needed. Batteries are inefficient for storing large amounts of electricity, but you can use the electricity to make $H_2$ at any time of day, storing the fuel for when you actually do need it. Estimates show that by 2015, wind-generated $H_2$ will cost no more than that made with solar photovoltaics.[35]

Solar is especially interesting because the total solar power that shines on the United States each day represents ten thousand times the electricity we now consume.[36] It would take 200,000 square kilometers of solar thermal or photovoltaics to generate 100 percent of the energy needs of the United States. For comparison, Alaska's North Slope region that has been the source of so much of the country's oil since the 1970s, is about that size. So is the state of

Nebraska.[37] Is that an absurd amount of land to dedicate to power generation? How many square kilometers of roofs do we already have in the United States? How many square kilometers of parking lots, which could be covered with solar panels, creating shade at the same time as energy, are there? How many square kilometers do we dedicate now to power generation of one kind or another?

How many square kilometers of flat roofs are there at just the Kmarts, Costcos, and Wal-Marts of the world? Many of these big-box retailers are selling gasoline nowadays, so considering the roof and parking lot space available at these retailers that might be used for solar panels, they may be the best bet for $H_2$ fueling stations in the future. To be sure, big-box retailers will sell $H_2$ because there's money to be made selling transportation fuel. In 2002, Wal-Mart/Sam's Club sold nearly 2.5 billion gallons of gasoline and Costco sold another billion.[38]

### *Hydrogen from Coal*
In the aftermath of the 1973 Arab oil embargo, NASA's Jet Propulsion Lab studied the potential of converting coal into a hydrogen gas; in the 1990s, the U.S. Department of Energy also studied the economics and technology of coal gasification.[39] In the end, with oil at less than $20 per barrel, it made no economic sense to produce fuels from coal, but the technology exists. At $60 a barrel, the economics change and the hydrogen produced from such gasification may cost no more than gasoline.

At any price, though, the problem of coal gasification lies in the volumes of greenhouse gases released in the process, mainly $CO_2$. Experiments are ongoing around the world to come up with a reliable way to sequester $CO_2$, but no one is sure how effective these measures will be or what unintended damage could occur in the process. As noted previously, $CO_2$ is currently pumped into oil wells to force more oil to the surface, but no one knows how much of the $CO_2$ remains in the ground. Work is also being done to sequester $CO_2$ in the seafloor and in saline aquifers, but much more research needs to be done to know if these concepts are effective, not to mention economical. Another intriguing prospect for $CO_2$ sequestration is to use it as a feedstock for producing even more fuel. Private companies and the State of Arizona are planning to feed $CO_2$ from a conventional power plant to algae, which in turn can be converted to biodiesel and ethanol.[40]

These various means of making hydrogen, all of which are being demonstrated throughout the world today, suggest that mass-produced hydrogen will soon compete favorably with today's petroleum fuels in terms of price and the necessary volumes. To be certain that $H_2$ fuel is also producing a net benefit for the environment, however, we must compare it with petroleum, or other fuels, on a "well-to-wheel" basis. Well-to-wheel calculations measure the energy consumed to make a particular fuel, and the emissions produced, from the source (the well) to the tailpipe (the wheel).

## Well-to-Wheel Measurements

A summary of the well-to-wheel science shows that for every vehicle type (ICE, battery-electric hybrid, or fuel cell), $H_2$ fuel is cleaner by far than petroleum fuels, especially when the $H_2$ is made from biomass or electrolysis of water (assuming the electricity is made from renewable sources). Making $H_2$ by gasification of coal can also be cleaner if the $CO_2$ is successfully sequestered. Reforming natural gas to obtain $H_2$ is about equal to petroleum fuels in terms of air emissions, although hydrogen may be significantly cleaner because none of the well-to-wheel studies includes all the pollution created when producing a gallon of gasoline.[41]

That's an important point, too often glossed over by those concerned with "green" versus "black" hydrogen. As noted in chapter 2, the vast majority of crude oil and refined petroleum products are moved around in ships that burn extremely dirty "bunker fuel," and there is no accurate way to estimate their contribution to air pollution and greenhouse gases. Other pollution sources from petroleum are also often overlooked, including diesel generators at oil wells and on ships, pollution from oil exploration, and the pollution effects when oil escapes both wells and wheels. For example, the cleanup of the *Exxon Valdez* oil spill required the services of a thousand boats and a hundred airplanes and helicopters, all of which generated unquantified petroleum pollution.[42]

There's also an important trend to consider in making well-to-wheel calculations. As described above, hydrogen can be made from a variety of locally available materials. Just about every community has its own electricity and water sources, for example, not to mention its own waste products. Hydrogen can also be made at home with small electrolysis units and water. Proton Energy Systems of Connecticut manufactures a home fueling appliance about the size of a dishwasher that uses any source of electricity (including solar panels) and water to make and compress hydrogen for vehicle use.

Thus, you could say that hydrogen production will move closer to the end users over time. Petroleum fuels, on the other hand, are moving farther away. Sixty percent of the 21 million barrels of oil used in the United States each day come from overseas. That's up from 40 percent from the 1980s. Think also about the refined petroleum products. California, for example, was a net exporter of refined fuels until 2000. The United States is now a net importer, bringing fuels from thousands of miles away because of the increasing demand and lack of new refinery capacity. In short, production of petroleum fuels is moving farther away from consumers, creating more air pollution and greenhouse gases to deliver them, as hydrogen "moves" closer and thereby becomes more efficient.

This concept of "moving" closer or farther away is important in another respect. A common rap on $H_2$ fuel is that it takes more energy to produce a unit of hydrogen than that unit returns as useful energy to the vehicle. Yes, that is true, but then no fuel falls off trees. The point is that you take raw materials and turn them into something useful. Chemicals don't power your radio until energy is expended to manufacture batteries. Crude oil can't power your car until energy is expended to extract it from the ground and refine it into gasoline. All these processes involve investing more energy than you will harvest, but you can't use the sources of energy in their raw form. So it is with hydrogen, too.

Because of all the different ways to make hydrogen, there are many variables to any energy "cost" calculation, but on average it takes 1.65 units of energy to produce 1 unit of useable energy in $H_2$ fuel.[43] The "unit" of measurement is irrelevant; you might measure kilowatts or British thermal units, but the ratio will still be approximately 1.65 to 1. For comparison, it takes on average 1.25 units of energy to make 1 useable unit of energy in the form of petroleum fuel, such as gasoline. As with well-to-wheel comparisons, this figure is misleading because it doesn't include all the energy expended on oil spills, wars and other oil defense costs, and the other externalities previously described. Nonetheless, setting aside the creative accounting that favors oil, let's stipulate that gasoline today takes less energy to produce than hydrogen fuel, but both take more input than you will ever get on the output side.

The 1.65 to 1 ratio for $H_2$ fuel, however, is going down, whereas the 1.25 to 1 ratio for petroleum is going up. $H_2$ production is moving quite literally closer to the end users, whereas petroleum fuel production is moving farther away. As we drain the pools of oil that nature left us, we also have to drill deeper than ever before, which takes more energy. The oil at the bottom of the pool contains more sulfur, which must be removed to make useful fuels, which therefore takes even more energy. As noted earlier, hydrogen is used to strip sulfur from petroleum, and, of course, it takes energy to make that hydrogen.[44] U.S. refineries consume more than 500 trillion cubic feet of natural gas every year, along with more than 30 trillion kilowatt hours of electricity.[45] Oil tankers are equally voracious.

One average oil tanker consumes 100,000 barrels of oil for fuel each year.[46]

The future of petroleum's 1.25 to 1 ratio looks even grimmer if we examine the latest technologies being used to tease the last drops from the ground. Oil embedded in shale deposits that lie hundreds of feet below the surface are a new target of oil explorers. To loosen the tar from the minerals, large metal tubes are inserted into the ground and heated to 700 degrees Fahrenheit for as long as four years before pumps can suck oil to the surface.[47] Tar sands, although found closer to the surface, carve enormous scars in the earth to extract them, leaving 9 tons of toxic debris for 1 ton of oil recovered.[48] Turning it into something akin to crude oil then takes a process that requires more than 900 degrees Fahrenheit of cooking.[49]

In both processes, extracting and cooking the oil consumes so much energy that the input/output ratio approaches 5 to 1, making hydrogen at less than 2 to 1 seem quite a bargain. Of the world's remaining oil, 85 percent is tied up in these oil shale and tar sand deposits.[50]

## How Do We Get from Here to There?

The promise of a clean energy evolution has led many to call for an "Apollo moon program" for hydrogen to accelerate commercialization. Ironically, the first man walked on the moon in 1969 thanks to hydrogen and fuel cell technology. Nonetheless, we don't need that kind of Herculean effort to make the same fuel available to those of us who simply need to get the kids to school or take a vacation.

No, there is no real need for an Apollo program for hydrogen, nor do we need to wait for colonies on Mars to prove the utility of the technology on Earth. There is a need, however, to break the monopoly on our transportation system that is the fruit of the National City Lines conspiracy, and all its petroleum-powered progeny, and for which we have paid so dearly from one day to another.

Are there strategies that can force oil companies and automakers to evolve so that we might survive to do likewise? Has society ever confronted such an entrenched, well-funded opposition—where the stakes were so high, both in terms of our public and economic health—and come out victorious?

---— CHAPTER 8 ——

# The Quality of Mercy

The quality of mercy is not strain'd,
It droppeth as the gentle rain from heaven
Upon the place beneath: it is twice blest;
It blesseth him that gives and him that takes. . . . [1]

*Shakespeare,* Merchant of Venice

Underlying Shakespeare's ode to justice, and the mercy that should guide it, is the notion of fairness. Is it fair that so many living things sacrifice physical, economic, and social well-being so that a few corporations and their shareholders might enjoy more financial wealth? Where is the justice in the Niger Delta? Where is the mercy in the impaired ability to breathe for millions of people harmed by the effects of preventable pollution?

Yes, we all use oil, directly or indirectly, and we all rely in many ways on engines that pollute, becoming unwilling participants in these injuries to ourselves, our neighbors, and our planet. The evidence shows, however, that oil companies and automakers have made persistent efforts to obscure the facts about the true cost of their products from the public and government regulators that has prevented the scales of justice from balancing. It is a decades-long smokescreen that has obstructed the path to cleaner, safer, healthier alternatives, including the loss of mass transit from many of our cities, the result of corporate collusion that was proven in federal courts.

Adding insult to these injuries, the evidence presented thus far also indicates that oil and auto lobbyists have used their vast wealth to protect their corporations from paying for many of the externalities attributable to their products, including health-care costs, defense costs, damages to our food and water supply, and even the erosion of our national monuments. In 2005, the top ten oil and auto companies reported revenues of nearly $2 trillion and profits of almost $100 billion.[2] Although we must continue to advocate that these same corporations deliver alternatives that are less harmful, isn't it only fair that they should disgorge some of these considerable profits to mitigate the true costs of their past and present business model? Can there be "gentle rain" upon Earth instead of petroleum's black, harsh rain?

Like tobacco companies, which were sued by state attorneys general and which ultimately agreed to pay more than $2 trillion to state governments over a twenty-five-year period to compensate taxpayers for public health-care costs and to fund anti-smoking campaigns, why shouldn't oil and auto companies "pay to play"?[3] Why shouldn't they allocate a fraction of their kingly wealth to compensate taxpayers for health-care costs and the enormous expense of cleaning up their toxic legacy in our air, water, and landscapes? Many agree that they should, including at least one representative of these polluting industries.

"It's not aggressive enough," said Bob Wyman, an attorney for the Regulatory Flexibility Group, which represents Chevron, Texaco, Toyota, Reliant Energy, and Northrop Grumman, when speaking about regulatory efforts to attain air quality standards in Southern California. "We're running out of time. It's time for the agencies to start thinking outside the box. We need to be more creative and use a different toolbox."[4]

Because the $2 trillion oil and auto industries are no more likely to offer compensation to their victims voluntarily than tobacco companies did, should tobacco-like litigation be one of the "creative" and "outside-the-box" solutions? Litigation may be an appropriate strategy on several levels. Like tobacco companies, the potential automakers and oil company defendants knew, or should have known, of the health effects related to their products and failed to take steps to reduce those harms. Instead, evidence shows that these corporations went to great lengths to prevent government regulators from reducing harms to the public, stalling improvements in CAFE regulations and undermining the California ZEV program, for example.

In 1953, scientists and doctors from Harvard Medical School, including the nation's leading pulmonologists, presented findings based on years of research that detailed the lung damage caused by smog.[5] In 1954, Los Angeles air pollution researchers concluded that smog was killing spinach, lettuce, and tomatoes grown in the region.[6] In the years leading up to these revelations, California scientists had shown that vehicle exhaust was responsible for more than half of that pollution.[7] Ironically, scientists had even reached the conclusion, as far back as 1939, that air pollution was severely damaging the leaves, and therefore the quality and yield, of one of the nation's most valuable agricultural products, tobacco.[8]

In 1971, California state researchers Alfred C. Hexter and John R. Goldsmith published one of the first studies to quantify the cost of air pollution in terms of human life.[9] They examined death records from a ten-day period of heavy smog in August 1955 and found 1,200 more deaths than normal for any comparable period. Death certificates said "heart attack," "heat stroke," and "lung disease," but the researchers concluded that the proximate cause was smog.

These few highlights, along with the detailed information presented in prior chapters, are just a few of the many persistent pieces of evidence that oil and auto companies ignored. How then might this problem be addressed in a courtroom? Let me start by saying that I am not a lawyer, but I have been a plaintiff in numerous successful lawsuits enforcing environmental laws against polluters, both as a citizen-activist and as secretary of California's Environmental Protection Agency. When looking at the tobacco cases and other related environmental litigation, lawyers with whom I have worked over the years have suggested several courses of action that a state or individual plaintiff might consider in seeking redress of grievances against the oil and auto industries.

These concepts, however, are not merely legal theory. California, New York, and a dozen other state and city governments have already banded together to sue the federal government to regulate greenhouse gas emissions, such as $CO_2$, or give states the right to do so.[10] Many of those same states have sued power plants for creating a nuisance by emitting tons of $CO_2$ each year, seeking payment of damages to state natural resources and termination of the pollution.[11] This growing coalition of state attorneys general is now looking at tobacco-like litigation against oil and auto companies for damages to natural resources, public health, and state treasuries.

Although these cases are making their way through the courts or are planned for future action, at least one adjudicated case suggests that this approach may yield results. In April 2002, a San Francisco jury found that gasoline with the additive MTBE is a "defective product" and the defendants—Shell Oil Co., Lyondell Chemical Co. (formerly Arco Chemical), Equilon Enterprises LLC, and Tosco Corp. (now part of Phillips Petroleum)—were fully aware of the additive's risks and harms to the public. The jury found "clear and convincing evidence" that Shell and Lyondell had acted with "malice," in part because of a failure to warn the public about the potential harms from MTBE.

"As a resort community, Lake Tahoe has built a reputation on a pristine lake, clean air and pure water," said Dennis Cocking, spokesman for the plaintiff, the South Tahoe Public Utilities District. "Who wants to save up their money and go on a vacation and drink water that tastes like paint thinner?"[12]

The oil and chemical companies settled that one case for $69 million.[13] Given the evidence already presented about the monetary damage to taxpayers at all levels of government, this case and others like it, along with the tobacco settlement model, suggest that there is a practical solution emerging to hold oil and auto companies accountable for the damages they have thus far forced others to subsidize. Here are a few causes of action that have been used or are under consideration to ultimately bring these companies as defendants before a judge and jury.

## Public Nuisance

On February 22, 2006, a jury in Providence, Rhode Island, decided that three former lead paint manufacturers were guilty of creating a "public nuisance" with the lead in their products and that, although lead had been banned in the United States in 1978, the company continued to knowingly poison the state's children. The companies could be held liable for millions of dollars in lead cleanup and mitigation costs.[14]

In North Carolina, the state's attorney general sued the Tennessee Valley Authority and its eleven power plants in early 2006 for causing a "public nuisance" that causes respiratory illness in residents of the state, kills trees, fouls waterways, and leaves a haze over the Great Smoky Mountains. That lawsuit asks the court to mandate that pollution control devices be installed at the coal-fired power plants to prevent the spread of sulfur dioxide, nitrogen oxides, and mercury that create the nuisance.[15]

A "public nuisance" is an act or circumstance that interferes with the rights of the public to pursue or enjoy surroundings or community. Typical examples are a vicious dog that makes it difficult for you to use a sidewalk or access your front door; blocking a street; drug trafficking that makes your neighborhood dangerous or lowers property values; and fouling a common water supply, such as polluting the water supply for Lake Tahoe communities with MTBE.[16]

Does preventable air pollution interfere with the rights of the public? Legally, air pollution has constituted a public nuisance under a variety of circumstances, such as smoke from a factory or dust from a construction site that permeates your home. Since the passage of the federal Clean Air Act and other federal and state environmental laws, however, courts tend to defer to the regulatory systems delegated to the USEPA (and its state counterparts) that were established by these laws, saying that other courses of action are "preempted."

One example of the preemption concept is currently being heard in federal court in relation to California's landmark law to reduce greenhouse gases from cars and light trucks. Automakers have sued California to prevent implementation of the regulations under that law, which require new cars beginning in 2009 to lower greenhouse gas emissions by a third. The plaintiff automakers, supported by the Bush administration, claim that the state is trying to regulate fuel economy, not simply greenhouse gas emissions, and that fuel economy regulation is the sole province of the federal government. In other words, they claim that states are preempted from taking action on pollution that the federal government has reserved for its own rulemaking. Numerous cases have upheld the original intention of Congress, repeatedly stating that the purpose of the preemption provisions of the Clean Air Act is not to hamstring local efforts to reduce air pollution, but rather to prevent the burden on interstate commerce resulting from a multiplicity of conflicting state and local exhaust emission standards.[17] Moreover, not all pollutants or harms from oil and auto products are regulated by these laws. Carbon dioxide and other greenhouse gas emissions, for example, are not regulated by the federal government, and states are therefore free to impose their own restrictions.

Nuisance is an attractive legal theory because it does not require one to prove that the offensive act is illegal; rather, one needs merely to prove that it is taking place and causing a harm. Moreover, if an act is found to be a nuisance, it is subject to abatement, and, if a defendant's conduct is particularly egregious, plaintiffs may be entitled to punitive damages. For example, a jury might consider fumes from refineries, gasoline pumps, and tailpipes that cause illness and cancer to be an egregious nuisance. Unlike tobacco use, wherein smokers had the choice to stop smoking and nonsmokers can usually move away from secondhand smoke, none of us has the choice to avoid petroleum air pollution. Even children, who have never driven a car or otherwise contributed to air pollution personally, are harmed.

## Fraud and Misrepresentation

In the tobacco litigation, addiction was the key. Courts were sympathetic to the plaintiffs' argument that tobacco companies had addicted consumers by manipulating the levels of nicotine in cigarettes to ensure continued consumption, which therefore increased illnesses and deaths.

In air pollution litigation, the practice of fraud and deceit that we have seen in previous chapters, including conspiracies that were proven in courts such as the National City Lines case, has economically addicted us. Our choices were taken away to further the goals of the oil and auto companies, including eliminating clean mass transit in forty-five cities, installing "defeat devices" on engines to bypass pollution controls, and stalling advancements in pollution prevention technology such as catalytic converters and zero emission vehicles. Those actions have made us addicts even more so than smokers, given that smokers have the choice to quit, which is impractical for drivers.

The general definition of fraud is an intentional misrepresentation that seeks to make someone rely on false or misleading statements. The victim of fraud must in fact be harmed by relying on the false or misleading statements. The evidence presented thus far shows that oil and auto companies have known for a very long time that their products and processes are harmful to human health and the environment. It shows that safer, effective, affordable alternatives—or less harmful versions of their current products— exist. Despite this knowledge, these industries have represented to governments, to the public, and to consumers that their products are safe to human and environmental health and that no better alternatives or less harmful versions of their current products exist or could be affordably manufactured. Many of these practices were discussed earlier, but two examples stand out that seem ripe for litigation and compensation: the sale of high-octane gasolines and the sale of "defective" vehicles.

### Octane Fraud

Recall that gasoline is generally sold in three grades, each with a different octane rating. The overwhelming majority of automobiles driven in the United States require gasoline with an octane rating of 87 or lower; for decades, however, petroleum companies have advertised and marketed to the public that the higher the octane rating, the better the car will operate and the cleaner the engine will become, and that these results will lead to reduced maintenance costs for the consumer. In fact, none of these representations is true for the overwhelming majority of cars.[18]

Nonetheless, the petroleum industry's marketing and advertising campaigns have thus far succeeded in misleading the driving public. Study after study shows that consumers purchase more high-grade and midgrade fuels than they can properly use. Even the *Oil & Gas Journal*, an industry publication, stated unequivocally that "octane demand is a situation forced on customers."[19] This situation is not a harmless status symbol, comparable with selling a $50 belt when a $5 belt will keep your pants in place equally well. Producing higher-octane fuel requires more energy, thus creating more refinery air and water pollution than would be needed for refining fuels of lower octane. Burning higher-octane fuels in engines that cannot do so efficiently actually results in increased engine deposits, which in turn make the vehicle operate less efficiently and therefore produce more pollution. All this pollution results in increased illness and premature deaths.

"A lot of consumers buy more expensive fuel on the mistaken belief it will enhance performance," said Sean Comey, a spokesman for the Automobile Association of America. "They might as well throw the money out the window and burn it."[20] Comey was equally unimpressed by automakers that "recommend" higher-octane fuels for luxury models. "If you shoot truth serum into the veins of car engineers," he said dryly, "they'll admit that 'recommended' means you don't really need it."

The cost of octane fraud is fairly easy to quantify based on the volume of high-octane fuels sold compared with the number of vehicles that actually need it. This cost could then form the basis for compensating victims.

### Fraud and ICE

Another product that could be the subject of a fraud claim is the petroleum internal combustion engine itself. Based on misleading representations that the automobile industry has made to governmental regulatory and legislative bodies about the industry's ability to make cleaner vehicles, the government has essentially protected the industry from regulations that would have otherwise forced them to make their products less polluting. Recall the evidence of how the oil and auto companies undermined both the CAFE and ZEV regulations, which would have resulted in cleaner vehicle choices for consumers.

Consumers, in turn, have had no real choice but to purchase petroleum-powered ICE automobiles. For instance, even after manufacturing and selling popular battery-electric cars, automakers not only fought to terminate those models, but recalled and scrapped many that were already in service on the roads. Many states also have unfair business practices laws to address fraudulent corporate behavior, which allow plaintiffs to recover damages, including disgorgement of ill-gotten profits by the offending companies. California's Business and Professions Code (sections 17200 and 17500 specifically) prohibits business practices that are "unfair" or illegal, including advertising and marketing that is false or misleading. These laws permit citizens to file suit for such violations, and they have already been successfully enforced in environmental cases, for both monetary and injunctive relief (an order to stop the offending action). When I sued a major polluter of waterways in California in 1995, for example, the ironically named Ecology Auto Wrecking, we included this cause of action because the company had an unfair business advantage over competitors that were spending money to clean up their facilities and prevent such pollution from fouling local waterways. That case was settled before going to trial and Ecology implemented a wide variety of pollution prevention measures at its numerous locations.

## Product Liability: Strict Liability and Negligence

Tobacco companies were held responsible for selling defective products, products that, when used as directed, killed or injured consumers. Petroleum products and the vehicles designed to use them may also be considered defective. The jury in the South Lake Tahoe case, where MTBE had contaminated the community's drinking water, found gasoline containing that additive to be "defective." As documented earlier, the mere act of pumping gasoline into the car—an intended use—

is known to expose consumers to fumes that cause cancer and reproductive harm. The combustion of petroleum products in vehicles produces emissions that cause similar harms, and, as we have learned, even
at rest, many of today's vehicles emit toxic vapors.

Product liability law was created to protect consumers from
unsafe products. Generally, a product is defective in design when the
foreseeable risks of harm from the product could be reduced or
avoided by the use of a reasonable alternative design. Just as in fraud,
a lawsuit alleging product liability is based on the oil and auto companies' long-time knowledge that their products and processes are
harmful to human health and the environment and that safer, effective, and affordable alternatives exist, including designs that use technology already deployed within the industry (as we will discover in
the discussion of PZEVs below). In product liability, lawsuits can be
brought under either strict liability or negligence theories. Under
"strict liability," a manufacturer will be held strictly liable when it
places a product on the market knowing that it is to be used without inspection for defects, and the product proves to have a defect
that causes injury. The plaintiff is not required to show that the
defendant did anything wrong; if the risks of the design outweigh
its utility, strict liability imposes liability without regard to whether
the manufacturer knew or should have known about those risks.

The risks inherent in the current design of the petroleum ICE
automobile arguably outweigh its utility, especially when compared
with alternative designs that are already available in some vehicles.
An example is found in evaporative emissions from petroleum ICE
automobiles, a significant source of pollution, caused by vaporizing
(as opposed to combusted) gasoline. These emissions typically occur
when the engine is not running and from sources other than the
tailpipe, such as the engine, tubes, and fuel system. The automobile
industry currently produces a partial zero emissions vehicle (PZEV)
that is designed to prevent such evaporative emissions. There are still
some harmful tailpipe emissions (thus "partial"), but eliminating

evaporative emissions significantly reduces toxic air pollution. All vehicles can be made with PZEV technology, but very few are.

Negligence, unlike strict liability, is concerned with reasonableness. To establish negligence, a plaintiff must prove that a duty of care was owed to the plaintiff by the defendant, that the defendant breached that duty, that the breach was a proximate cause of the plaintiff's damages, and that the plaintiff was harmed as a result.

Recent case law, involving MTBE contamination and handguns, supports the notion that a duty of care is owed not only to actual users of automobiles and gasoline, but to bystanders—the public—as well.[21] That is because it is reasonably foreseeable by oil and auto companies that the entire public is exposed to the harms of gasoline and automobile pollution, not just their own consumers. Therefore, the oil and auto industries have a duty of care, consisting of producing safe automobiles and safe fuels. They have breached that duty of care by continuing to produce harmful petroleum fuels and internal combustion engine vehicles instead of safer, effective, and affordable alternatives that exist today. Safer state-of-the-art technology includes zero emission and partial emission vehicles and battery-electric, hybrid, natural gas, biofuel, hydrogen internal combustion, hydrogen fuel cells, and other alternative-fuel engines that are technically and economically feasible.

## Antitrust Conspiracy

A case in antitrust conspiracy might charge that the oil and auto industries have agreed to unlawfully restrain the development and marketing of alternative cars and fuels and that the competitive market has suffered as a result. Various technology companies, and indeed the oil and auto industries themselves, have developed better alternatives to the petroleum internal combustion engine and gasoline fuel, including cleaner fuels, PZEVs and electric, hybrid, natural gas, and hydrogen-powered vehicles.

Even with the demand for such improvements, however, the oil and auto industries have collectively prevented successful development and sale of these products to the public. They have stalled the introduction of cleaner-petroleum vehicles by fighting fuel economy standards, and they have hindered the introduction of alternative fuel automobiles by misleading regulators and consumers, as we have seen in the fight over the ZEV mandate. In both cases, they have zealously lobbied lawmakers against mandates to offer these products to the public and have deceived lawmakers, regulators, and the public about the technology, utility, and cost of such alternatives.

## Public Trust Doctrine

In the early 1900s, Southern California water agencies bought the rights to rivers that fed Northern California's Mono Lake. By diverting the water to cities in the south, the lake began to dry up. Residents around the lake sued these water agencies under the public trust doctrine, claiming that everyone has the right to use a natural resource such as water, but not in a way that it diminishes the ability of others to do so. The water agencies violated the public trust, the plaintiffs argued, and the state had failed in its duty as trustee. In 1989, a California Supreme Court judge ordered a halt to the water diversions, and in 1994, the state performed its duty as a trustee by ordering the defendants to restore the lake.[22]

The Mono Lake case was successful because the public trust doctrine in California and most other states provides that the state holds its natural resources, such as wildlife, minerals, air, and water, in trust for public use and that the government owes a fiduciary duty to manage such resources for the common good of the public as beneficiary. The Court of Appeals of California recently confirmed that the public trust doctrine has been expanded beyond its traditional common-law emphasis on commerce, navigation, and fisheries and that it is today construed flexibly to encompass changing public needs, such as concern for the environment, expanding recreational uses, and aesthetic preservation.[23]

The state, as the public trustee, is obliged to protect the environment and to restore natural resources, as exemplified by the Mono Lake decision. A strong case could be made that our federal and state governments are failing to fulfill their trustee responsibilities. The Clean Air Act by itself fails to adequately regulate air pollution, which continues to cause grave injury to the human, ecological, and financial health of society.

For example, in early 2006, the USEPA released its National-Scale Air Toxics Assessment, which showed that despite decades of air pollution regulation, residents of urban areas, such as Los Angeles and New York, suffer an air pollution–related cancer incidence that is twice the national average.[24]

"People should understand that [vehicle emissions] have very large impacts on health," said Melanie Marty, chief of air toxicology and epidemiology at the California Office of Environmental Health Hazard Assessment. "It's not just asthma and heart disease. It's cancer too."[25]

Marty and my other former colleagues at California's Environmental Protection Agency went on to report that the air pollution–related cancer risk in places like Los Angeles is actually as much as fifteen times greater than the National-Scale Air Toxics Assessment reports. That's because USEPA did not include risks associated with particulate matter in the assessment even though the particulate matter in diesel exhaust poses one of the greatest threats to human health. About 70 percent of the Los Angeles area's air pollution–related cancer risk comes from diesel exhaust, 20 percent from automotive gasoline exhaust, and only 10 percent from industrial sources.[26]

Both federal and state officials do agree that the air pollution causing these illnesses comes mostly from vehicles. Benzene and butadiene were ranked by the assessment as the most dangerous airborne carcinogens, emitted mostly from vehicle exhaust, and are responsible for 35 percent of the cancer risk posed by air pollutants. Both these toxins have been linked to leukemia in humans and animals.[27]

Using such information, governments, public interest organizations, and any member of the public may sue to enjoin violations of the public trust as it relates to our air. A successful lawsuit against the trustees could force them to further regulate emissions from the oil and auto industries, including emissions at refineries and from tailpipes, using the most up-to-date scientific evidence of the illnesses caused by these emissions.

## Compensation of Victims

If litigation is successful, what would plaintiffs seek in compensation? Local, state, and federal governments could seek restitution of health-care costs and other subsidies to these industries. Oil companies could also be forced to disgorge ill-gotten profits, such as the extra millions of dollars they make from selling high-octane fuel to consumers whose vehicles can't benefit from it or are actually harmed by it.

There is also injunctive relief. Courts can order defendants to stop the harmful behavior. A court could demand, for example, that automakers immediately apply the evaporative emission controls found on some makes and models to all new vehicles. They could also mandate that a growing percentage of new vehicles and fuels sold be zero emission models.

One of the most significant benefits of the tobacco litigation was the restitution to states of the costs they incur for health-care programs related to cigarette smoking. Relief in oil and auto cases could be similarly focused. One study suggests that 4.5 percent of all health-care costs are for air pollution–related illness.[28] Another study estimated that air pollution–related health-care costs in the United States each year are at least $55 billion.[29] In March 2006, a California State University Fullerton study revealed that residents of the San Joaquin Valley, an agricultural region with worsening air pollution, spend more than $3 billion per year for costs related to smog.[30]

Plaintiffs might prefer to seek restitution of natural resource damages such as water pollution, crop damage, or forestry damages from, for example, the ozone-related fires that torched the forests of Southern California in 2003. Studies are also beginning to quantify the cost of greenhouse gas pollution–related effects to water supply, crops, and coastal erosion.[31] Regardless of the accounting method or the damages being calculated, local, state, and federal governments stand to recover billions of dollars in actual out-of-pocket costs every year for their taxpayers.

Another approach to compensation is for defendants to contribute to a general relief fund. A percentage of sales or profits could be contributed to the fund, which would then be disbursed to government agencies to deal with their most pressing oil and auto pollution-related expenses, such as health care, assistance to farmers for crop damage, oil spill cleanup, groundwater cleanup, and mass transit.

Could the oil and auto industries afford to compensate public or private victims on the same scale as tobacco company settlements with state and federal governments? Recall that in 2005, the top ten oil and auto companies had a combined profit of almost $100 billion.

## Wartime Strategies?

To be sure, there are strategies other than litigation to accomplish the goals of reducing air pollution–related illness and moving toward energy independence. Given the history of oil and auto companies, however, it is likely that any attempt to hold them financially accountable would also end up in court, so, in essence, even these efforts become legal strategies.

Policy makers, for example, might consider regulating transportation fuels like they do the other essential resources of water and electricity. In California, as in other states, a public utilities commission sets electricity rates and other aspects of a marketplace that is not fully subjected to competition. Unlike cigarette or soft drink manufacturers, utilities provide products that are essential to our lives and economies, and because of the large investment and long lead time required for new facilities, there are fewer competitors in the utility marketplace to ensure fair pricing and supply.

Transportation fuel is no different than electricity. Large industrial facilities are needed to manufacture the product, elaborate transmission systems are needed to ensure reliable supplies to consumers, and shortages—both real and created—can lead to crippling economic consequences. Refineries and the products they produce could be regulated like electricity, ensuring fair profits and genuine competition in the marketplace. A state's fuel prices could also be set by regulators to provide conservation incentives.

In conjunction with the regulatory approach, another strategy worth serious consideration is legislation that would enable fuel rationing. It worked in World War II and ensured that sufficient fuel at fair prices was available for everyone who really needed it. Rationing, if properly structured, ensures adequate supplies at low prices for real necessity, but restricts wasteful uses (as might be defined by legislation or a regulatory authority).

Although there is no major shortage yet that would create the political will for such a system, having it on the books would prepare us for more difficult times when they come. For example, rationing might only be implemented, like the military draft, when certain national fuel emergencies existed. I can think of one: when an air district fails to attain federal air quality standards by mandated deadlines. Rationing would reduce fuel use and almost certainly bring the region into compliance with health-based air quality objectives. A rationing system might allocate fuel to each household based on some reasonable formula. If, for instance, someone chose to live in a sprawl suburb or drive a SUV that gets low gas mileage, the allotment would not be enough to commute each day and thus that person would have to make other choices.

We should also examine and repair a federal tax system that rewards the purchase of three-ton living rooms on wheels. States might also consider increasing taxes on petroleum fuels to fund programs like the hydrogen commercialization projects that are being implemented in many parts of the country. Such revenues might also be used to pay for more mass transit or, as is being discussed in Melbourne, Australia, making public transit completely free to riders.[32] In that city alone, it would take some $340 million a year to pay for that plan, but considering the benefits, it may well be worth it.

These taxes might be considered "taxpayer protection fees" rather than taxes because they force the producer or user of the product to pay its full cost to society, rather than burdening all taxpayers. Such taxes might be levied at the gas pump or as "severance" taxes, a fee on each barrel of oil that is taken (or severed) from state lands. Either way, although some will argue that raising the price of petroleum products will hurt a petroleum-dependent economy, higher prices may change the behavior of consumers for the better of all.

"Gas is cheaper than bottled water," said Eron Shosteck of the Alliance of Automobile Manufacturers. "There is no incentive for people to use less."[33]

Regardless of the regulatory approach or legal cause of action adopted, or the compensation sought, it is time to hold oil and auto corporations responsible for their actions, if for no other reason than to deter the next tobacco, oil, auto, Enron, or other corporate robber baron. As always, Shakespeare found a way to capture it succinctly: "What makes robbers bold but too much leniency."[34]

# The Seventh Generation

A new source of power, called gasoline . . . is exploded inside the cylinder of the . . . so-called "internal combustion engine." The dangers are obvious. Stores of gasoline in the hands of the people interested primarily in profit would constitute a . . . hazard of the first rank. Horseless carriages propelled by gasoline engines might attain speeds of 14 or even 20 miles per hour . . . hurtling through our streets and poisoning our atmosphere.

*Summary of the report of the Congressional*
*Horseless Carriage Committee of 1875*

T hat excerpt from the report to Congress in 1875 by the Horseless Carriage Committee shows that our ancestors faced a dilemma similar to our own concerning the promises and dangers of a paradigm shift in transportation technology. We might wish that they had known more about the real dangers of petroleum and the machines that use it, but the purple prose and the quaint view of the speed limit do bring into sharp focus the fears and the practical hurdles of any major technological transformation. Our ancestors overcame those challenges, although it is unlikely that the horse and buggy lobby was as wealthy, politically connected, and resistant to change as are the oil and auto industries.

Therein lies the real challenge for the twenty-first century. Whether we use invention, the courtroom, or the court of public opinion, can we redirect industries that are so powerful, products that are so ubiquitous, and a political system that rewards profit over the common good? Perhaps we can, if we can educate a wider audience about the Faustian deal we have made and the means by which we can now extricate ourselves from that fool's bargain.

Think for a moment of the sacrifices we will *not* make for locally produced biofuels and hydrogen:

- In the United States alone, tens of thousands of our citizens will not die prematurely each year.

- Tens of thousands more will avoid hospitalizations.

- Millions will be spared asthma attacks.

- Diesel exhaust will no longer cause tens of thousands of new cases of cancer every year.

- On the day that petroleum use becomes the exception rather than the rule, minorities and the poorest among us will no longer suffer five times more asthma and lung cancer than everyone else simply because they live near freeways, railroads, and refineries.

- We will no longer consider despoiling our most valuable natural resources for securing a few more days worth of oil.

- There will be little or no petroleum-related amounts of lead, benzene, toluene, xylene, MTBE, and other toxins in our food and drinking water.

- Tens of millions of gallons of oil will no longer wash up upon our shores each year from spills and polluted roadways.

- The United States will no longer send $612,500 every minute to largely anti-American foreign countries to buy their crude oil.

- Billions in potential tax revenues will not be drained from local, state, and federal treasuries every year when tax exemptions and subsidies for some of the richest corporations in the world are ended.

- Farmers will no longer lose as much as a third of their crops to petroleum-related air and water pollution, but will again reap what they sow.

- Consumers will no longer waste millions of dollars on fraudulent grades of fuel for their vehicles.

- Though global warming will still affect us because of the hundred-year buildup of greenhouse gases, we will no longer face a future that promises to grow worse and worse, especially if we help other nations move away from burning fossil fuels at the same time we do so ourselves.

- The ways of life of villagers from the Colombian countryside to the Niger River delta will no longer be distorted by oil pipelines and drilling rigs that transect their landscapes.

- Our sons and daughters will not die in foreign wars to protect our access to oil.

To end our addiction to the petroleum economy and to accomplish these optimistic outcomes, each of us will need to begin making different personal choices now and our government will need a new generation of visionary leaders. I remember being inspired, although skeptical, when Joseph Califano, secretary of the Department of Health, Education and Welfare, called for a tobacco- and smoke-free society by the year 2000. In the late 1970s when he said that, it seemed an impossible dream, but today, public places in California, New York, and many other states are now virtually smoke-free.

Tailpipe emissions are chemically similar to tobacco smoke, so isn't it time to create a truly "smoke-free" society, ending the tyranny of petroleum pollution as well? How about starting with a surgeon general's report, like the landmark 1964 report on the effects of smoking, about the dangers of exposure to petroleum and vehicle exhaust?[1] Then how about encouraging one of our political leaders to offer a Califano-like vision of a date for the phased elimination of this dangerous, dinosaur technology that costs us so dearly? Sweden apparently has that leadership, announcing in 2006 that the country will phase out not only petroleum-powered vehicles, but petroleum-powered heating systems, becoming oil-free by 2020.[2] At least one automaker thinks that a similar future lies ahead for the United States. "I wouldn't be at all surprised if you couldn't buy a new [petroleum] internal combustion engine car 25 years from now," predicted Gary Stottler, a senior engineer for GM.[3]

Neither government nor corporate America can make the necessary changes alone, however. Indeed, the real reason that the Hopi survive today while the islanders of Easter Island (Rapa Nui) did not is that the Hopi understand that their survival depends on personal, individual responsibility and action. They guide their actions by the ancient concept of the seventh generation: they consider the effect of their actions today on the progeny of a time so far in the future that they will not live to see it. In this manner, they have thrived for more than ten thousand years.

Yet we often unwittingly emulate the islanders of Rapa Nui. We consume as if there's a prize for consumption itself, like the pie-eating contest at the county fair. We don't see the incremental losses from one generation to the next, just as the residents of Rapa Nui failed to do so. Members of each generation accept as "normal" the state of affairs they inherit, from which they feel it is acceptable to take their share. The late Donella H. Meadows, a professor of environmental studies at Dartmouth College, called this DLP: the drift to low performance. She observed:

> Our environment is suffering badly from DLP. Once we would have been outraged to find *any* sewage on our beaches. Now we just ask for a standardized warning when it's present. President Bush has just dropped the goal of wetland protection from a firm "no net loss" to a declaration that it's OK to lose a third of our remaining wetlands after all. We have stopped expecting that local streams should run truly clear. Our new Clean Air Act asks for a reduction in acid rain emissions, but not for rain that's normal. The most damaging drift to low perform- ance is in our politics—which is why we're seeing DLP in so many other places. We have come to expect cam- paigns to be mean and stupid, and politicians to be unre- sponsive, self-seeking, and for sale to the highest bidder. We make jokes about our vice-president; all we ask of a president is that he be likeable. We seem to have given up on the Pentagon's corrupt use of our tax dollars.[4]

Meadows could have written that yesterday, but she was actually writing nearly two decades ago, during the administration of the first President George Bush. We have drifted for decades, accepting what oil has done for us but conveniently ignoring what oil has done to us. Ours will certainly be remembered as the Oil Age, and it will likely be recalled as the most destructive force our planet has ever known, thanks in part to politics. Geopolitics have certainly shifted because of oil. Would the Middle East be of such significance to every presidential administration without it?

Where might we be if we had continued to make progress with fuel economy standards each year instead of stalling on them in the mid-1980s? How different might the world be today if we had simply adopted the federal government's plan to save 80,000 barrels of oil per day by eliminating unnecessary high-octane fuels from the marketplace? We have had nearly two decades to act on those simple, practical, painless proposals—put forth, ironically, by a Bush administration—but our political leaders have not been able to stand up to the oil lobby to make even that modest progress.

At its peak in 1994, AIDS killed 50,000 Americans in one year, a number that has declined to 10,000 annually.[5] Rightfully, we hold star-studded galas to raise funds to fight this disease, we persuade pharmaceutical companies to offer drugs to impoverished African nations at a reduced price, and our government sets forth a plan to spend $15 billion fighting AIDS over many years.

Yet more than 100,000 Americans died, or died early, of air pollution–related illness in 1994 and at least that many every year since, as described in chapter 1. In September 2004, the University of Southern California released the results of a decade-long study that concluded that children who live in smoggy areas lose 1 percent of their lung capacity every year.[6] Think about that. Preventable air pollution robs our children of 5 percent of their ability to breathe by the age of 5, 10 percent of their ability to breathe by the age of ten, and so on. Nonetheless, no one speaks out against it in the United Nations and few ask oil and auto companies to absorb the external costs that their products impose on the rest of us. Instead, our government spends billions of dollars to subsidize these industries, in turn subsidizing our addictive self-destruction.

So who will join the growing ranks of those who declare that they can do with a little less so that our children might have a little more? Who will join those whose success is not only measured by the number on the bottom of the balance sheet but by the balance of clean air, water, and land that we bequeath to our children? Who will join those that think not just of ourselves and our children, but seven generations into the future, and act accordingly?

Let us declare our energy independence now and break our addiction to oil by making three simple changes in the way we think and act. First, each of us must accept personal responsibility for the good of the community, as the Hopi have done for millennia. Drive less. Walk more. Use mass transit. Buy a hybrid or an alternative fuel vehicle and follow fuel-saving practices. Ask your friends and colleagues at work to do likewise.

Second, make energy policy a critical test when you step into the voting booth. Demand that candidates take up the energy independence banner with actions to end our use of oil within a generation and urge elected officials to support legislation that will deliver energy independence now.

Third, send every message you can to the corporations that have encouraged our addiction in the first place to say that you want them to change. You can do so with your next vehicle purchase, but you can also inform yourself about which oil and auto companies are seriously attempting to reduce greenhouse gas emissions and are introducing cleaner products like improved battery technology, biofuels, hydrogen, and the vehicles that run on these products. Patronize the best companies and shun the worst. If you are fortunate enough to own stock, divest yourself of oil and auto company stocks until you see evidence that the companies are responding. If you are part of a retirement fund, urge the portfolio managers to do the same.

If today is the day we take these steps, and many more like them to gain true energy independence, history will not need to remember us. Our descendants will still be here, healthy and prosperous, to give testimony for us about the foresight and strength of character their ancestors displayed at the dawn of the twenty-first century, seven generations ago.

# ACKNOWLEDGMENTS

I am deeply grateful to a number of people who have given me the opportunity to work on the issues presented in this book and by doing so, I hope to make our future on this planet healthier and more sustainable than our past. My appreciation and admiration go to Governor Arnold Schwarzenegger, Maria Shriver, Karen Borell, and the team at Environment Now (Luanne Wells, Frank Wells, Rob Wells, and Kevin Wells).

Many other people and organizations have contributed to the ideas and information presented in this book. I owe a great debt of gratitude to all of them, but special thanks to a few. For technical support, I thank Daniel Emmett and Rick Margolin of EnergyIndependenceNow.org; Dr. Alan Lloyd, former secretary of the California Environmental Protection Agency; Ralph Cavanagh of the Natural Resources Defense Council; and Tim Carmichael and Wendy James of the Coalition for Clean Air. For legal advice. I thank Portia Cohen and Steve Fleischli. For content advice and editing help, I thank Drew Bohan and my terrific editor, Jonathan Cobb and his colleagues Emily Davis and Cecilia González; Paul R. Epstein, associate director of the Center for Health and the Global Environment at Harvard Medical School; Jonathan Patz, associate professor of Environmental Studies and Population Health Sciences at the University of Wisconsin at Madison; Vic Sher, my old environmental advocacy colleague-in-arms; and for the title, I thank Jake Rubin.

Finally, there are always a few people who inspire you to write or give you the courage to face the computer screen day after day. My love and thanks go to Leslie Mintz, Norman and Lisette Ackerberg, Geri and Dennis Weaver, Bonnie Reiss, David Crane, Laurie David, and Robert F. Kennedy Jr.

# NOTES

## PROLOGUE

1   President George W. Bush, "State of the Union Address," January 31, 2006.

2   Black Mesa Trust, March 2006, http://www.blackmesatrust.org/.

3   Jared Diamond, "Easter's End," *Discover* August 1995, 64.

4   Diamond, "Easter's End."

5   "Questions of Mass Extinction," Norman Myers, *Biodiversity and Conservation,* 2:2–17, 1993.

6   Richard Leakey and Roger Lewin, *The Sixth Extinction* (New York: Doubleday, 1995). Excerpted at The WELL, http://www.well.com/~davidu/sixthextinction.html.

7   Leakey and Lewin, *The Sixth Extinction.*

## CHAPTER 1. *The Breath of Our Fathers*

1   David Suzuki, *Sacred Balance* (Vancouver, British Colombia, Canada: Greystone Books, 1997), 37.

2   *Evidence for Mechanisms of Particulate Matter Cardiovascular Mortality Observations* (Sacramento, CA: California Air Resources Board, 2004).

3   *Protocol to the 1979 Convention on Long-Range Transboundary Air Pollution.* Available online at United Nations Economic Commission for Europe, http://www.unece.org/env/lrtap/full%20text/1979.CLRTAP.e.pdf (updated March 3, 2006).

4    As quoted in "Smog," *Encyclopedia Brittannica.* Available online at http://www.britannica.com/eb/article-9068319 (accessed April 1, 2005).

5    Jack Doyle, *Taken for a Ride* (New York: Four Walls Eight Windows, 2000), 23.

6    Doyle, *Taken for a Ride,* 23, 25.

7    Doyle, *Taken for a Ride,* 25.

8    *Air Pollution Sources, Health Effects, and Controls* (Sacramento, CA: California Air Resources Board, October 1998); USEPA, March 1, 2006, http://www.epa.gov/oar/oaqps/; and California Air Quality Data, January 3, 2006, http://www.arb.ca.gov/aqd/aqdpage.htm.

9    *Air Pollution Research* (Sacramento, CA: California Air Resources Board, June 1998), 102.

10   Charles A. S. Hall, Cutler J. Cleveland, and Robert Kaufmann, *Energy and Resource Quality* (Boulder, CO: University Press of Colorado, 1992), 418.

11   *National Air Quality and Emissions Trends Report* (Triangle Park, NC: USEPA Office of Air Quality Planning and Standards, September 2003). Available online at http://www.epa.gov/airtrends/.

12   *National Air Quality and Emissions Trends Report.*

13   As quoted in *Exposure to Hazardous Air Pollution in Los Angeles,* report prepared for Representative Henry Waxman, Special Investigations Division, Committee on Government Reform, U.S. House of Representatives, March 1, 1999.

14   *State of the Air: 2006* (New York: American Lung Association, 2006), 5.

15   Information for the entire section on petroleum secondhand smoke, except as noted, is taken from *Air Pollution Sources, Health Effects, and Controls* (Sacramento, CA: California Air Resources Board, October 1998); USEPA, March 1, 2006, http://www.epa.gov/oar/oaqps/; and California Air Quality Data, January 3, 2006, http://www.arb.ca.gov/aqd/aqdpage.htm.

16   Even though vehicles may not be the biggest contributor of total PM by mass, they do contribute the majority of the finest particles (PM 2.5). Both PM 10 and PM 2.5 can be created in the atmosphere from a reaction of other pollutants such as nitrogen and sulfur oxides.

17   Francine Laden and others, "Reduction in Fine Particulate Air Pollution and Mortality: Extended Follow-up of the Harvard Six Cities Study,"

*American Journal of Respiratory Critical Care Medicine* 173:667–672; and as reported by Nicholas Bakalar, "Cleaner Air Brings Drop in Death Rate," *New York Times*, March 21, 2006.

18  Ami Patel and others, *Chronic Low Level Exposure to Gasoline Vapors and Risk of Cancer: A Community-Based Study* (Pittsburgh, PA: University of Pittsburgh, Archives of Environmental Health, November 2004); and Mark Roth, "Leukemia Tied to Benzene Exposure," *Pittsburgh Post-Gazette*, February 8, 2006.

19  Timothy Begany, "Study: Fewer Cars Equal Fewer Asthma Exacerbations," *Respiratory Reviews*, 6, no. 5, (May 2001). Available online at http://www.respiratoryreviews.com/may01/rr_may01_fewer.html.

20  Joe E. Heimlich, *CDFS-193-97: Lead* (Columbus, OH: Ohio State University, 2006). Available online at http://ohioline.osu.edu/cd-fact/0193.html.

21  Boyden Gray and Andrew R. Varcoe, *Octane, Clean Air, and Renewable Fuels: A Modest Step Toward Energy Independence* (Washington, DC: Energy Future Coalition, January 2006).

22  Devra Davis, *When Smoke Ran Like Water* (New York: Basic Books, 2002), 157.

23  Anthony Ham, "Spain Chokes under 'Grey Beret,'" *The Age*, February 11, 2006.

24  Adianto P. Simamora, "Good Air Hard to Find in Smog-Filled Jakarta," *The Jakarta Post*, February 27, 2006.

25  Rachel L. Miller and others, *Polycyclic Aromatic Hydrocarbons: Environmental Tobacco Smoke, and Respiratory Symptoms in an Inner-City Birth Cohort* (New York: Columbia Center for Children's Environmental Health, 2004); and Melissa P. McNamara, "Double Dose of Bad Air Puts Fetuses at Risk," *New York Times*, January 27, 2004.

26  B. Ritz and others, "Ambient Air Pollution and Risk of Birth Defects in Southern California," *American Journal of Epidemiology* 155, no. 1 (January 2002): 17–25; and Gary Polakovic, "Air Pollution Harmful to Babies, Fetuses, Studies Say," *Los Angeles Times*, December 16, 2001.

27  *Failing the Grade: How Diesel School Buses Threaten Our Children's Health* (Los Angeles, CA: Coalition for Clean Air, November 1999), 6.

28  Gina M. Solomon and others, *No Breathing in the Aisles: Diesel Exhaust*

*Inside School Buses* (Los Angeles, CA: Natural Resources Defense Council and the Coalition for Clean Air, January 2001), 1.

29  K. Berhane and others, "Statistical Issues in Studies of the Long Term Effects of Air Pollution: The Southern California Children's Health Study," *Statistical Science* 19, no. 3:414–449; and as quoted in "Kids' Asthma Cases on Rise in Southern California," *Los Angeles Daily News*, February 23, 2004.

30  As quoted in *Regulatory Impact Analysis: Heavy Duty Engine and Vehicle Standards and Highway Diesel Fuel Sulfur Control Requirements*, USEPA, December 2002. Available online at http://www.epa.gov/otaq/regs/hd2007/frm/exec-sum.pdf.

31  *Danger in the Air: The 2001 Ozone Season Summary* (Washington, DC: U.S. PIRG Education Fund August, 2002); and Don Hopey, "State's Air Ranked Fourth Worst in U.S.," *Pittsburgh Post-Gazette*, January 14, 2000.

32  W. James Gauderman and others, "Childhood Asthma and Exposure to Traffic and Nitrogen Dioxide," *Epidemiology* 16, no. 6 (November 2005): 737–743; Ira B. Tager and others, "Chronic Exposure to Ambient Ozone and Lung Function in Young Adults," *Epidemiology* 16, no. 6 (November 2005): 751–759; Rob McConnell and others, "Asthma in Exercising Children Exposed to Ozone: A Cohort Study," *The Lancet* 359, no. 9304 (February 2, 2002): 386–391; and D. Schoch, "Study Links Freeway to Asthma Risk," *Los Angeles Times*, September 21, 2005.

33  *Exhausted by Diesel* (Los Angeles, CA: Natural Resources Defense Council, April 1998); and Larry Pynn, "Life Next to the Fast Lane Full of Health Hazards," *Vancouver Sun*, December 31, 2005.

34  "AQMD Fact Sheet: Study of Air Pollution Levels Inside Vehicles," South Coast Air Quality Management District, June 10, 1999. Available online at http://www.aqmd.gov/news1/in_car_facts.htm.

35  *Measuring Concentrations of Selected Air Pollutants Inside California Vehicles* (Sacramento, CA: Research Division, California Environmental Protection Agency Air Resources Board, December 1998).

36  S. Kaur, M. Nieuwenhuijsen, and R. N. Colvile, "Pedestrian Exposure to Air Pollution along a Major Road in Central London, UK," *Atmospheric Environment* 39, no. 38 (December 2005): 7307–7320.

37  "Taxi Travel Pollution Highest," *BBC News*, January 10, 2006.

38  *Regulatory Impact Analysis: Heavy Duty Engine and Vehicle Standards and High-*

*way Diesel Fuel Sulfur Control Requirements*, USEPA, December 2000. Available online at http://www.epa.gov/otaq/regs/hd2007/frm/exec-sum.pdf.

39  *Exhausted by Diesel*, v. The same report (p. vii) quotes the American Automobile Manufacturers Association admitting that "diesel engines account for an estimated 26% of the total hazardous particulate pollution in our air, and 66% of the particulate pollution from on-road sources."

40  N. Li and others, "Comparison of the Pro-oxidative and Proinflammatory Effects of Organic Diesel Exhaust Particle Chemicals in Bronchial Epithelial Cells and Macrophages," *Journal of Immunology* 169, no. 8 (October 15, 2002): 4531–4541; as reported in D. L. Laskin, *Peroxides and Macrophages in Toxicity of Fine Particulate Matter* (Los Angeles, CA: Health Effects Institute, January 2004); and as reported by Gary Polakovic, "Air Particles Linked to Cell Damage," *Los Angeles Times*, April 7, 2003.

41  William C. Hinds, *Southern California Environmental Report Card 2001* (Los Angeles: University of California Los Angeles, 2001), 10.

42  *No Breathing in the Aisles*, 4; and *Crude Reckoning: The Impact of Petroleum on California's Public Health and Environment* (Sacramento, CA: Center for Energy Efficiency and Renewable Technologies, August 2000), 40.

43  National Air Toxics Assessment, USEPA, February 2006; and as quoted in Dan Stockman, "Benzene from Auto Emissions Drives Indiana's Cancer Danger," *Ft. Wayne Journal Gazette*, March 26, 2006.

44  Agnes B. Bodnar, Randy L. Maddalena, and Thomas E. McKone, *The Contribution of Locally Grown Foods in Cumulative Exposure Assessments* (Berkeley, CA: Lawrence Berkeley National Laboratory, September 2002).

45  Hilary F. French, *Clearing the Air: A Global Agenda*, Worldwatch Paper 94 (Washington, DC: Worldwatch Institute, January 1990), 23.

46  P. R. Miller and J. R. McBride, eds., *Oxidant Air Pollution Impacts in the Montane Forests of Southern California: A Case Study of the San Bernardino Mountains* (New York: Springer-Verlag, 1999).

47  Michael Jerrett and others, "Spatial Analysis of Air Pollution and Mortality in Los Angeles," *Epidemiology* 16, no. 6 (November 2005); and as reported by Janet Wilson, "Study Doubles Estimate of Smog Deaths," *Los Angeles Times*, March 25, 2006.

48  Polakovic, "Air Pollution Harmful."

49  G. Solomon, *Manganese in Gasoline: Potential Public Health Effects* (Boston, MA: Greater Boston Physicians for Social Responsibility, 1995).

## CHAPTER 2. *A Losing Proposition*

1    *Crude Reckoning: The Impact of Petroleum on California's Public Health and Environment* (Sacramento, CA: Center for Energy Efficiency and Renewable Technologies, August 2000), 13.

2    Paul R. Epstein and Jesse Selber, *Oil: A Life Cycle Analysis of Its Health and Environmental Impacts* (Boston, MA: Center for Health and the Global Environment, Harvard Medical School, March 2002).

3    Robert L. Hauser and William F. Guerard Jr., *A History of Oil and Gas Well Blowouts in California, 1950–1990* (Sacramento, CA: California Department of Conservation, Division of Oil, Gas, and Geothermal Resources, 1992).

4    *Crude Reckoning*, 13.

5    Personal communication with Bud Leland, Chief Operations Officer, California Office of Oil Spill Prevention and Response, November 29, 2005. Data reported to the California Department of Conservation, Division of Oil, Gas, and Geothermal Resources, from oil operations on the Outer Continental Shelf between 1994 and 1997.

6    California Integrated Waste Management Board, www.ciwmb.ca.gov/usedoil/facts/htm/.

7    *Crude Reckoning*, 14.

8    *Save Our Shores: Florida's Shores at Risk* (Tallahassee, FL: Florida Public Interest Research Group, 2006). Available at http://floridapirg.org/FL.asp?id2=2614&id3=FL&.

9    Ben Raines, "Gulf Rigs: Islands of Contamination," *Mobile Register*, December 30, 2001; and University of West Florida professor Enid Sisskin, "Analysis of the Draft Environmental Impacts Statement, Destin Dome 56, Unit Development and Production Plan and Right of Way Application," IV-20, Gulf Coast Environmental Defense, September 13, 1999, New York.

10   Jonathan Wills, *Muddied Waters: A Survey of Offshore Oilfield Drilling Wastes and Disposal Techniques to Reduce the Ecological Impact of Sea Dumping* (Yuzhno-Sakhalinsk, Russia: Sakhalin Environment Watch, May 25, 2000).

11   Wills, *Muddied Waters*.

12   *Shell Mounds Environmental Review* (Sacramento, CA: California State Lands Commission, March 2001).

13   Epstein and Selber, *Oil: A Life Cycle Analysis*.

14  "Mexico Strikes Oil under Sea," *Los Angeles Times*, March 14, 2006.

15  David Moffat and Olof Lindén, "Perception and Reality: Assessing Priorities for Sustainable Development in the Niger River Delta," *Ambio: A Journal of the Human Environment* (Royal Swedish Academy of Sciences 24, nos.7–8 (December 1995).

16  *Oil Rigs in the Santa Barbara Channel: The Silent Polluters* (Santa Barbara, CA: Santa Barbara ChannelKeeper, 2001). The rigs in Santa Barbara also generate 4 tons of smog, producing reactive organic gases (ROG) and 6 tons of nitrogen oxides ($NO_x$) each day. Some three hundred oil pump engines in the county generate more than 2 tons of $NO_x$ each day by themselves, according to *Crude Reckoning*, 14.

17  "Odor Tied to Capped Oil Well in South L.A.," *Los Angeles Times*, February 15, 2002.

18  *Largest Oil Spills* (New South Wales, Australia: Southern Cross University, March 2006); Water Education Foundation with California Integrated Waste Management Board, www.watereducation.org; and Netstate.com, www.netstate.com/states/geography/ak_geography.htm.

19  Kim Murphy, "Exxon Oil Spill's Cleanup Crews Share Years of Illness," *Los Angeles Times*, November 5, 2001.

20  Epstein and Selber, *Oil: A Life Cycle Analysis*.

21  *Crude Reckoning*, 21

22  U.S. Energy Information Agency and The Mariner Group, http://www.marinergroup.com/main.htm.

23  As quoted in *Crude Awakenings: Could an Exxon Valdez Spill Happen in Southern California?* (Santa Monica, CA: Environment Now Foundation, August 2000), 8.

24  *Crude Awakenings*, 1.

25  *Crude Awakenings*, 47.

26  Office of Pipeline Safety, Research and Special Programs Administration, pipeline statistics. Available online at http://ops.dot.gov/stats/lq_sum.htm.

27  "U.S. Sues Pipeline Companies," *Los Angeles Times*, May 31, 2002.

28  "Nearly 19,000 Gallons of Crude Oil Spills into Tributary of Lake Superior," Associated Press, January 28, 2003.

29  South Carolina Waterfowl Association, Pinewood, SC, as reported April 1, 2006 at http://www.scwa.org/habitat/reedy%2oriver.html.

30  "Colonial Pipeline Fined $34 Million for Oil Spill," Environment News Service, March 1, 2003; and "U.S. Reaches Landmark Settlement with Colonial Pipeline for Oil Spills in Five States—$34 Million Civil Penalty Is the Largest Paid by a Company in EPA History," USEPA press release, April 1, 2003.

31  Epstein and Selber, *Oil: A Life Cycle Analysis.*

32  *Crude Reckoning*, 16

33  Sam Howe Verhovek, "Crude Leak Plugged in Alaska Pipeline," *Los Angeles Times*, March 9, 2006; and Sam Howe Verhovek, "Bigger Estimate of Alaska Oil Leak Adds Fuel to Debate," *Los Angeles Times*, March 11, 2006.

34  Epstein and Selber, *Oil: A Life Cycle Analysis.*

35  "State of Denial," *Sacramento Bee*, April 27, 2003.

36  "State of Denial."

37  *Foreign Sources of Crude Oil Imports to California 2002* (Sacramento, CA: California Energy Commission, May 5, 2003).

38  *California's Refineries* (Sacramento, CA: California Energy Commission, 2006); and *Crude Reckoning*, 25. On average, 43 percent of the output from these facilities is vehicle fuel.

39  "Oil Refineries Fail to Report Millions of Pounds of Harmful Emissions," report prepared for Representative Henry Waxman, Special Investigations Division, Committee on Government Reform, U.S. House of Representatives, November 10, 1999.

40  "Oil Refineries Fail to Report Millions."

41  *Effects on Our AIR!* (San Francisco, CA: Institute for Global Communications, 2002). Available online at www.igc.apc.org/cbesf/air.html.

42  *Crude Reckoning*, 32

43  *2005 Estimated Annual Average Emissions (Statewide)* (Sacramento, CA: California Air Resources Board, 2006).

44  "Sulfur Release in Martinez Triggers Alerts," *Contra Costa Times*, January 27, 2002

45  "Oil Refineries Fail to Report Millions."

46  Statement of Carlos J. Porras, Communities for a Better Environment,

before the U.S. Senate Committee on Environment and Public Works, April 5, 2001.

47 "Shell, Texaco to Fork Over Thousands to Settle with EPA," *Bakersfield Californian*, August 25, 1994.

48 Jack Doyle, "Riding the Dragon," Addendum no. 3, Environmental Health Fund, November 2002; and Refinery Reform Campaign, www.refinery reform.org/News_DMN_100100.html.

49 Doyle, "Riding the Dragon"; and Legal Affairs, www.legalaffairs.org/ issues/May-June-2003/story_bazelon_mayjun03.msp.

50 Information for the list of examples is taken from *Crude Reckoning*, 29, except as noted.

51 Dennis A. Lemly, "Assessing the Toxic Threat of Selenium to Fish and Aquatic Birds," *Environmental Monitoring and Assessment* 43 (1996): 19–35.

52 "Energy Assurance Daily," U.S. Department of Energy, Office of Electricity Delivery and Energy Reliability, December 21, 2005.

53 *Crude Reckoning*, 33

54 *Crude Reckoning*, 23

55 *Crude Reckoning*, 23

56 *Crude Reckoning*, 33, 35

57 *Crude Reckoning*, 35

58 *Methyl Tertiary Butyl Ether ("MTBE") Products Liability Litigation: This Document Relates to All Cases*, U.S. Dist. LEXIS 12192, MDL No. 1358, August 2001; James W. Weaver and Matthew C. Small, "MTBE: Is a Little Bit OK?" presented at the National Ground Water Association's Petroleum Hydrocarbons and Organic Chemicals in Ground Water: Prevention, Assessment, and Remediation, November 6–8, 2002, Atlanta, GA, 206–219; and *Crude Reckoning*, 37.

59 Jack Doyle, *Taken for a Ride* (New York: Four Walls Eight Windows, 2000), 236.

60 *Crude Reckoning*, 11; and *Exposure to Hazardous Air Pollution in Los Angeles*, report prepared for Representative Henry Waxman, Special Investigations Division, Committee on Government Reform, U.S. House of Representatives, March 1, 1999; and *National-Scale Air Toxics Assessment* (Washington, DC: USEPA, February 2006).

61 U.S. Department of Energy, Energy Information Agency, as described online May 2006 at http://www.eia.doe.gov/oiaf/1605/ggccebro/chapter1.html.

62 U.S. Department of Energy, Energy Information Agency, as described online May 2006 at http://www.eia.doe.gov/oiaf/1605/ggccebro/chapter1.html.

63 *Air Quality Trends Report 2000,* USEPA. Available online at http://www.epa.gov/airtrends/carbon.html.

64 R. Guderian, *Air Pollution: Phytotoxicity of Acidic Gases and Its Significance in Air Pollution Control* (New York: Springer-Verlag, 1977); P. B. Reich, R. G. Amundson, and J. P. Lassoie, "Reduction in Soybean Yield after Exposure to Ozone and Sulfur Dioxide Using a Linear Gradient Exposure Technique," *Water, Air Soil Pollution* 17 (1982): 29–36; R. J. Oshima and others, "Reduction of Tomato Fruit Size and Yield by Ozone" *Journal of the American Society for Horticultural Science* 102 (1977): 287–293; H. E. Heggestad and J. H. Bennett, "Photochemical Oxidants and Potential Yield Losses in Snap Beans Attributable to Sulphur Dioxide," *Science* 213 (1981): 1008–1010; and B. Hileman, "Crop Losses from Air Pollutants," *Environmental Science and Technology* 16 (1982): 495A–499A.

65 John S. Reuge and Pierre J. Schuurmans, *Policy Implications of Hybrid-Electric Vehicles* (Stanford, CT: NEVOR, Inc., April 22, 1996).

66 Paul Hawken, Amory L. Lovins, and Hunter Lovins, *Natural Capitalism— Creating the Next Industrial Revolution* (New York: Little, Brown, 1999), 24.

67 *Air Pollution Research* (Sacramento, CA: California Air Resources Board, June 1998), 16.

68 Personal communication with Tom Cackette, Deputy Director, California Air Resources Board, January 20, 2006.

69 Gina M. Solomon and others, *No Breathing in the Aisles: Diesel Exhaust Inside School Buses* (Los Angeles, CA: Natural Resources Defense Council and the Coalition for Clean Air, January 2001), v.

70 *Crude Reckoning,* 11, 43.

71 *Particulate Air Pollution and Daily Mortality: Replication and Validation of Selected Studies,* phase I report of the particle epidemiology evaluation project (Boston, MA: Health Effects Institute, 1995).

72 *Crude Awakenings,* 125.

73 *Used Oil Facts* (Sacramento, CA: California Integrated Waste Management Board, 2002).

74  "The Devices on Cars That Keep Polluting Emissions from Reaching Air Are Spewing Out Other Potentially Toxic Substances," Environmental News Network, November 27, 2001.

75  University of North Dakota, Energy and Environmental Research Center, www.eerc.und.nodak.edu/features/EBAF.html.

76  American Coalition for Ethanol, www.ethanol.org/in_the_news/sky-high. html.

77  Randolph E. Schmid, "Most Oil Polluting the Oceans Comes from Runoff, Rivers, Small Boats, Not Tanker Spills," Associated Press, May 24, 2002.

78  Andre Mele, *Polluting for Pleasure* (New York: W. W. Norton, 1993); *2-Stroke Engine Fact Sheet* (San Francisco, CA: Bluewater Network, 2002); and Andrew C. Revkin, "Offshore Oil Pollution Comes Mostly as Runoff, Study Says," *New York Times*, May 24, 2004.

79  Revkin, "Offshore Oil Pollution;" and California Air Resources Board, www.arb.ca.gov/msprog/offroad/recmarine/recmarine.htm.

80  "Worldwide Snowmobile Sales: Estimated Retail Sales," International Snowmobile Manufacturers Association. Available online at www.snow mobile.org.

81  *Clean Snowmobile Facts: Frequently Asked Questions* (Helena, MT: Montana Department of Environmental Quality, 2006).

82  Constantinos Sioutas, *Physical and Chemical Characteristics of PM Near Freeways Impacted by Heavy and Light-Duty Traffic* (Los Angeles, CA: University of Southern California School of Engineering, Southern California Particle Center and Supersite, October 5, 2005).

83  As quoted in Kerry Cavanaugh, "Big Trouble from Tiny Particles," *Los Angeles Daily News*, March 7, 2004.

84  Sioutas, *Physical and Chemical Characteristics*.

85  N. Li and others, "Comparison of the Pro-oxidative and Proinflammatory Effects of Organic Diesel Exhaust Particle Chemicals in Bronchial Epithelial Cells and Macrophages," *Journal of Immunology* 169, no. 8 (October 15, 2002): 4531–4541; as reported in D. L. Laskin, *Peroxides and Macrophages in Toxicity of Fine Particulate Matter* (Los Angeles, CA: Health Effects Institute, January 2004); and as reported by Gary Polakovic, "Air Particles Linked to Cell Damage," *Los Angeles Times*, April 7, 2003.

86  Sioutas, *Physical and Chemical Characteristics*; and as quoted in Cavanaugh, "L.A.'s Toxic Freeways."

87  Kerry Cavanaugh, "L.A.'s Toxic Freeways," *Los Angeles Daily News*, September 29, 2003.

88  Ben Harder, "My Own Private Bad-Air Day: Outdoor Data Underrate Pollutant Exposure," *Science News* 165, no. 1 (January 3, 2004): 4.

89  Data provided by the California Office of Environmental Health Hazard Assessment, January 2004.

90  Thomas H. Maugh II, "'Safe' Lead Levels Lower IQ in Children, Study Finds," *Los Angeles Times*, April 17, 2003.

91  Maugh, "'Safe' Lead Level."

92  Maugh, "'Safe' Lead Levels."

93  Riki Ott, Charles Peterson, and Stanley Rice, *Exxon Valdez Oil Spill (EVOS) Legacy: Shifting Paradigms in Oil Ecotoxicology* (Cordova, AK: Alaska Forum for Environmental Responsibility, 2002); and Murphy, "Exxon Oil Spill's Cleanup Crews."

94  Ott, Peterson, and Rice, *Exxon Valdez Oil Spill (EVOS) Legacy*; and Murphy, "Exxon Oil Spill's Cleanup Crews."

## CHAPTER 3. *Desperate Enterprise*

1  Christopher Marlowe, *The Tragicall History of the Life and Death of Doctor Faustus*, act I, scene 1 (from the quarto of 1616).

2  Tom Plenys, "Health Care Costs in California Due to Petroleum Related Processes and Byproducts," *Environment Now*, December 1, 2003, 12.

HEALTH COST SUMMARY OF PETROLEUM-RELATED STAGES IN CALIFORNIA (COST ESTIMATES IN BILLIONS OF DOLLARS, 2003)

| Cost Component Description | Direct Costs | Indirect Costs | Total Costs |
|---|---|---|---|
| *"Nontailpipe" Stages* | | | |
| Crude oil extraction and field production, accidents | — | $0.01 | $0.01 |
| Crude oil transport | — | $0.05 | $0.05 |

| Cost Component Description | Direct Costs | Indirect Costs | Total Costs |
|---|---|---|---|
| Storage of crude oil and gasoline (including MTBE water pollution) | $0.4 to $1.7 | $0 to $0.04 | $0.4 to $1.7 |
| "Upstream" emissions | $0.5 to $2.7 | $1.4 to $8.0 | $1.9 to $10.7 |
| Oil refinery accidents (Contra Costa County only) | – | $0.005 | $0.005 |
| **Total nontailpipe costs** | **$0.9 to $4.4** | **$1.5 to $8.1** | **$2.4 to $12.5** |
| *'Tailpipe' Stages* | | | |
| Criteria pollutants from evaporative vehicle emissions | $1.1 to $57.3 | $5.9 to $169.6 | $7.0 to $226.9 |
| Toxic pollutants from evaporative vehicle emissions | $0.03 to $0.45 | $0.03 to $0.45 | $0.05 to $0.9 |
| **Total tailpipe costs** | **$1.1 to $57.8** | **$5.9 to $170.1** | **$7.1 to $227.8** |
| Grand total costs | $2.0 to $62.2 | $7.4 to $178.2 | $9.4 to $240.3 |

3   Leonard S. Miller and others, "State Estimates of Total Medical Expenditures Attributable to Cigarette Smoking," *Public Health Reports* (September/ October 1998): 447–458.

4   See table of direct costs in note 2.

5   W. Max and others, *The Cost of Smoking in California* (Sacramento, CA: California Department of Health Services, 2002).

6   As cited in Tom Plenys, "Health Care Costs in California due to Petroleum Related Processes and Byproducts," *Environment Now*, December 1, 2003.

ANNUAL NATIONAL COSTS BY POLLUTANT DUE TO MOTOR-VEHICLE-RELATED EMISSIONS BASED ON A 100 PERCENT REDUCTION IN MOTOR-VEHICLE-RELATED EMISSIONS (COST ESTIMATES IN BILLIONS OF DOLLARS, 2003)

| Ambient Pollutant | Motor Vehicles | Motor Vehicles plus Upstream | Percentage of Total (Based on high estimate of "motor vehicles plus upstream") |
|---|---|---|---|
| PM 10 | $22.6 to $360.3 | $25.7 to $377.9 | 94.2% |
| Ozone | $0.3 to $2.6 | $0.3 to $2.6 | 0.7% |

ANNUAL NATIONAL COSTS BY POLLUTANT DUE TO MOTOR-VEHICLE-RELATED
EMISSIONS BASED ON A 100 PERCENT REDUCTION IN MOTOR-VEHICLE-
RELATED EMISSIONS (COST ESTIMATES IN BILLIONS OF DOLLARS, 2003), CONT'D

| Ambient Pollutant | Motor Vehicles | Motor Vehicles plus Upstream | Percentage of Total (Based on high estimate of "motor vehicles plus upstream") |
|---|---|---|---|
| Nitrogen dioxide | $1.4 to $7.4 | $1.4 to $7.4 | 1.8% |
| Carbon monoxide | $1.2 to $11.0 | $1.2 to $11.0 | 2.7% |
| Toxics | $0.1 to $2.2 | $0.1 to $2.2 | 0.6% |
| **Total** | **$25.6 to $383.5** | **$28.7 to $401.1** | **100%** |

Mark A. Delucchi, James J. Murphy, and Donald R. McCubbin, "The Health and Visibility Cost of Air Pollution: A Comparison of Estimation Methods," *Journal of Environmental Management* 64 (2002): 139–152, and table 3.

7   Renee Sharp and Bill Walker, *Particle Civics* (Washington, DC: Environmental Working Group, 2003), 5; Gary Polakovic, "Air Particles Linked to Cell Damage," *Los Angeles Times*, April 7, 2003; and N. Li and others, "Comparison of the Pro-oxidative and Proinflammatory Effects of Organic Diesel Exhaust Particle Chemicals in Bronchial Epithelial Cells and Macrophages," *Journal of Immunology* 169, no. 8 (October 15, 2002): 4531–4541; and as reported in D. L. Laskin, *Peroxides and Macrophages in Toxicity of Fine Particulate Matter* (Los Angeles, CA: Health Effects, January 2004). Some scientific debate revolves around the emissions contribution made by motor vehicles to the aggregate total of PM pollution. For example, road dust has been found to contribute a significant share of PM, but this dust is primarily the larger-sized particles. As the evidence in these citations shows, the most important effects occur from PM of less the 2.5 microns (PM 2.5) because the finer particles penetrate deeper into lung tissue. Almost all PM 2.5 is attributable to vehicle exhaust.

8   *Homicide in California 2002* (Sacramento, CA: California Department of Justice—Division of California Justice Information Services, Bureau of Criminal Information and Analysis, Criminal Justice Statistics Center, 2004); and Steven Shippen, *Human Immunodeficiency Virus Disease Deaths California 2002* (Sacramento, CA: California Department of Health Services, Center for Health Statistics, June 2004).

9   *Regulatory Impact Assessment for Petroleum Refineries* (Washington, DC: USEPA, 1995); and *Crude Reckoning: The Impact of Petroleum on California's*

*Public Health and Environment* (Sacramento, CA: Center for Energy Efficiency and Renewable Technologies, August 2000), 32.

10  Cecilia Parsons, "Winds, Warmth, Emissions Combine to Choke Valley," *Porterville Recorder,* June 12, 2003; R. Guderian, *Air Pollution: Phytotoxicity of Acidic Gases and Its Significance in Air Pollution Control* (New York: Springer-Verlag, 1977); P. B. Reich, R. G. Amundson, and J. P. Lassoie, "Reduction in Soybean Yield after Exposure to Ozone and Sulfur Dioxide Using a Linear Gradient Exposure Technique," *Water, Air, and Soil Pollution* 17 (1982): 29–36; R. J. Oshima and others, "Reduction of Tomato Fruit Size and Yield by Ozone," *Journal of the American Society for Horticultural Science* 102 (1977): 287–293; H. E. Heggestad and J. H. Bennett, "Photochemical Oxidants and Potential Yield Losses in Snap Beans Attributable to Sulphur Dioxide," *Science* 213 (1981): 1008–1010; and B. Hileman, "Crop Losses from Air Pollutants," *Environmental Science and Technology* 16 (1982): 495A–499A.

11  As quoted in Parsons, "Winds, Warmth, Emissions Combine to Choke Valley."

12  Mark A. Delucchi, "Environmental Externalities of Motor-Vehicle Use in the US," *Journal of Transport Economics and Policy* 34, part 2 (December 1999): 135–168; Arthur Winer and others, *Valuing the Health Benefits of Clean Air* (Washington, DC: American Association for the Advancement of Science, 1992); and Donald R. McCubbin and Mark A. Delucchi, "The Health Costs of Motor-Vehicle-Related Air Pollution," *Journal of Transport Economics and Policy* (1996): 122–131.

13  Roland Hwang, *Money Down the Pipeline: The Hidden Subsidies to the Oil Industry* (San Francisco, CA: Union of Concerned Scientists, 2002); D. Koplow, *Federal Energy Subsidies: Energy, Environmental, and Fiscal Impacts* (Washington, DC: Alliance to Save Energy, 1993); and J. W. Loper, *State and Local Taxation: Energy Policy by Accident* (Washington, DC: Alliance to Save Energy, 1994).

14  *Oil and Gas: Long-Term Contribution Trends* (Washington, DC: Center for Responsive Politics, March 2006).

15  "The Best Energy Bill Corporations Could Buy: Summary of Industry Giveaways in the 2005 Energy Bill," *Public Citizen,* August 2005; and *The Energy Policy Act of 2005: What the Energy Bill Means to You* (Washington, DC: U.S. Department of Energy, August 2005).

16  The Energy Policy Act of 2005, sections 311, 322-323, 344-346, 353-354,

1323, 1325-1326, 1329, Title IX, Subtitle J; and as described in "The Best Energy Bill".

17  "The Best Energy Bill."

18  Rob Nixon, "A Dangerous Appetite for Oil," *New York Times*, October 29, 2001.

19  Ruth Morris, "U.S. Aims to Stem Pipeline's Flow of Trouble," *Los Angeles Times*, February 6, 2002.

20  *The Hidden Cost of Oil* (Washington, DC: National Defense Council Foundation, October 2003); and Evan Harrje, *The Real Price of Gasoline* (Washington, DC: International Center for Technology Assessment, 2000); and Mark Mazzetti and Joel Havemann, "Bush's Bill for War Is Rising," *Los Angeles Times*, February 3, 2006.

21  As quoted in Robert Baer, *Sleeping with the Devil* (New York: Crown-Random House, 2003), 34.

22  Frida Berrigan, "Smart Defense," TomPaine.com, May 18, 2006.

23  *Review of Studies of the Economic Impact of the September 11, 2001, Terrorist Attacks on the World Trade Center* (Washington, DC: Government Accounting Office, May 29, 2002).

24  According to the U.S. Department of Energy, the United States consumes 375 million gallons of petroleum fuels each day or approximately 137 billion gallons per year. Divide 137 billion into the dollar estimates compiled in the table "Annual Costs to U.S. Consumers of Oil and Auto Industry Subsidies and Externalities" to arrive at the cost per gallon. See Energy Information Administration, http://www.eia.doe.gov/oil_gas/petroleum/info_glance/petroleum.html.

25  The National Coalition on Health Care, http://www.nchc.org/facts/cost.shtml.

26  National Clearinghouse for Educational Facilities, *2006 School Construction Survey* (New York: McGraw-Hill Construction, 2006)

27  Jane V. Hall and others, "Valuing the Health Benefits of Clean Air," *Science* 255, no. 5046 (February 14, 1992): 812–817.

28  *Impacts of the SAMI Strategies: An Independent Analysis of the Benefits and Economic Impacts* (Washington, DC: USEPA, April 2002).

29  *Informing Regulatory Decisions: 2003 Report to Congress on the Costs and Ben-*

*efits of Federal Regulations and Unfunded Mandates on State, Local, and Tribal Entities* (Washington, DC: Office of Management and Budget, Office of Information and Regulatory Affairs, 2003); and Luis Cifuentes and others, "Hidden Health Benefits of Greenhouse Gas Mitigation," *Science* (August 17, 2001): 1257–1259.

30  As quoted in Devra Davis, *When Smoke Ran Like Water* (New York: Basic Books, 2002), 114.

31  "Fortune Global 500—2005," *Fortune*, March 2006, 25.

32  Compensation data in this chapter are taken from filings with the Securities and Exchange Commission.

33  Compensation data in this chapter are taken from filings with the Securities and Exchange Commission.

34  Mike Lewis, "Exxon Still Owes for Valdez Spill," *Seattle Post-Intelligencer*, March 13, 2006.

35  James Flanigan, "Big Three Face Hard Road Even with Union Help," *Los Angeles Times*, September 21, 2003.

36  "Toyota Tops J. D. Power's Annual Report," Associated Press, May 7, 2003.

37  J. D. Power Consumer Center, http://www.jdpower.com/news/releases/pressrelease.asp?ID=2005069.

38  *Consumer Reports, Automotive Edition*, April 2006; and John O'Dell, "Japanese Brands Sweep Top 10 Auto List," *Los Angeles Times*, March 2, 2006.

39  "A Hummer-Sized Loophole," *Los Angeles Times*, May 30, 2003.

40  Toyota Motor Company, http://www.toyota.com/prius/tax.html.

41  David Goodstein, *Out of Gas* (New York: W. W. Norton, 2004), 23.

42  "Probe: Shell Hid Lies on Reserves for Years" and "Shell's Challenge: Regain Trust After Reserves Scandal," *Sacramento Bee*, April 2004.

43  Colin J. Campbell and Jean H. Laherrere, "The End of Cheap Oil," *Scientific American*, March 1998, 79.

44  Campbell and Laherrere, "The End of Cheap Oil."

45  "Geologists Say World's Oil Supply May Run Dry," *Sacramento Bee*, May 29, 2005.

46  Goodstein, *Out of Gas*, 29.

47  Jay Palmer, "Clearing the Air," *Barron's*, December 16, 2002.

48  Goodstein, *Out of Gas*, 33.

49  "Statistical Review of World Energy 2005," BP. Available online at http://www.bp.com/genericsection.do?categoryId=92&contentId=7005893, June 2005.

50  As quoted in Richard Heinberg, "The End of the Oil Age," *Earth Island Journal*, Autumn 2003, 25.

51  William Shakespeare, *Julius Caesar*, act 4, scene 3.

52  Jack Doyle, *Taken for a Ride* (New York: Four Walls Eight Windows, 2000), 8.

53  Doyle, *Taken for a Ride*, 239.

54  Doyle, *Taken for a Ride*, 240; and James P. Barrett and J. Andrew Hoerner, *The Impacts of Increased Corporate Average Fuel Economy (CAFE) Standards on the U.S. Auto Sector* (Washington, DC: Redefining Progress, 2005).

55  John O'Dell, "Big Autos' Big Profits Make a Shift Unlikely," *Los Angeles Times*, June 27, 2004

56  Doyle, *Taken for a Ride*, 7.

57  Neela Banerjee, "Tight Oil Supply Won't Ease Soon," *New York Times*, May 16, 2004; and Elizabeth Douglass, "Upward Pressure at the Pump," *Los Angeles Times*, July 8, 2003.

58  D. J. Peterson and Sergej Mahnovski, *New Forces at Work in Refining* (Santa Monica, CA: Rand Corporation, 2003), 16; and Elizabeth Douglass, "Study Predicts More Volatility in Gas Prices," *Los Angeles Times*, August 28, 2003.

59  Elizabeth Douglass, "A Refinery's Fever Pitch," *Los Angeles Times*, July 28, 2003.

60  Douglass, "A Refinery's Fever Pitch."

61  Flex Your Power, http://www.fypower.org/pdf/Katrina_Impact.pdf.

62  Jennifer Coleman, "Gas Prices Soar Due to Rupture of Pipeline," Associated Press, August 20, 2003.

63  *Reducing California's Petroleum Dependence* (Sacramento, CA: California Energy Commission and California Air Resources Board, August 2003).

64  Campbell and Laherrere, "The End of Cheap Oil."

65 "Global Expansion Fuels Rapid Gains in Demand for Oil," *Wall Street Journal,* June 11, 2004.

66 "Stronger Rise in Oil Demand Seen," *Los Angeles Times,* February 8, 2006.

67 Bruce Stanley, "World's Thirst for Oil Expected to Rise," Associated Press, November 14, 2003.

68 *The National Security Implications of the Economic Relationship Between the United States and China* (Washington, DC: US–China Security Review Commission, July 2002), chapter 7, p. 1; and as reported in Gail Luft, "U.S., China Are on a Collision Course Over Oil," *Los Angeles Times,* February 2, 2004.

69 Don Lee, "China Making Big Oil Moves," *Los Angeles Times,* January 23, 2006.

70 "In the Pipeline," *The Economist,* May 1, 2004.

71 Kristi Heim, "Energy Reshapes China's Priorities," *Seattle Times,* February 9, 2006.

72 Ching-Ching Ni, "China's New Love of Cars Can Be a Fatal Attraction," *Los Angeles Times,* May 22, 2004.

73 "China's Growing Love Affair with Cars Poses Energy and Environmental Hazards." May 11, 2004, Agence France-Presse.

74 Keith Bradsher, "GM Raises its Wager in China," *New York Times,* June 8, 2004.

75 Joseph B. White, "China's SUV Surge," *Wall Street Journal,* June 10, 2004.

76 *2005 Air Pollution Forecast,* China's State Environment Protection Administration; and as reported in "China's Growing Love Affair with Cars Poses Energy and Environmental Hazards."

77 White, "China's SUV Surge."

78 Elizabeth Douglass, "14-Day Gas Price Jump Sets Record," *Los Angeles Times,* August 26, 2003.

79 Kelly Hearn, "Woes Mount for Oil Firms in Ecuador," *Christian Science Monitor,* February 9, 2006.

80 Solomon Moore, "Attack Jolts Iraq Oil Business as Civilian, Troop Tolls Rise," *Los Angeles Times,* February 3, 2006.

81  Mark Mazzetti and Joel Havemann, "Bush's Bill for War Is Rising," *Los Angeles Times*, February 3, 2006.

82  "Nigeria Rebels Warn of More Hits on Oil Sites," *Los Angeles Times*, January 19, 2006.

83  Douglass, "Upward Pressure at the Pump."

84  Douglass, "Upward Pressure at the Pump."

## CHAPTER 4. *All That Glitters*

1   William Shakespeare, *Merchant of Venice*, act 2, scene 7.

2   As quoted in Robert Baer, *Sleeping with the Devil* (New York: Crown-Random House, 2003), 80.

3   Daniel Yergin, *The Prize* (New York: Touchstone/Simon and Schuster, 1992), 13–14.

4   "President Bush Discusses the Iraqi Interim Government," White House Audio News Archive, June 1, 2004.

5   Ed Shaffer, "Oil and the Middle East," *The Outlook*, September 1, 1999.

6   Baer, *Sleeping with the Devil*, 209; and Robert Tucker, "Oil: The Issue of American Intervention," *Commentary* 59, no. 1 (January 1975).

7   David Runk, "Abraham: U.S. Committed to Mideast Partners, Investment," Associated Press, September 29, 2003; and John Gallagher, "Oil, Gas Tighten U.S. Connection to Mideast," *Detroit Free Press*, September 30, 2003.

8   Paul R. Epstein and Jesse Selber, *Oil: A Life Cycle Analysis of its Health and Environmental Impacts* (Boston, MA: Center for Health and the Global Environment, Harvard Medical School, March 2002), 43–50; and Carbon Dioxide Record from the Hawaiian Mauna Loa Observatory from NOAA's Climate Monitoring and Diagnostics Laboratory, available online at http://www.cmdl.noaa.gov/info/testimony.html.

9   John Pickrell, "Oceans Found to Absorb Half of All Man-Made Carbon Dioxide," *National Geographic News*, July 15, 2004.

10  *Global Population Profile: 2002* (Washington, DC: U.S. Department of Commerce, Agency for International Development, Bureau for Global Health, March 2004), A-10; and *International Energy-Related Environmental Informa-*

*tion—Carbon Dioxide Emissions* (Washington, DC: U.S. Department of Energy, Energy Information Administration, November 2004).

11  Epstein and Selber, *Oil: A Life Cycle Analysis*, 43–50.

12  "NASA Blames Diesel Soot in Global Warming," *Los Angeles Times*, December 27, 2003.

13  Aaron Katzenstein and others, "Extensive Regional Atmospheric Hydrocarbon Pollution in the Southwestern United States," *Proceedings of the National Academy of Sciences* 100, no. 21 (October 14, 2003): 11975–11979.

14  As quoted at The Climate Group, http://www.theclimategroup.org/index .php?pid=428.

15  Phil Couvrette, "Inuit Leaders Blame U.S. for Global Warming," Associated Press, December 25, 2005; and personal communication with Sheila Watt-Cloutier, April 1, 2006.

16  Online edition of the *Los Angeles Times*, September 23, 2003.

17  Ian Gary and Terry Lynn Karl, *Bottom of the Barrel: Africa's Oil Boom and the Poor* (Baltimore, MD: Catholic Relief Services, June 2003).

18  "The Devil's Excrement—Is Oil Wealth a Blessing or a Curse?" *The Economist*, May 22, 2003, 78.

19  As quoted in "The Devil's Excrement," 78.

20  As quoted in Epstein and Selber, *Oil: A Life Cycle Analysis*; and Gal Luft, "Africa Drowns in a Pool of Oil," *Los Angeles Times*, July 1, 2003.

21  As quotedin Epstein and Selber, *Oil: A Life Cycle Analysis*.

22  Bob Egelko, "Nigerian Villagers Allowed to Sue ChevronTexaco," *San Francisco Chronicle*, March 26, 2004.

23  Terence Chea, "Chevron Fights Allegations of Human Rights, Environmental Abuses," Associated Press, January 1, 2006.

24  Rory Carroll, "Shell Told to Pay Nigerians $1.5bn Pollution Damages," *The Guardian*, February 25, 2006.

25  *Nigeria Fact Book* (Langley, VA: U.S. Central Intelligence Agency, 2006).

26  T. Christian Miller, "The Politics of Petroleum," *Los Angeles Times*, May 16, 2004.

27  Miller, "The Politics of Petroleum."

28  Miller, "The Politics of Petroleum."

29  Miller, "The Politics of Petroleum."

30  Miller, "The Politics of Petroleum."

31  Miller, "The Politics of Petroleum."

32  Miller, "The Politics of Petroleum."

33  Miller, "The Politics of Petroleum."

34  Miller, "The Politics of Petroleum."

35  Miller, "The Politics of Petroleum."

36  Tyche Hendricks, "Ecuador Tribe Battles Chevron on Oil Spill," *San Francisco Chronicle*, April 29, 2004.

37  Tyche Hendricks, "Ecuador Tribe Battles Chevron."

38  Tyche Hendricks, "Ecuador Tribe Battles Chevron."

39  Epstein and Selber, *Oil: A Life Cycle Analysis.*

40  Chea, "Chevron Fights Allegations."

41  Chea, "Chevron Fights Allegations."

42  Ken Silverstein, "Oil Adds Sheen to Kazakh Regime," *Los Angeles Times*, May 12, 2004.

43  Silverstein, "Oil Adds Sheen."

44  Silverstein, "Oil Adds Sheen."

45  Silverstein, "Oil Adds Sheen."

46  Silverstein, "Oil Adds Sheen."

47  Silverstein, "Oil Adds Sheen."

48  Baer, *Sleeping with the Devil*, 31–32.

## CHAPTER 5. *Wealth Seems Rather to Possess Them*

1   Wayne Leonard, Chief Executive Officer, Entergy Corp., Southern Governor's Conference Speech, August 25, 2002. Available online at http://www.entergy.com/corp/speeches/leonard_08_25_02.asp.

2   Michael Orey, *Assuming the Risk: The Mavericks, the Lawyers, and the Whistle-Blowers Who Beat Big Tobacco* (New York: Little, Brown, 1999), 36ff.

3   Adam Levy and others, *The People vs. Big Tobacco: How the States Took on the Cigarette Giants* (New York: Bloomberg Press, 1998); and JeffreyWigand.com, www.jeffreywigand.com/insider.

4   As quoted in Jack Doyle, *Taken for a Ride* (New York: Four Walls Eight Windows, 2000), 29.

5   Devra Davis, *When Smoke Ran Like Water* (New York: Basic Books, 2002), 58; Doyle, *Taken for a Ride*, 47–48; "Let George Do It," *American Lawyer*, May 7, 1990, 33; "Fighting the Big Lie about General Motors," *American Lawyer*, May 21, 1990; *U.S. v. National City Lines*, U.S. Supreme Court, 1955; and Peter Montague, "Tire Dust," *Rachel's Environment and Health News* (Environmental Research Foundation), April 27, 1995.

6   Davis, *When Smoke Ran Like Water*; and "Tire Dust."

7   "Fortune Global 500—2005," *Fortune*, March 2006, 25.

8   "Fortune Global 500—2005."

9   Riki Ott, *Sound Truth and Corporate Myth$: The Legacy of the* Exxon Valdez *Oil Spill* (Cordova, AK: Dragonfly Sisters Press, 2005).

10   Personal communication with Dr. Riki Ott, January 1, 2002.

11   Ott, *Sound Truth*.

12   Kim Murphy, "Exxon Oil Spill's Cleanup Crews Share Years of Illness," *Los Angeles Times*, November 5, 2001.

13   "Ads for Exxon Gasoline Are Deceptive, FTC Charges" and "Exxon Settles FTC Charges," U.S. Federal Trade Commission press releases, Washington DC, September 17, 1996 and June 24, 1997; and *FTC Facts for Consumers: The Low Down on High Octane Gasoline*, (Washington, DC: U.S. Federal Trade Commission, October 2003). Exxon settled the charges by agreeing to end the deceptive practices, to conduct a public education campaign that included television ads and point-of-purchase literature, and to cooperate with the FTC oversight that would prevent such misreprentations in the future.

14   Jack Doyle, *Crude Awakening* (Washington, DC: Friends of the Earth, 1994), 206.

15  Elizabeth Douglass, "Octane's Allure Hurt by High Cost," *Los Angeles Times*, November 28, 2005.

16  As quoted in Doyle, *Crude Awakening*, 206.

17  *Administrator's Medium Term Energy Measures* (Washington, DC: U.S. Department of Energy, September 13, 1990).

18  Boydon Gray and Andrew R. Varcoe, *Octane, Clean Air, and Renewable Fuels: A Modest Step Toward Energy Independence* (Washington, DC: Energy Future Coalition, January 2006).

19  Doyle, *Crude Awakening*, 208.

20  T. Nishizaki, "The Effects of Fuel Composition and Fuel Additives on Intake System Detergency of the Japanese Automobile Engine," SAE Technical Paper 790203, Society of Automotive Engineers, 1979.

21  "Fuels and Fuel Additives," USEPA, March 6, 2006. Available online at www.epa.gov/otaq/fuels.htm.

22  As quoted in Doyle, *Crude Awakening*, 208.

23  Beth Gardiner, "Probe—Shell Hid Lies on Reserves for Years," Associated Press, April 20, 2004.

24  "The Devil's Excrement," *The Economist*, May 22, 2003, 78.

25  Robert Winnett, "Saddam 'Bought UN Allies' with Oil," *Sunday Times of London*, October 3, 2004.

26  As quoted in Doyle, *Taken for a Ride*, 145.

27  As quoted in Doyle, *Taken for a Ride*, 20.

28  Doyle, *Taken for a Ride*, 20.

29  As quoted in Doyle, *Taken for a Ride*, 22.

30  Doyle, *Taken for a Ride*, 70.

31  *Efforts to Discourage/Eliminate Alternative Vehicles or Cleaner Technologies* (Santa Barbara, CA: Energy Independence Now, 2002).

32  Doyle, *Taken for a Ride*, 100.

33  As quoted in *Efforts to Discourage/Eliminate Alternative Vehicles or Cleaner Technologies*.

34  As quoted in Doyle, *Taken for a Ride*, 104.

35  Doyle, *Taken for a Ride*, 26.

36  Doyle, *Taken for a Ride*, 104.

37  Doyle, *Taken for a Ride*, 119.

38  Doyle, *Taken for a Ride*, 135.

39  Personal communication with Beth Lowery, January 10, 2003.

40  Conference call for GM's announcement of a settlement in the ZEV litigation, August 11, 2003. Participants included Jason Mark (Union of Concerned Scientists), Sierra Club representatives, staff of the California Air Resources Board, and the author; GM representatives on the call were Beth Lowery, Dave Barthmuss, and Tim McCann.

41  HybridCars.com, http://www.hybridcars.com/silverado-sierra.html.

42  Meeting of GM officials, CARB officials, and the author at CalEPA in Sacramento, CA, June 20, 2004.

43  "U.S. Announces $45 Million Clean Air Settlement with GM," U.S. Department of Justice press release, Washington, DC, November 30, 1995; and Doyle, *Taken for a Ride*, 515–532.

44  Doyle, *Taken for a Ride*, 27. Although the automakers and their trade association admitted no guilt, they agreed in the settlement that they would not obstruct the further development and installation of pollution control devices.

45  "American Honda Agrees to $267 Million Settlement to Resolve Clean Air Act Violations," U.S. Department of Justice press release, Washington, DC, June 8, 1998.

46  Personal communication with Rich Kassel and Gail Ruderman Feuer, Natural Resources Defense Council, and Tom Cackette, California Air Resources Board, September 2004.

47  *Fuels and Fuel Additives* (Washington, DC: USEPA, March 2006).

48  Jamie Kitman, "Hidden History of Leaded Gasoline Reveals Industry Conspiracy to Conceal Dangers: Lethal Product Still Marketed Throughout World," *Lead Action News* 8, no. 1 (2001): 12; and Gray and Varcoe, *Octane, Clean Air, and Renewable Fuels.*

49  Lead Exposure to Animals and Plants, www.rst2.edu/ties/LEAD/university/resources/experts/leadinanimals/animal1.htm.

50  Lead Exposure to Animals and Plants, www.rst2.edu/ties/LEAD/university/resources/experts/leadinanimals/animal1.htm.

51  ECO-USA, www.eco-usa.net/toxics/lead.shtml.

52  Jamie Lincoln Kitman, "The Secret History of Lead," *The Nation*, March 20, 2000.

53  Kitman, "The Secret History of Lead."

54  Colby College, www.colby.edu/personal/t/thieten/air-lead.html.

55  Paul N. Cheremisinoff and Nicholas P. Cheremisinoff, *Lead: A Guidebook to Hazard Detection, Remediation, and Control* (Englewood Cliffs, NJ: Prentice-Hall, 1993).

56  Cheremisinoff and Cheremisinoff, *Lead.*

57  "Lead Levels in Preindustrial Humans," *New England Journal of Medicine* (May 7, 1992), as referenced in John D. MacArthur, "Lead and the Brain." Available online at www.xs4all.nl/~stgvisie/VISIE/lead.html and www.nejm.org.

58  Global Lead Network, www.globalleadnet.org/advocacy/initiatives/nation.cfm; and Kitman, *Secret History of Lead.*

59  Colby College, www.colby.edu/personal/t/thieten/air-lead.html.

60  Viv Bernstein, "NASCAR Plans to Switch to Unleaded Fuel in '08," *New York Times*, January 20, 2006.

61  Greg Steele, and Joe O'Neill, *Measuring Blood Lead Levels in NASCAR Racing Team, MPH Newsletter* (Indiana University School of Medicine, Department of Public Health), Fall 2005.

62  As quoted in Doyle, *Taken for a Ride*, 348.

63  As quoted in Doyle, *Taken for a Ride*, 348.

64  As quoted in Doyle, *Taken for a Ride*, 349.

65  As quoted in Doyle, *Taken for a Ride*, 349.

66  As quoted in Doyle, *Taken for a Ride*, 349.

67  Doyle, *Taken for a Ride*, 349.

# CHAPTER 6. *Worse Poison to Men's Souls*

1   Dick Morris, "Hydrogen Cars and Fuels Survey: Results and Analysis," Washington, DC, survey conducted by Vote.com, April 2003.

2   As quoted in Devra Davis, *When Smoke Ran Like Water* (New York: Basic Books, 2002), 45.

3   Davis, *When Smoke Ran Like Water*, 46.

4   Davis, *When Smoke Ran Like Water*, 55–56.

5   Robert L. Fischman and others, *An Environmental Law Anthology* (Cincinnati, OH: Anderson Publishing, 1996). The Clean Air Act of 1970 is actually an extension of a federal law first passed in 1963. It requires the USEPA to develop and enforce regulations to protect the general public from exposure to airborne contaminants that are known to be hazardous to human health. The Clean Air Act was made federal law in 1970 (42 U.S.C.A. §§7401) and is the first major environmental law in the United States to include a provision for citizen suits. The USEPA, which began operation on December 2, 1970, is the agency of the federal government charged with protecting human health and with safeguarding the natural environment: air, water, and land. The National Environmental Policy Act was signed into law on January 1, 1970 (although it was enacted on January 1, 1970, its actual title is the National Environmental Policy Act of 1969) by President Richard Nixon. The preamble reads: "To declare a national policy which will encourage productive and enjoyable harmony between man and his environment; to promote efforts which will prevent or eliminate damage to the environment and biosphere and stimulate the health and welfare of man; to enrich the understanding of the ecological systems and natural resources important to the Nation."

6   Davis, *When Smoke Ran Like Water*, 90.

7   As quoted in Davis, *When Smoke Ran Like Water*, 95.

8   Davis, *When Smoke Ran Like Water*, 97.

9   Davis, *When Smoke Ran Like Water*, 140.

10  *Recommendation for an Ambient Air Quality Standard for Ozone* (Sacramento, CA: California Office of Environmental Health Hazard Assessment, June 2004), 2.

11  *Ambient Air Quality Standards* (Sacramento, CA: California Air Resources Board, November 29, 2005). The California twenty-four-hour exposure standard for respirable particulate matter (PM 10), for example, is 50 parts

per billion (ppb), whereas the federal standard is 150 ppb, or 300 percent higher.

12   Elizabeth Shogren, "EPA Proposal Targets Tractors, Bulldozers," *Los Angeles Times*, April 16, 2003.

13   Kerry Cavanaugh, "Choking on Air," *Los Angeles Daily News*, February 21, 2004.

14   As quoted in Cavanaugh, "Choking on Air."

15   Bluewater Network, Cavanaugh, "Choking on Air"; and http://blue waternetwork.org/press_releases/pr2004jun7_cv_annex.pdf.

16   Cavanaugh, "Choking on Air."

17   "Auto Workers Favor Greater Fuel Efficiency," Environment News Service, January 31, 2002.

18   About the Alliance of Automobile Manufacturers, see www.autoalliance.org. The alliance represents all major U.S. and foreign automakers with the notable exceptions of Honda of Japan and Hyundai/Kia of Korea.

19   The history of the CAFE regulation in this section is based on information taken from several sources: Richard Byrne, *Life in the Slow Lane: Tracking Decades of Automaker Roadblocks to Fuel Economy* (Cambridge, MA: Union of Concerned Scientists, July 2003); Kenneth E. Train and Clifford Winston, *Vehicle Choice Behavior and the Declining Market Share of U.S. Auto Makers* (Berkeley, CA: University of California Berkeley and the Brookings Institution, January 2004); Richard Simon, "Plan to Toughen Fuel-Mileage Rules Thwarted," *Los Angeles Times*, July 30, 2003; and *Effectiveness and Impact of Corporate Average Fuel Economy (CAFE) Standards* (Washington, DC: National Academy of Sciences, National Research Council, Transportation Research Board, 2002). The Pinto was a small sedan, and the Maverick was a midsized version. According to the National Highway Traffic Safety Administration, the Energy Policy Conservation Act, enacted into law by Congress in 1975, added Title V, "Improving Automotive Efficiency," to the Motor Vehicle Information and Cost Savings Act and established CAFE standards for passenger cars and light trucks. The act was passed in response to the 1973–1974 Arab oil embargo. The near-term goal was to double new car fuel economy by model year 1985. See www.nhtsa.gov/cars/rules/CAFE/overview.htm.

20   As quoted in Richard Byrne, *Life in the Slow Lane*.

21  Richard Byrne, *Life in the Slow Lane.*

22  As quoted in Richard Byrne, *Life in the Slow Lane.*

23  As discussed in Richard Byrne, *Life in the Slow Lane.*

24  As quoted in Richard Byrne, *Life in the Slow Lane.*

25  "High-Tech Driver Distractions," CBSNews.com, January 15, 2003. Available online at www.cbsnews.com/stories/2003/01/15/national/main 536583.shtml.

26  Simon, "Plan to Toughen Fuel-Mileage Rules Thwarted."

27  Simon, "Plan to Toughen Fuel-Mileage Rules Thwarted"; and "Bond Floor Speech on His CAFE Amendment to the Energy Bill," July 24, 2003, available online at http://bond.senate.gov/atwork/recordtopic .cfm?id=206803.

28  Train and Winston, *Vehicle Choice Behavior.*

29  "Tighter Fuel Rules Set for Bulky SUVs," Associated Press, March 30, 2006.

30  As quoted in *Evidence of a Conspiracy to Hinder Introduction of Electric Vehicles*, Preston, Gates & Ellis and Sierra Club Legal Defense Fund, as presented to the Antitrust Division of the U.S. Department of Justice, January 17, 1996, 2–3.

31  *Evidence of a Conspiracy*, 5.

32  *Evidence of a Conspiracy*, 5.

33  As quoted in *Evidence of a Conspiracy*, 6.

34  *Evidence of a Conspiracy*, 1.

35  *Evidence of a Conspiracy*, the Department of Justice did not act on SCLDF's evidence.

36  *Evidence of a Conspiracy*, 6.

37  Jack Doyle, *Taken for a Ride* (New York: Four Walls Eight Windows, 2000), 315.

38  As quoted in *Evidence of a Conspiracy.*

39  As quoted in *Evidence of a Conspiracy.*

40  *Evidence of a Conspiracy*, 6.

41  *Evidence of a Conspiracy*, 2.

42 Doyle, *Taken for a Ride*, 316.

43 Doyle, *Taken for a Ride*, 318.

44 *Evidence of a Conspiracy*.

45 Doyle, *Taken for a Ride*, 313; and *Evidence of a Conspiracy*.

46 Doyle, *Taken for a Ride*, 313.

47 *Evidence of a Conspiracy*, 2–3.

48 *Efforts to Discourage/Eliminate Alternative Vehicles or Cleaner Technologies* (Santa Barbara, CA: Energy Independence Now, 2002).

49 Bob Pool, "Drivers Find Outlet for Grief Over EV1s," *Los Angeles Times*, July 25, 2003.

50 Pool, "Drivers Find Outlet for Grief Over EV1s."

51 Pool, "Drivers Find Outlet for Grief Over EV1s."

52 Jack Doyle, *Crude Awakening* (New York: Friends of the Earth, 1994), 154–155.

53 Doyle, *Crude Awakening*, 164.

54 As quoted in Doyle, *Crude Awakening*, 164.

55 Doyle, *Crude Awakening*, 169.

56 William Shakespeare, *Romeo and Juliet*, act V, scene 1.

## CHAPTER 7. *Postcards from the Year 2025*

1 James Flanigan, "Russia Is World's Key to Having Oil to Burn," *Los Angeles Times*, May 30, 2004.

2 "The End of the Oil Age," *The Economist*, October 23, 2003.

3 *Frequently Asked Questions about Flex Your Power* (San Francisco: Flex Your Power, California Efficiency Partnership, June 21, 2005). Available online at http://www.fypower.org/about/faq.html.

4 Keith Schneider, "A New Green Coat for an Old Grey Factory," Great Lakes Bulletin News Service, December 12, 2002; and personal communication with William Ford Jr. in 2004.

5 Eric Schlosser, *Fast Food Nation: The Dark Side of the All-American Meal* (New York: Harper Perennial, 2002).

6   Energy Information Administration, USEPA, U.S. Department of Agriculture, U.S. Department of Energy, National Biodiesel Board, National Renewable Energy Laboratory, as reported in "Why $5 Gas is Good for America," *Wired*, December 2005, 239–347.

7   "President Delivers 'State of the Union,'" Office of the Press Secretary, the White House, January 28, 2003.

8   Peter Hoffmann, *Tomorrow's Energy* (Cambridge, MA: MIT Press, 2002), 19.

9   Hoffmann, *Tomorrow's Energy*, 53

10  "Nine European Cities to Get Fuel Cell Buses," Environment News Service, December 20, 2001. Available online at http://ens.lycos.com/ens/dec2001/2001L-12-20-02.html.

11  "Chevron Fuels AC Transit's HyRoad Hydrogen Fuel Cell Demonstration Program," Chevron Corporation press release, March 13, 2006.

12  Dr. Michael R. Swain, *Fuel Leak Simulation* (Washington, DC: U.S. Department of Energy, 2001). Available online at www.energyindependencenow.org.

13  Hoffmann, *Tomorrow's Energy*, 241.

14  Hoffmann, *Tomorrow's Energy*, 233–234.

15  Hoffmann, *Tomorrow's Energy*, 214–215.

16  Hoffmann, *Tomorrow's Energy*, 236.

17  "2005 Honda FCX with Breakthrough Honda Fuel Cell Stack Earns EPA and CARB Certification," Honda Motor Company, July 28, 2004.

18  As quoted in Jay Palmer, "Clearing the Air," *Barron's*, December 16, 2002.

19  As quoted in Palmer, "Clearing the Air."

20  The Bellona Foundation http://www.bellona.no/en/energy/hydrogen/report_6-2002/22898.html.

21  Amory B. Lovins, *Twenty Hydrogen Myths* (Snowmass, CO: Rocky Mountain Institute, 2003).

22  Lovins, *Twenty Hydrogen Myths*.

23  "Delivered fuel cost alone is not a good indicator of the economic competitiveness of hydrogen as a transportation fuel," notes Joan Ogden. "Even if hydrogen is much more expensive than other fuels on an energy basis, it

may be able to compete on a lifecycle cost basis for applications where it can be used with higher efficiency than other fuels . . . because fuel cell vehicles would be two to three times as energy efficient as gasoline vehicles, would have a longer lifetime, and lower maintenance costs." It is also worth noting that the hydrogen used as fuel for ICEs is less expensive than the hydrogen needed for fuel cells because it doesn't need to be as pure. As quoted in Hoffmann, *Tomorrow's Energy*, 74. "Hydrogen is not inherently an expensive fuel," BP's fuels project manager, James Uihlein says. "At the refinery gate (the price of hydrogen or other fuels before taxes and retailer profit are added), hydrogen costs are comparable to conventional fuel costs. Using the refinery gate cost for hydrogen, the cost per mile driven is actually significantly less than conventional fuel due to the very high efficiency of the fuel cell engine." U.S. House of Representatives, www.house.gov/science/ hearings/energy02/jun24/uihlein.htm.

24  "2005 Honda FCX."

25  "BMW to Start Serial Output of Hydrogen-Powered Cars," Reuters, March 14, 2006.

26  California Hydrogen Highway Network, full details and updates are available at http://www.hydrogenhighway.ca.gov/.

27  As quoted in Palmer, "Clearing the Air."

28  "Planned BP Station Will Make and Sell Fuel from Water," *Singapore Straits Times*, July 20, 2004.

29  "Planned BP Station."

30  "Sierra Nevada Brews Up Environmentally Friendly Fuel Cell Electricity," *FuelCellWorks*, July 28, 2005. Available online at http://www.fuelcellsworks.com/Supppage3136.html.

31  "Other State Hydrogen and Fuel Cell Initiatives," Energy Independence Now, March 2006. Available online at www.energyindependencenow.org.

32  Joan Ogden, *Developing an Infrastructure for Hydrogen Vehicles: A Southern California Case Study* (Princeton, NJ: Center for Energy and Environmental Studies, Princeton University, 1999), as reported in the *International Journal of Hydrogen Energy* 23 (1999): 709–730.

33  "Waste to Hydrogen," Pyromex process, Innovative Logistics Solutions, Inc., presented to the National Hydrogen Association Annual Conference, Long Beach, CA, March 2006.

34  *California Energy Plan II*, September 2005, issued jointly by the California Energy Commission and the California Public Utilities Commission.

35  Hoffmann, *Tomorrow's Energy*.

36  David Goodstein, *Out of Gas* (New York: W. W. Norton, 2004), 40.

37  Carl Benson, "Alaska's Size in Perspective," *Alaska Science Forum*, Article 1404, September 2, 1998.

38  Elizabeth Douglas, "Getting Pumped Up," *Los Angeles Times*, September 21, 2003.

39  Hoffmann, *Tomorrow's Energy*, 69.

40  Personal communication with Raymond S. Hobbs, P.E., Senior Consulting Engineer for Arizona Public Service Company, and Daniel J. Rabun, Business Development Engineer, Air Products Corporation, March 2006.

41  "How Do Hydrogen Fuel Cell Vehicles Compare in Terms of Emissions and Energy Use? A Well to Wheel Analysis," Energy Independence Now, March 2006. Available online at http://www.energyindependencenow .org/pdf/fs/EIN-Well-to-Wheel-Analysis.pdf.

42  Stefan Lovgren, "Exxon Valdez Spill, 15 Years Later: Damage Lingers," *National Geographic News*, March 22, 2004.

43  California Energy Commission and USEPA as reported March 2006 at Energy Independence Now, www.energyindependencenow.org.

44  Jack Doyle, *Crude Awakening* (Washington, DC: Friends of the Earth, 1994), 197.

45  U.S. Energy Information Agency statistics, as cited in Doyle, *Crude Awakening*, 195.

46  Tanker Advisory Service, New York, NY, as cited in Doyle, *Crude Awakening*, 200.

47  Bureau of Land Management and Shell, as reported in "Ending the End of Oil," *Business 2.0*, December 2005, 167–175.

48  Personal communication with Jack Jenkins, engineer for the Western Oil Sands project, Alberta, Canada, February 6, 2006.

49  Suncor, as reported in "Ending the End of Oil."

50  U.S. Department of the Interior, Minerals Management Service, U.S. Geological Survey, as reported in "Why $5 Gas Is Good for America."

## CHAPTER 8. *The Quality of Mercy*

1   William Shakespeare, *Merchant of Venice*, act 4, scene 1.

2   "Fortune Global 500—2005," *Fortune*, March 2006, 25.

3   *Funds, by State, from Settlement Agreement Reached in November, 1998 by 46 State Attorneys General and the Tobacco Industry* (Ann Arbor, MI: Center for Social Gerontology, 1998).

4   Gary Polakovic, "Smog Woes Back on Horizon," *Los Angeles Times*, July 15, 2003.

5   Devra Davis, *When Smoke Ran Like Water* (New York: Basic Books, 2002), 71.

6   Davis, *When Smoke Ran Like Water*, 81.

7   Davis, *When Smoke Ran Like Water*, 79.

8   Davis, *When Smoke Ran Like Water*, 82.

9   Davis, *When Smoke Ran Like Water*, 86.

10  Office of California Attorney General, October 23, 2003. The other governments are California, Connecticut, Illinois, Minnesota, Massachusetts, New Jersey, New Mexico, New York, Oregon, Rhode Island, Vermont, Washington, the District of Columbia, American Samoa, and the Cities of New York and Baltimore.

11  *State of Connecticut, et al. v. American Electric Power Company, Inc., et al.*, U.S. District Court, Southern District of New York, 2005.

12  Jane Kay, "Two Oil Giants Deceived Public on MTBE's Hazards, Jury Finds," *San Francisco Chronicle*, April 17, 2002.

13  "Oil Companies Settle for $69 Million in Tahoe MTBE Case," *U.S. Water News Online*, August 2002. Available online at http://uswaternews.com/archives/arcrights/2oilcom8.html.

14  "Three Lead Paint Makers Are Found Guilty," Associated Press, February 22, 2006.

15  "New Strategy on Clean Air, *New York Times*, March 4, 2006.

16  South Texas College of Law, www.stcl.edu/faculty_pages/faculty_folders/steiner/nuisance/nuisance/sld028.htm.

17  Congressional Records state the purposes of the motor vehicle emissions

preemption provision, CAA, 42 U.S.C. § 7543, 42: [To] "prevent a chaotic situation from developing in interstate commerce in new motor vehicles." S. Rept. No. 192, reprinted in 1967 U.S.C.C.A.N. 1956; and [Preemption is] "necessary in order to prevent a chaotic situation from develping in interstate commerce in new motor vehicles." H.R. Rept. No. 728, 90th Cong., 1st Sess. 21 (1967); and to [protect motor vehicle manufacturers from] "fifty different sets of [State] requirements relating to emissions controls. . . . H.R. Rept. No. 294, reprinted in 1977 U.S.C.C.A.N 1077, 1388; and ". . . vehicle manufacturers not be subject to fifty different sets of requirements relating to emission controls which would unduly burden interstate commerce" H.R. Rept. No. 294, 95th Cong., 1st Sess. (1977); and (italics added) ". . . *When the States by their union made the forcible abatement of outside nuisances impossible to each, they did not thereby agree to submit to whatever might be done. They did not renounce the possibility of making reasonable demands on the grounds of their still remaining quasi-sovereign interests."* *Georgia v. Tennessee Copper Co.*, supra 206 U.S. at 237–38.

18 "Ads for Exxon Gasoline Are Deceptive, FTC Charges" Washington, DC, U.S. Federal Trade Commission press release, September 17, 1996; and *FTC Facts for Consumers: The Low Down on High Octane Gasoline* (Washington, DC: U.S. Federal Trade Commission, October 2003).

19 Jack Doyle, *Crude Awakening* (Washington, DC: Friends of the Earth, 1994), 206.

20 Matt Richtel, "With So Many Gasoline Choices, What's a Driver to Do?" *New York Times*, July 11, 2004.

21 An example of relevant MTBE litigation was described earlier in this chapter. An example of a growing number of cases against gunmakers is reported by Jeff Chorney, "9th Circuit Won't Rehear Gun Liability Case," *The Recorder*, June 2, 2004: "The case, *Ileto v. Glock Inc.*, 04 C.D.O.S. 4631, was filed by victims of a Southern California shooting rampage. The victims sued Austrian handgun manufacturer Glock and Chinese manufacturer China North, as well as other entities involved in the making, marketing and distribution of seven illegally obtained weapons. Alleging the manufacturers were negligent and that they created a public nuisance, the victims' families argued that the companies were to blame for promoting a secondary market for illegal gun distribution. The case was tossed out by U.S. District Judge Audrey Collins in Los Angeles, but reinstated in November 2003 by a divided 9th Circuit panel. Senior Judge Cynthia Holcomb Hall dissented from Judges Sidney Thomas and Richard Paez, who wrote the majority opinion. On Friday, the court declined to take the

case en banc. Eight judges dissented, saying the court should not only rehear the case, but remand it to California courts. They also predicted an upswell in [similar] litigation." Available online at http://www.law.com/ jsp/law/LawArticleFriendly.jsp?id=1085626360685.

22 *The Los Angeles Aqueduct and the Owens and Mono Lakes Cases* (Washington, DC: American University). Available online at http://www.american .edu/ted/mono.htm (accessed May 2006).

23 *National Audubon Society v. Superior Court of Alpine, Department of Water and Power of the City of Los Angeles,* et al. 33 Cal.3d 419, 433-435 (1983). "The principal values plaintiffs seek to protect, however, are recreational and ecological—the scenic views of the lake and its shore, the purity of the air, and the use of the lake for nesting and feeding by birds." Also, under *Marks v. Whitney,* it is clear that protection of these values is among the purposes of the public trust. "[The] public uses to which tidelands are subject are sufficiently flexible to encompass changing public needs. In administering the trust the state is not burdened with an outmoded classification favoring one mode of utilization over another." (*Marks v. Whitney,* 6 Cal.3d 251, 259–260).

24 National-Scale Air Toxics Assessment, USEPA, February 2006, available online at http://www.epa.gov/ttn/atw/nata1999/index.html; and Marla Cone, "State's Air Is Among Nation's Most Toxic," *Los Angeles Times,* March 22, 2006.

25 Cone, "State's Air is Among Nation's Most Toxic."

26 South Coast Air Quality Management District, diesel risk reduction program, 2000; and Cone, "State's Air."

27 National-Scale Air Toxics Assessment, USEPA, February 2006, available online at http://www.epa.gov/ttn/atw/nata1999/index.html; and Cone, "State's Air."

28 Davis, *When Smoke Ran Like Water,* 103

29 Mark A. Delucchi, "Environmental Externalities of Motor-Vehicle Use in the US," *Journal of Transport Economics and Policy* 34, part 2 (December 1999): 135–168; Donald R. McCubbin and Mark A. Delucchi, "The Health Care Costs of Motor-Vehicle-Related Air Pollution," *Journal of Transport Economics and Policy* (1996): 122–131; and Jane V. Hall and others, "Valuing the Health Benefits of Clean Air," *Science* 255, no. 5046 (February 14, 1992): 812–817.

30 Janet Wilson, "A Valley's Smog Toll Tallied," *Los Angeles Times*, March 30, 2006.

31 *2006 California Climate Action Team Final Report to the Governor and Legislature*, April 2006. Available online at www.climatechange.ca.gov/ climate_action_team/index.html.

32 William Birnbauer, "A Radical Idea," *The Age*, March 5, 2006.

33 Richard Simon, "Plan to Toughen Fuel-Mileage Rules Thwarted," *Los Angeles Times*, July 30, 2003; and as quoted in Richard Byrne, *Life in the Slow Lane: Tracking Decades of Automaker Roadblocks to Fuel Economy* (Cambridge, MA: Union of Concerned Scientists, July 2003), 9.

34 William Shakespeare, *Henry VI*, part 3, act 2, scene 6.

## EPILOGUE. *The Seventh Generation*

1 Devra Davis, *When Smoke Ran Like Water* (New York: Basic Books, 2002), 87.

2 "Sweden Aims for Oil-Free Economy," *BBC News*, February 8, 2006.

3 As quoted in Jay Palmer, "Clearing the Air," *Barron's*, December 16, 2002.

4 "The Drift to Low Performance," Donella Meadows Archive, Sustainability Institute, Hartland, VT. Available online at http://www.sustainer.org/ dhm_archive/index.php?display_article=vn396drifted.

5 The United Nations, http://www.un.org/ecosocdev/geninfo/afrec/ vol15no1/aideaths.htm.

6 W. James Gauderman and others, "The Effect of Air Pollution on Lung Development from 10 to 18 Years of Age," *New England Journal of Medicine* 351, no. 11 (September 9, 2004); and as reported by Miguel Bustillo, "Smog Harms Children's Lungs for Life, Study Finds," *Los Angeles Times*, September 9, 2004.

# INDEX

Abraham, Spencer, 85
"Abrupt Climate Change Scenario and
 Its Implications for U.S. National
 Security, An," 90
AC Transit, 169
Addiction to oil, 1–2, 82, 85, 131, 211
 steps to energy independence,
  *see* Energy independence,
  three steps to
Ade, Sunny, 94
Adgate, John, 47–48
Africa, leaded–gasoline sold in, 125
Agip oil company, 78
Aguinda, Toribio, 101
AIDS, 210
Airplane fuel, 43, 49, 134
Air pollution, vehicle exhaust and,
 2, 3, 9–26, 40–42, 116, 128–30,
 208
 in China, 76
 in confined vehicles, 21
 fake pollution control by auto
  makers, 118–25
 federal standards, 10
 financial benefits of reducing, 61–63
 history of smog, 11–13
 illnesses related to, *see specific illnesses*
 largest single source of, 10
 most dangerous pollutants in smog,
  13–17
 national monuments and, 23–24
 as public nuisance, 192
 similarities between tobacco smoke
  and vehicle exhaust, 17–19

studies of health effects of, 25,
 189–90
 true costs of, 57, 189–90
Akinboboye, Wanle, 94, 96
Alaskan North Slope region, 180–81
Alban, Jorge, 101
Alcala, Paul, 76
Alfonso, Juan Pablo Pérez, 93
Alliance of Automobile Manufacturers,
 138, 144
Amazon Watch, 102
American Automobile Manufacturers
 Association, 109, 118–19, 148, 150
American Council of Government and
 Industrial Hygienists, 134
American Lung Association, 12–13
American Petroleum Institute, 20, 38,
 39, 129
Anglo-Persian Oil Company, 84
 as BP, *see* BP
Angola, 93, 117
Antitrust conspiracy, 198–99
Aquinda, Chief, 101
Arab oil embargo of 1963, 70, 93, 137,
 159
Arms trafficking, 74–75
Arndt, Art, 3–4
Aspland, Jerry, 33
Asthma, 2, 11, 12, 31, 40, 112, 129, 200
 ozone and, 14–15, 20–21
Atwood, Sam, 47
AutoChoice, 140
Automobile Association of America,
 195